JOIN!

THE ALLIANCE NEEDS YOU!
HUMANITY NEEDS YOU!
EARTHFORCE NEEDS YOU!
SEE YOUR LOCAL EARTHFORCE RECRUITER

Earthforce Sourcebook

A Supplement for the Roleplaying Game Based on BABYLON 5,
the Warner Bros. Television Series Created by J. Michael Straczynski

Written by Joseph Cochran, Jon Tuffley, Dale MacMurdy,
Charles Ryan, and Zeke Sparkes

Ship combat system designed by Jon Tuffley based upon his *Full Thrust* ship combat system, with additional design by Zeke Sparkes

Illustrated by Theodore Black, Audrey Corman, Darryll Elliot, John Gronquist,
Chris Impink, Mark Poole, Douglas Shuler and Christina Wald

Edited by Charles Ryan, with additional editing by Ronald Jarrell and Joseph Cochran

The Babylon Project roleplaying game line developed by Joseph Cochran and Ronald Jarrell

Graphic design by Charles Ryan

Art Coordination by Matthew Tice

Ship Combat System Playtesting by Tim Johnson, with additional playtesting by Paul Duke, Josh Durham, John Franklin, Chris Impink, Kevin Johnson and Josh Reid

ISBN 1 85286 861 9

First Edition October 1997

10 9 8 7 6 5 4 3 2 1

British Library Cataloguing-in-Publication Data. A catalogue record for this book is available from the British Library.

The Babylon Project is produced under license by Wireframe Productions Inc., and is co-published by Titan Books/Chameleon Eclectic Entertainment, Inc. BABYLON 5, names, characters, and all related indicia are trademarks of Warner Bros. ™ and © 1997 Warner Bros.

Titan Books
42-44 Dolben Street
London SE1 0UP

Printed and bound in Great Britain by Stephens and George Ltd, Merthyr Industrial Estate, Dowlais, Merthyr Tydfil.

Contents

Introduction

David looked up and down the busy, narrow street of the colony. The pale orange light of the noon sun filtered through the dome, mixing with the artificial lighting to give the false appearance of a sunset to the heavy lunchtime foot traffic. He eased his way through the crowd of people, men and women of all trades rushing back and forth, intent on their own business, ignoring his passing.

The young man, barely eighteen, looked over across the crowd at a squat brown building bearing the Earth Alliance logo above its door. He looked again at the note clutched in his hand. He couldn't tell his parents face to face, but he had to let them know. "I'm not running away," he had written, "but I don't want to sit back and let others do the work for me. I want to help others, I want to be a part of something important."

He walked over to the public mail station and dropped the letter into the box. Checking his pocket for the data crystal with his school records on it, he took a deep breath and walked into the crowd, toward the EA building on the far side of the street.

"Are you sure about this?" he asked himself under his breath, as he walked. Dodging a fast moving woman who wasn't watching where she was going and threading between two groups of men talking about trade alliances, he nodded to himself. "It's now or never."

He paused at the door, looking back at the street for a moment, and stepped into the quiet calm of the building.

The offices inside were unremarkable. Drab institutional walls of the same textured gray materials common to most EA colonial buildings and stations framed a government issue desk and chairs across from the door, with a comm station set into the wall behind it. Behind the desk was an older man, slightly balding, in the blue uniform of an Earthforce lieutenant. He looked up as David entered.

"Can I help you, son?" asked the officer as he rose and offered his hand, a professional smile on his face.

David crossed to the officer, shaking his hand and taking an offered seat. Pulling the data crystal and his identicard out, he handed them over to the man.

"Yes sir. I'd like to enlist."

The older man scanned the card with a handheld reader, while giving his visitor a cursory look. "Well, Mr. Corwin, I think we can help you out."

The year is 2250. The Earth Alliance is still recovering from its devastating war with the Minbari and trying to keep the peace with its neighboring races. The most hard-hit, however is Earthforce, the military arm of the Alliance.

This book is about that military. It details the history of Earthforce, a large organization, entrusted with the lives of humans throughout known space, from its inception as a multinational peacekeeping force to the current integrated military over its 143-year history. This book also explores that military's role in the interstellar community of today.

The Babylon Project

BAB COM

This book is a supplement for *The Babylon Project* roleplaying game. It contains additional fictional information about the BABYLON 5 setting, as well as optional rules for use with the rules presented in the main rulebook. While the fictional history in this book can be enjoyed and some rules can be used without the base rulebook, it is not intended to be a fully playable game. Many rules and situations assume that you have read or can refer to information in the base rulebook.

The Earth Alliance

The Earth Alliance was formed as a political and economic conglomerate in 2075 after the success of the Armstrong Colony, the first civilian colony on Earth's Moon, in 2064. The founding of the small Luna Colony by the United States and the European Community in 2018, and of the orbital Station Prime in 2047, had been the first steps in a process that would change the way humanity viewed itself forever. The effort to build Armstrong Colony—the first sizable human settlement on a world other than Earth —was undertaken by all civilized nations of the world with unprecedented cooperation.

After the Armstrong Colony's successful completion, many people began to agree with the visionaries who believed that it was possible for humans to become a true spacefaring civilization. The collective sight of the world shifted from the Earth to the Moon, and then beyond to Mars. A project to settle Mars was created, and chartered under this new cooperative organization called the Earth Alliance. The United States of America, the United Kingdom, France and Australia were the largest benefactors in the formation of this new Alliance, devoting funds and manpower to the new organization, but they were far from the only members. The realistic goal of colonization drew most of the world's nations into the Alliance, and by 2088 its membership exceeded that of the United Nations. Work proceeded quickly on the colonization of the red planet, and true to the goal the first colony ship left Earth's orbit from Station Prime in August 2089, arriving in Mars' orbit in the spring of 2090. The success of this effort prompted a worldwide rush to join the Alliance among those nations who had not yet done so, creating for the first time an Earth with a single united purpose.

The nations of the world were not the only ones profiting from this renaissance in space travel. With the need for steady production of space ships, aerospace companies began to build them in greater number. Several also began to utilize these new vessels in mining and survey operations on the moon. The most elite of the rich and famous even braved the dangers of space travel for the sheer thrill of it. Traffic in space began to expand.

However, not all humans shared the peaceful goals of exploration and settlement fostered by the Alliance. Many representatives within the governments of the Earth felt that too many of the resources of the Earth and Moon were being squandered in a fruitless effort. Several of them even went as far as ordering covert acts against ships and people who were going to Mars. These small acts of terror were especially frequent in the first five years of the colony's existence.

The Earth Alliance, realizing that something needed to be done, petitioned its member nations for military support. Again the core nations of the Alliance were ready to support the organization, devoting troops and technology to the effort of defense of Station Prime and the invaluable transport ships to the Moon and Mars. By 2097 most acts of terror had been eliminated, and mass transport to Mars began.

However, those who were not content with the colony did not cease their efforts. History never recorded who was responsible or how it was done, but over the next year a series of small explosives was shipped to the colony and planted within the central dome. On February 16, 2099, at 6:34 A.M. Earth Standard Time, those explosives detonated inside the central dome, killing over five hundred colonists, destroying the dome and disabling life support systems all across the colony. Before the next scheduled transport could arrive to help the survivors, seven hundred more died from injuries and life support failure. Four different terrorist groups claimed credit, but the actual culprit was never found.

The Earth Alliance responded to the terrorism by redoubling its efforts to colonize Mars. With the full support of its core nations, the EA began to rebuild the colony immediately. As space travel was becoming more common, the Alliance needed a way to ensure the safety of those who traveled. Private corporations had taken over the roles of transit, building ships that could transfer people and cargo to and from Mars and sending exploration vessels into the asteroid belt and the outer planets. To regain some measure of control, the EA set up customs stations, and instituted more stringent security inspections of those traveling to and from Earth.

Not all of the ships being sent into space were there for the betterment of humanity. The bottom line in many cases was profit, and competition for the Mars to Earth run became fierce. In July of 2102 the EA sanctioned TransitCorp when one of the company's survey crews mounted a mining laser on their vessel to use as a makeshift weapon when a claim dispute arose. Though the situation was resolved before anyone was killed, the idea had already spread, and before long space would become a dangerous place to travel unless something was done. Using the resources of its member nations, it undertook construction of a new breed of space ship, the combat vessel. Designing and constructing small armed patrol craft it was (using manpower drawn largely from the militaries of its core nations) able to enforce the peace during the recolonization of Mars. The permanent Mars Colony, founded in June of 2105, prospered under the protection of the Alliance and its member nations' militaries.

The success of the Mars Colony galvanized the Alliance and assured many that it was a worthwhile organization. It acted as the protector and government of the colony, and maintained the safety of the space lanes. Over the next two years, many of the world's smaller nations, realizing that the Alliance was stronger, began to send more of their efforts there rather than to the old United Nations. The Alliance, growing stronger and getting more funding, had

begun to expand its humanitarian actions on Earth as well as in space. The weakened UN, provided with fewer resources than ever before, began to collapse, and was disbanded in favor of the EA in 2107.

As more attention and resources were given to the EA, its role expanded. It established Station Aphrodite in orbit of Venus in late 2111 and began to lay out plans to set up commercial mining operations in the asteroid belt with several large corporations. It also began to plan the full exploration of the Jovian system and the colonization of two of Jupiter's moons, Europa and Ganymede.

The Alliance Expands

While no nation on Earth wanted to give up sovereignty over its own lands, in the years that followed most realized that these new EA offworld territories needed a real government capable of serving the needs of the colonists. Conflicts between nations were on the rise, crime was becoming a systemwide problem and terrorist activity was still rampant back on Earth. The solutions to these problems were found in the same spirit of cooperation on which the Alliance was founded. In a historic summit

in Geneva, the leaders of the member nations met personally and on July 2, 2122, after three weeks of intense negotiations, they voted to make the Alliance the formal government of all non-sovereign lands controlled by human beings anywhere. The EA Senate was formed, made up of the leader of each nation (or a duly appointed proxy), and headed by a President elected from within the Senate's ranks.

This change in its charter gave the Alliance control over emigration to the colonies, as well as the ability to set up official administrations for the colony worlds. It also had the unforeseen side effect of giving the EA much stronger arbitration rights among nations on Earth over time, as international affairs now fell under its auspices —although this right was not actually realized until two member nations found themselves at odds over foreign overseas shipping rights thirty-two years later.

Under its new charter, the Alliance began to enact legislation to restructure the until then haphazard administrative structure of the Mars Colony into a government which could serve the colonists. While some of the most avid of the pioneers felt that the colony did not need a formal EA structure ruling them, the vast majority of the colonists appreciated the added benefit that the new government brought to the frontier world.

The Founding of Earthforce

With the economic and social power that it was given, the EA realized that it needed much more manpower to enact its goals, and began to recruit its own volunteer corps to help in all facets of space travel and interplanetary communication. One of these corps was a security force whose mission was to protect lives from the criminals, terrorists and miscreants who still tried to plague the Earth's settlements in space, as an expansion of the old UN's multinational peacekeeping force. This militia, called Earthforce, was seeded with manpower from the armed forces of some of the core nations in the Alliance, particularly the United States and Australia. As its enrollment grew, Earthforce became more

multinational, eventually including members from all nations of the Alliance.

At first more a police service than a military force, its role was to protect the liberty and property of all who traveled in space, and its main job tended to be keeping the peace on the Mars colony and in the transport lanes to and from the colony. As Earth's settlements in the solar system expanded, so did Earthforce's responsibility. Disputes over claims for mineral rights in the asteroid belt, now much more accessible due to the Mars settlements, started to grow more heated. In response the Alliance built the Skywalker Asteroid Base in 2230 as the first of a series of bases that would become both claim registration offices and bases for operations when police actions were needed. As the Alliance reached beyond the asteroid belt toward the outer planets, Earthforce provided both the manpower and the ships to ensure safe travels.

In 2145 the Ganymede Outpost was formed with the intention of settling a civilian colony either there or on Europa as space travel time allowed. However, before those plans could be enacted, the next few years changed the way humanity would look at itself and changed the Alliance's plans and Earthforce's role permanently.

The Decade of Change

The ten-year period between 2147 and 2157 was a pivotal point for the course of humanity. Three momentous events had a heavy impact on the mission of Earthforce. Early on in the decade, Earthforce became a police organization almost exclusively, protecting humanity against itself. As Earthforce took over these duties, many nations began to turn their attention elsewhere, increasing the workload on the already overtaxed peacekeeping force. The first event that impacted Earthforce's mission was its failure to prevent the detonation of a nuclear warhead by terrorists in San Diego. The EA member nations, the United States in particular, realized that they had been relying on Earthforce to police terrorism for them, and began to once again crack down on these issues within their own borders.

The second event that affected Earthforce was the assassination attempt on EA President Robinson, an event that brought the existence of telepaths to the fore. From the time she formed the Psi-Corps as a governmental organization in 2152, telepaths from all walks of life began to register for legal protection. When President Bullock re-chartered the Corps in 2161 into its present form as an independent organization, all of the telepaths currently serving in Earthforce left to join the Corps as per the new laws.

The third and most important event that led to changes in Earthforce was the discovery of Humanity by the Centauri Republic. This proof of alien races had a unifying effect on Humans. The knowledge that there were other races out there —and that wars among them were not uncommon— forced the Alliance to consider the possibility of invasion as more than a popular fictional concept. The structure of Earthforce changed over the next few years from a piecemeal militia to a real military. The main proponent of these changes was the United States, who encouraged them not only with funds, but also a large troop and supply commitment. This western influence is still reflected in today's Earthforce, though it is now truly a multinational organization.

The Formation of the Fleet

When Earthforce was founded as a peacekeeping militia, the majority of its members were deployed in countries or on colonies to control terrorist aggression on the ground. This changed only a little during the next few years as the Alliance expanded into the asteroid belt and beyond, as EF built some few ships to patrol the trade routes. But once Earth had the technology to travel among the stars with other races, it became a top priority to build ships that could defend human settlements from attack. Over the next twenty years, the Earthforce Fleet division grew from a small group of officers to the largest service branch of the military.

Alien Skirmishes

The purchase of jump technology from the Centauri gave humanity a vast frontier to explore, and men and women flocked to the unknown by the thousands, lured by curiosity and the quest for wealth, much like the gold rush in the old west. By 2165 the Earth Alliance had established three outposts in nearby systems in addition to the Proxima Colony. The neighboring races began to notice humanity. Most saw the fledgling race as a new opportunity for commerce and trade, opening relations with Earth's government and sending ambassadors to meet with the humans. Some, however, saw this newly expanding race as something else.

The Koulani, a nearby race holding just their own homeworld, saw the expansion of the humans as a threat to their own security. Rather than let the humans get a foothold near their own world, they decided to negotiate a treaty with the humans. Unfortunately, their philosophy was to attack a target and then bargain from a position of strength. Thus, when the humans set up a hyperspace beacon pair directly between Signet Outpost and their homeworld in April of 2169, they struck. The EA ships of the

---

The Starfury Program

BABCOM

In the decades after first contact with the Centauri, one of the plans the fleet had for defense was a specialized space fighter, capable of standing up to the fighters of the Centauri and Narn races. Looking at the designs of earlier alien fighters, the Human engineers realized that most to date had been designed to operate both in space and in atmospheric conditions. To give it an edge over the others, the new fighter was created to be completely maneuverable in space, without any regard to aerodynamics. Since it would only be used against alien aggression, the EA Senate felt that the lack of ability to maneuver in an atmosphere was a small price to pay for a competitive fighter. The Starfury program was instituted in 2161 just after the Alliance bought jump technology. "The ultimate war machine" according to the EA press releases, the Starfury Aries was projected to begin active fleet service in 2171.

time were no match for the Koulani forces, and it was only by good fortune that the outpost survived until the Koulani ambassador and the EA Senate reached an agreement (one that included the permanent deactivation of the beacon between the two systems).

The following year, another neighboring race, the Ch'lonas, set their sights on the Alliance. Unlike the Koulani, however, they saw humanity not as a threat, but as prey. In January 2170, the EA discovered a system they named Leonis, a unique system in that it was both rich in Quantium-40 (the mineral essential in jump gate technology) and had two suitable candidates for colonies. The Ch'lonas, a race more interested in taking things than exploring to find them, wanted to take the system resources for their own. The young human race's defeat at the hands of the Koulani was a well-known secret among diplomatic circles, and the Ch'lonas smelled an easy victory. Unknown to the Ch'lonas, however, the Koulani battle prompted the Alliance to accelerate its starfury program, and production on the Aries had already begun.

In May of 2170, the Ch'lonas attacked, going for the settlement on Leonis IV. The Alliance, not surprised at the attack on the Q-40 rich system, had the carrier *Avenger* on patrol in the system with a full complement of fighters including three squadrons each of the new Starfuries. The superior maneuverability of the 'fury changed the battle from a rout to an even fight, and the Ch'lonas were forced to retreat when the destroyers *Merrimac* and *Lincoln* arrived a few hours later.

The Fleet Takes Shape

With the addition of the starfury to its forces, the EA fleet began to grow rapidly. The continual rumors of rebellion among the Centauri subject worlds as well as the threat of attack from other races made the defense of Earth and her territories one of the most important things in the Earth Government's budget. Funding the construction of new destroyers and carriers was relatively easy, and by the turn of the century the Alliance had one of the most formidable fleets in the region.

The Earth Alliance Becomes a Power

When the EA learned the secrets of interstellar travel, it learned of the alien community and the long history of the Centauri aggression in this region of space, although the Centauri had never been aggressive toward the human race. The rise of the Narns and the weakening of the Centauri Republic in the early 2200's triggered the formation of the League of Non-Aligned Worlds. Since the League was a group designed to protect the smaller races from the larger powers in the region, they only invited less powerful races into their ranks. Although the Narns were invited to join the League, they refused, expanding in only a few years to take over many of the old Centauri worlds and becoming a major power.

By this time the Earth Alliance had fourteen colonies and seven outpost worlds and a fleet rivaling the fading Centauri war machine, making them far too large a race for the League to consider. This de facto recognition of the Alliance's status as a power was ignored by the Centauri and rapidly growing Narn, neither of whom wanted to acknowledge the young race as a threat. Soon, however, the stage would be set for the young human race to assert its power.

One of the older races far enough away from the Centauri Republic to be ignored by the League during its formation was the Dilgar. In late 2229, the secretive race inexplicably began taking over worlds from their neighbors, expanding their empire into space already settled by others. This aggression was unforeseen and unwelcome, and the League tried unsuccessfully to fight back, but the combination of ships that had never fought together before, along with the different styles of command left the League forces largely powerless against the well-prepared Dilgar. The League asked for aid from the Centauri, the Narns and even the Minbari, but no help was forthcoming. Finally, in desperation they asked the young Alliance for help. The EA tried to negotiate with the Dilgar to no avail, and finally, realizing that the Dilgar would not stop unless defeated, declared war on them in March of 2231. With the fleet power of the Alliance and the newest Starfury Nova, as well as the unified command of the well-oiled

to watch events rather than use their technology to force others to obey them, the Minbari leaders had become aware of the existence of the Earth Alliance some time before the Dilgar War, but had dismissed humans as just another League race. In the aftermath of the War, however, some among the Minbari realized that this new race was more than that. While most Minbari continued about their business, a few watched the Alliance.

By 2245, the Alliance had eclipsed the Centauri as the dominant race in this area of the galaxy, with a fleet rivaling any of the other younger races, led by the powerful *Hyperion*-class cruisers and *Nova*-class dreadnoughts, along with the effective Starfury *Nova* and *Aurora* models. The fleet was the first line of defense from aggression against the Earth Alliance and the best deterrent to aggression against her allies.

In addition to its support of the League during the Dilgar War, the Alliance had become a mediator in differences among League worlds. Orion VII became home to many of these efforts, and a number of peace treaties were negotiated there, including the Brakiri-Markab Pact of 2237, the Gaim Non-Aggression Treaty of 2240 and the Ch'lonas Agreement of 2243.

The Minbari, cautious around new races, had made no overture toward the humans, preferring to remain apart and watch. To most humans, the Minbari seemed a myth, no more than the alien version of the boogey-man. The popular rumors said that they were a powerful old race of watchers who roamed the galaxy in giant ships wielding the power to destroy entire planets. But those within the upper ranks of the Alliance knew better, and gathered what little information the could on the Minbari.

The Minbari had barely begun to learn about the humans, and vice versa, when the two races met by accident. Had the meeting been a formal one, the two races might have been friends. But it was not, and because of it, the greatest tragedy in human history occurred.

The Earth Alliance Battle Group *Demosthenes* was on exploratory patrol in a new system near the Vega colony when the meeting occurred. Consisting of the

EA war machine, the League-EA forces were able to drive the Dilgar back and win the war.

With its success in war over a hostile race with higher technology, the EA could no longer be ignored. The Centauri and the Narns, as well as the League, all recognized the Alliance as a major power, and humanity truly took its place among the stars.

The Watchers and the War

The establishment of Earth as a major power in this area of the galaxy prompted a number of changes in the Alliance's relations with other races. Ambassadors from more races began to arrive at the diplomatic centers on Orion VII and Ganymede. Word of humanity's existence and accomplishments spread all through the known galaxy.

Among its highest council, the Minbari also began to take notice of this new race of humans. An older race that was content

Hyperion-class cruisers *Amundsen* and *Hyperion* led by the *Nova*-class dreadnought *Prometheus*, the group was assigned to look for signs of Minbari activity in nearby systems and determine whether the unknown race had any hostile intentions toward Humanity. Skirting Minbari space, they were to make long-range scans of suspected Minbari systems and determine where their forces were deployed.

The battle group jumped into a system designated Gamma Omega (later claimed by the Minbari and called *Drala Toth*) on July 12, 2245—a day, as the saying goes, that would live in infamy. As they jumped into the system, they detected several unfamiliar alien ships at the edge of their scanner range, well outside known Minbari borders. Their scanners having problems locking onto the ships, the group moved closer, drawing the notice of the Minbari.

Diverted from their mission, the Minbari cruisers changed course to meet the EA vessels, approaching with gun ports open in a gesture of respect, as was their custom. Blinded by the powerful electromagnetic charges from the Minbari scanners, the EA ships took the gesture as a hostile action, and opened fire.

The Minbari were not ready to start a fight, but it didn't take them long to respond when provoked. Humanity would not learn until much later that in those precious first seconds before the Minbari could respond, the EA's initial barrages disabled the lead Minbari ship and damaged one of the others, killing the leader of the Grey Council, Dukhat, and several others in the Council. Once they could return fire, the volleys from the Minbari vessels, even in their damaged state, were fierce. The *Hyperion* was heavily damaged and the *Amundsen* disabled by the first barrage. The second finished off the *Amundsen*, and damaged the *Prometheus*. The tide of battle changed in mere moments.

The *Hyperion* began laying down immediate covering fire for the *Prometheus* as they retreated, while the Minbari response continued. As soon as they were able to, the battered Earth ships opened a jump point and fled. In a matter of minutes, the battle was over. Both sides had lost ships, and each thought that it was due to the ag-

gressiveness of the other. It was the beginning of the fiercest war the younger races had ever seen, and the costliest humankind had ever fought.

The Earth-Minbari War

The undamaged Minbari escort ship from the EA attack located the frequencies for the human hyperspace beacons and two days later was able to follow it back to human space, attacking the Vega colony the week after the initial battle. It destroyed the small fleet that it encountered at Vega, but word had gotten back to EA command, and the war was on. The Minbari had done likewise, and had become a race intent on destroying those who had killed its leader.

Neither race had been prepared to fight, but both were now committed to the course of history. From the outset, the war was one-sided. The Minbari ships carried superior firepower and maneuverability, as well as having electronic countermeasures so far

The Evolution of the Starfury

The Starfury Aries was a very good idea. Its maneuverability gave it a better advantage than the designers had anticipated, and its effect on the battle with the Ch'lonas was seen as a great success. However, within the first few months of use, it became clear that the design was not durable. The wings experienced an incredible amount of shear, and were prone to cracking in combat or during maneuvers, and the cockpit was too far back, giving poorer visibility than pilots preferred. By 2180, the next model of the Starfury, the Fox, was in production, sporting a split wing that greatly reduced stress on the ship and featuring more forward visibility.

The Starfury Fox proved to be a good design that became the prevalent fighter for the next two decades, but it was still more limited than the engineers preferred. Back at the drawing board, they were beginning to design newer, better heavy warships, and as they did, they also designed a better Starfury.

The result was the Tiger, a new concept. Instead of aligning the engines horizontally, the maneuvering engines were aligned vertically, giving it the familiar X-shaped pattern seen in later models. With the engines out of view, the pilots could see and react much more quickly, and with the cockpit more open, an ejection mechanism was possible in case the ship was damaged but not destroyed. Introduced in 2203, it replaced the Fox as fast as production allowed.

The Tiger was the primary fighter for the Alliance all the way into the Dilgar War. By then, advances in technology had made it possible to remove the two primary-thrust engines from the design and make the four outer engines accelerate the ship. This resulted in a more fuel-efficient ship with slightly better maneuverability, and right before the Dilgar War the Starfury Nova was introduced. During the war, several ships used squadrons of Novas, but most were still the older Tiger model. Full scale production of the Nova resumed after the war, and the Tigers were slowly phased out.

The newest model of the Starfury in production is the Aurora. While physically very similar to the Nova, its internal technology is a generation beyond, with twice the acceleration and maneuverability, as well as twice the fuel capacity and better weapon control. It was introduced in 2244, shortly before the Minbari War, and is now the primary fighter in the fleet.

The two-seat Badger model is projected to make its appearance in the fleet in 2255. This long range fighter will allow EA ships to extend their range of protection with fighters that can travel a jump ahead of the ship without requiring refueling, as well as giving the Alliance a better reconnaissance craft.

Finally, the EA's newest Starfury project, only just entering the modeling and prototype phases, is the Thunderbolt. Like the Badger, the Thunderbolt will seat two crewmembers, and will primarily be long range. In a first for the Starfury program, however, the Thunderbolt will include mobile control surfaces that will allow it to maneuver in atmospheric environments.

AURORA

superior to humanity's as to make their ships invisible. The EA, forced to use holding measures and stalling tactics, fell back at terrible cost as the Minbari advanced. The pattern never changed during the course of the war: the Minbari were the hunters and the Humans the hunted.

The war began in earnest at Signet. Warned of aggression this time, the Alliance was able to hold the system against the Minbari for almost two months using guerrilla stalling tactics. It wasn't until a large Minbari task force arrived in October of 2245 that the attackers took the system.

During the Signet siege, civilians and other personnel were being evacuated from the Delphi IV Colony through Signet, the only safe route from that colony to the rest of the Alliance. Losses were heavy, but over sixty percent of Delphi's population eventually made it to safety.

When the Minbari attack force arrived, the bulk of the Alliance forces retreated, leaving a small diversionary force behind. The beacon between Signet and Cooke was deactivated, and the diversionary fleet retreated to Delphi IV, leading the Minbari away from Earth. The diversion worked, as the Minbari had little knowledge of EA space. The invaders were drawn into a dead end, giving the Alliance precious time.

The Minbari rediscovered Alliance space just after New Year's in 2246, launching an assault on Berlin II. Desperate measures allowed the EA to evacuate some of the civilians from the area, but the Minbari were ruthless. Within weeks Berlin, Myoto and Canton fell. Delaying tactics on New London bought barely enough time for the Alliance to get reinforcements out to Dakota. When New London fell in February of 2246 there was a fleet waiting at Dakota to meet the Minbari charge.

The initial assault at Dakota was the only victory the Alliance attained during the war. The Minbari had been sending small scout fleets into the Dakota system taking out EA patrols during the last two weeks of the Berlin assault. Rumors of an "ace cruiser" stalking the area had been reported to EA Command, and the Battle Group *Independence* was dispatched to investigate, headed up by the *Nova*—class dreadnought *Lexington*.

With contact from New London cut off, the Alliance fleet had no way of knowing that it had fallen and that the Minbari were about to begin their first assault on Dakota. Lured into an ambush, the *Lexington* and her escorts were the first targets of the advance Minbari task force, led by the flagship cruiser *Drala Fi*. Caught by surprise, the battle group was all but destroyed, with the exception of the *Lexington*, which was able to escape to a nearby asteroid field.

Her captain killed, badly damaged herself, the apparently dead *Lexington* was ignored by the Minbari fleet while it completed its annihilation of the remainder of the *Independence* group. Rather than sit by and wait while the Minbari took more Human lives, the XO mined the nearby asteroids with the nuclear warheads that *Nova*

—class ships were being armed with because of the war. Since the powerful weapons could not be aimed at a Minbari ship, the *Lexington* planned to bring the Minbari near the warheads.

The ship sent out a distress call, alerting the Minbari that it was still alive. The *Drala Fi*, being the closest ship, closed for the kill. When the cruiser was close enough, the *Lexington* detonated its warheads, destroying the *Drala Fi* and scoring Earth's first real victory against the Minbari. With no clear command structure, the remaining Minbari cruisers retreated to hyperspace to receive new orders.

Although they suffered relatively few casualties, the Minbari had momentarily lost the psychological advantage, and news spread quickly of the embarrassment. For the Alliance, this was the high point of the war and for a moment it seemed that victory might be possible after all.

Then the Minbari came for Dakota in force. The battle was quick and bloody.

Twelve *Nova*—class dreadnoughts and seven *Hyperion*—class heavy cruisers were turned into no more than floating debris in mere hours, and the Alliance was again forced to fight a guerrilla war. Now that the Minbari had reached the EA's inner systems, they could attack on several fronts, following the Human beacons to multiple systems.

The Alliance fought heroically. Although it was clear that resistance was ultimately futile, they made the Minbari fight for every system. Hundreds of thousands of men and women fearlessly marched and flew into the Minbari's path, facing certain death to defend their homes and families, though they knew the fight to be in vain.

Over the next two years the Minbari surgically attacked, whittling away the Alliance. Khandi, Leonis and Ross fell early on, followed by Sirius, Orion and Ceti. Once a colony could put up no further resistance, it was left under Minbari Martial Law and they proceeded to the next system. They were slowly stripping Earth of all her holdings before closing in for the kill. The fight at Wolf was bloody and brutal, its massive shipyards and proximity to Sol providing Earth with more reinforcements quickly. The siege there was the longest of the war, taking seven months and forcing the Minbari to fight them to the last man and woman on the base.

Earth was down to its last defenses. Endgame was near. EA Command received word that the Proxima III Colony and the Beta Durani Colony at Cooke II had fallen. Then Earth lost communication with the Io outpost . There was only one conclusion left.

The Minbari were coming to Earth.

The Battle of the Line

There was no retreat. The Minbari were going to end the war at last, and their fleet was on its way. The Joint Chiefs worked feverishly to pull together all that the Alliance had left. In an all-night planning session, Chairman Mazuk and Admiral Singh, Chief of Fleet Operations, charted the battle. They would hold on a line in Earth orbit. They could not win, but every minute they could hold meant that more civilians could escape to neutral space.

In reserve would be a heavy cruiser squadron led by the *EAS Hornet* backed by a full ten squadrons of starfuries. The 21st EA Cavalry Brigade was sent to Luna to defend the supply stations there.

The main Minbari armada emerged from hyperspace just inside Mars' orbit, and carefully formed up for the attack. Arcing straight for Earth, they met wave after wave of ineffectual human fighters backed by every capital ship the EA fleet could scrounge.

Minbari fighters, disgorged from giant angelfish-shaped cruisers, cut the defending starfuries to shreds. Unable to see the enemy fighters on their sensors, the starfuries went after the larger Minbari ships instead, on suicidal attack runs into the depth of the Minbari fleet. The Earth cruisers engaged, concentrating firepower on just a few enemy ships, hoping to hurt the Minbari fleet badly enough to get breathing room.

It was not enough—that became apparent early in the fight. The *Hornet* and her squadron were sent to stop a flanking maneuver by half a dozen Minbari corvettes. They were overwhelmed and destroyed in less than twenty minutes of fighting. Finally, as the cruisers closed, a flanking squadron of cruisers jumped into battle behind the line, despite the jammers the Alliance had hoped would prevent that. As the powerful Minbari cruisers began firing their weapons, the EA Fleet Command structure simply ceased to exist as ship after ship fought on gallantly but to no avail.

The Line had been destroyed. Earth was open to invasion, or worse. But the Minbari armada waited, amidst the wreckage of the EA fleet. Something was happening.

EA Command received a signal from the Minbari armada. The enemy wanted to talk. Fleet Admiral Mazuk, stunned, barely able to keep the tears from his eyes, opened the relay to discuss Earth's surrender, the president at his side. And then the truly unbelievable happened.

The Minbari fleet offered terms of their own surrender. The unstoppable Minbari were inexplicably admitting defeat. Without any explanation, the most destructive war in Alliance history was over. And

Earthforce was left with a question it has yet to answer:

Why?

Recovery from the War

In the two years since the War, the Alliance has been rebuilding. Restoring the fleet, decimated at the Line, has been a top priority. The remaining *Hyperion*—class cruisers that could be salvaged and repaired were pressed into service defending Alliance borders from opportunistic aliens almost immediately. The shipyards have been hard at work constructing *Hyperion II*—class cruisers, with better weapons systems and maneuverability and *Omega*—class destroyers, based on the *Nova*—class. The *Omegas* are small cities in space complete with rotating sections with positive gravity. In addition, the EA is recruiting heavily to replace the brave men and women lost during the war. While the planetary draft started during the war is over, there is still a massive

---

The Joint Chiefs of Staff BABCOM

The Joint Chiefs of Staff is the council of military advisors to the President of the Earth Alliance. In many ways, they are the final authority on how Earthforce is deployed. The Chiefs were formed in 2172 as Earthforce began to take on its current shape as a true military, and consisted of a Chairman, Vice Chairman, Chief of Fleet Operations and Chief of Ground Operations. In 2221 the post of Chief of Colonial Forces was added as National Guard type colonial fleets and ground troops were called upon more often during border skirmishes with the Narns. Finally, the Director of Military Intelligence was added in 2226. The Chairman of the Joint Chiefs is Fleet Admiral Garik Mazuk, Vice Chairman is Lieutenant General Kelly Ashe, Chief of Fleet Ops is Admiral Jason Ashvin Singh, Chief of Ground Ops is General Jennifer Romano, Chief of Colonial Forces is General Felipe Arturo Ruiz and Director of Military Intelligence is Admiral Lee Hwan Kim. For more information on the Joint Chiefs, see p. 123.

campaign underway to get volunteers to enlist.

The colonies of the Alliance have been rebuilding as well. While the Minbari didn't actively try to destroy property (merely the men and women who lived on that property), much was lost on the eight colonies and outposts attacked in their merciless advance. Rebuilding efforts in those systems were begun a few months after the war ended, but it will be several years before the process is complete.

Diplomatic relations have begun between the Minbari and the other younger races. Although the Centauri and a few of the Non-Aligned Worlds have had contact with the Minbari over time, the older race had long kept its own counsel rather than dealing with younger races. Among other races, the Alliance is now beginning to talk with the Minbari, and some of the differences between the two peoples are being solved. It is hoped that the Babylon Project will aid this effort when Babylon 3 comes online.

The Alliance is recovering. The aftermath of the war with the Minbari still dominates all aspects of human society, but in the end, humanity will endure.

Section 1: Background

In the aftermath of the Minbari War, as Humanity rebuilds its devastated interstellar network, the reaches of Human space are filled with the men and women of the military—of Earthforce. Many are new to service, eager to help reconstruct devastated systems and face down the threats of aliens who would follow the Minbari example. Many more are veterans of the war, some disillusioned, others hopeful, but all grateful that the conflict never set them directly in the path of the onslaught. The potential for Earthforce characters is unlimited.

The Structure of Earthforce

Earthforce is a combined arms force, which includes all elements of a modern military organization in a single command: an interstellar fleet; a ground force that includes atmospheric attack craft and assault

capabilities for almost any environment; an extensive network of military facilities; and full logistics and intelligence capabilities.

Earthforce's primary mandate is the protection of Humanity's holdings from alien threats, and as such its primary em-

Earthforce Rank

As with many of its traditions, the system of rank adopted by Earthforce is an extension of those used by the militaries of Earth's major powers in the twentieth century. Unlike most of those armies, however, Earthforce brings together the traditions of naval, air, and ground forces into a single structure–as well as the rank systems of all of these backgrounds. This can cause some confusion on the surface, but the underlying system is fairly straightforward.

Officer ranks are rated on a scale of 1-10 (preceded by an "O," to distinguish from enlisted ranks), as follows:

Rank	Fleet Officer Title	Ground Forces Officer Title	Fleet	Ground Forces
O1	Ensign	Second Lieutenant		
O2	Fleet Lieutenant	First Lieutenant		
O3	Lieutenant Commander	GF Captain		
O4	Commander	Major		
O5	Fleet Captain	Colonel		
O6	Rear Admiral	Brigadier General		
O7	Vice Admiral	Major General		
O8	Fleet Admiral	Lieutenant General		
O9	Admiral	General		
O10	Admiral of the EA Fleet	General of the EA Ground Forces		

An officer's title is a formality–the rank level is what really counts. Thus, a Fleet Captain outranks a Major, even though a Major outranks a GF Captain. This two-title system can be a little difficult for civilians to decipher, especially since the service branch in which an officer began his or her career determines the titles used for that entire career. The commander of the EAS Praxis, for example, is Colonel Bretagne–she began her career as a Ground Forces Lieutenant, and kept the Ground Forces rank title when she switched to Fleet.

As if that isn't confusing enough, there's also the chain of command. An officer outranks all those beneath his or her position in the chain of command. It's very rare that an officer of low rank will sit higher in the chain of command than one of higher rank—but it's not uncom-

(continues)

phasis is on its interstellar fleet. Ground Forces make up the largest single chunk of Earthforce manpower (by a fairly wide margin), but they rely on the Fleet for mobility and support. In combat they're generally tasked around the Fleet's strategic objectives.

In addition to its military mandate, Earthforce fills a number of civilian and governmental roles in the far reaches of Human space. It runs many stations and outposts. Earthforce maintains law and order in areas where no civilian government has a strong presence. It's personnel man customs stations in EA territory. Earthforce technicians monitor and keep up jump gates and beacon routes. Earthforce officers must often carry out diplomatic missions when civilian officials are not available.

Characters serving in or coming out of Earthforce might hail from either of the main service branches (Fleet or Ground Forces), and might have served in any of hundreds of capacities. They may have been officers, enlisted men or women, or NCOs (non-commissioned officers—sergeants and others of authority who aren't actual officers). Many of these roles are elaborated on in this chapter—but before these roles can best be understood, one has to understand Earthforce's is structure and operation.

The EA Fleet

Earthforce is a huge organization, with over five million officers and soldiers. It's somewhat ironic, though, that of the two major service branches (Fleet and Ground Forces), the one generally thought of as the core of Earthforce—its very image—is by far the smaller. In fact, only about a third of Earthforce's personnel—less than two million people—are actually part of the Earth Alliance Fleet.

Nevertheless, Fleet deserves its image as the heart of Earthforce. The mighty ships of the Earthforce armada—one of the most successful in the galaxy, despite the setback of the Minbari War and Humanity's relative youth as a spacefaring people—are the backbone that supports its far-flung interstellar empire. Without the Fleet, the Earth Alliance could not hold together, let alone face down the many threats that linger at the edge of Human space. And without the Fleet, all of Earthforce's other capabilities would be for naught.

The EA Fleet is composed of capital ships (mostly destroyers and cruisers), ship- and station-based fighter wings, and the support vessels to keep these craft in action. Additionally, the Fleet runs most of the stations, outposts, and other facilities owned or operated by Earthforce.

Fleet's mandate is concerned only with extra-planetary actions—combat against the space forces of aggressive aliens. Fleet ships often transport ground units and support EA Ground Forces operations, providing insystem screening and even orbital fire support for planetary assaults—but Fleet ships and fighters do not actually land or fight alongside Ground Forces troops. There

---

(continued from previous page)

mon for an officer to sit higher in the chain than another officer of equal rank. Furthermore, officers are traditionally promoted not before, but after being assigned to a new, higher position. Thus, an officer in an O4 slot (say, the Executive Officer on a destroyer) might be reassigned to the command of another ship–a job normally held by an O5. That officer's promotion to O5 will follow the reassignment–but for several months, he might still hold the same rank as his second in command.

Like officers, enlisted personnel (generically referred to as "soldiers," regardless of whether they're ground pounders, mechanics, communications specialists, etc.) are ranked on a numbered system. Enlisted ranks run from E1 to E9, and also have separate titles depending on service branch. Unlike officers' titles, however, a soldier that switches service branches does not keep the rank of his or her original branch, but switches to the title of the new branch.

Rank	Fleet Enlisted Title	Ground Forces Enlisted Title
E1	Crewman	Private
E2	Crewman First Class	Private First Class
E3	Petty Officer Third Class	Corporal
E4	Petty Officer Second Class	Sergeant
E5	Petty Officer First Class	Staff Sergeant
E6	Chief Petty Officer	Sergeant First Class
E7	Senior Chief Petty Officer	Master Sergeant
E8	Master Chief Petty Officer	Sergeant Major
E9	Command Chief Petty Officer	Command Sergeant Major

There is a third, much less commonly-encountered rank scale: Warrant Officers. Warrant Officers are generally personnel with specific, important technical skills but no command authority; or they are civilian contractors attached to Earthforce stations or colonies who need a military rank but don't fit into the conventional chain of command. Warrant Officers are considered officers in terms of military courtesy–they outrank enlisted personnel but are outranked by officers. However, they may only command those enlisted personnel directly assigned to them and are immune to the authority of officers not directly in their chain of command. Because of their unique status, Warrant Officers are not specifically assigned to Ground Forces or Fleet, but wear the uniform of the service branch they happen to be attached to at a given time.

Rank	Warrant Officer Title
W1	Warrant Officer Second Class
W2	Warrant Officer First Class
W3	Chief Warrant Officer
W4	Senior Chief Warrant Officer

is some debate over the development of an semi-atmospheric fighter for deployment in the EA Fleet—if such a class of craft is brought back into Earthforce service, Fleet may find itself more closely involved in Ground Forces actions.

The issue of direct involvement in planetary actions aside, the truth is that the Ground Forces make few moves without Fleet. Although Ground Forces transports, like most spacecraft, can travel the beacons of hyperspace between systems, those slow, lightly armed transport vessels are extremely vulnerable to attack in transit and during landing operations. Without Fleet ships and fighters at their backs, no Ground Forces operation can expect to succeed against a serious defense.

Earthforce bases its fleet units around ships, fighter wings, and facilities. A typical capital ship—say, a *Hyperion*-class cruiser—is manned by around 250 personnel, including about twenty officers. Such a ship is captained by a commanding of-

ficer (or "CO") of O5 rank, assisted by an executive officer ("XO," the second in command) of O4 rank. Department heads, such as the chief engineer, chief medical officer, and tactical officer, are generally O3 or O4 in rank. Most Earthforce capital ships carry one or more squadrons of fighters, each of which has its own CO and XO, usually O4 and O3 in rank, respectively. Although fighter units attached to capital ships are under the nominal command of the ship's CO, their true chain of command extends up through their wing commanders back at their home stations.

Individual ships are organized into battle groups, which can vary in size, but generally include at least ten (and often as many as twenty-five) capital ships along with a like number of support vessels. Battle groups are headed by a battle group commander (generally an O7) who, along with his or her staff and executive officer, takes up offices on one ship within the battle group. This ship is the centerpiece of the battle group, usually its largest vessel, and is termed the flagship. Battle groups do not always operate as a whole—individual ships or small groups are often tasked to missions that separate them from the rest of the group. A small group on such a mission is often called a task force, though that is merely a designation—the term doesn't signify a formal unit or command structure.

Earth Alliance stations, outposts, and other facilities vary greatly in size, from a few dozen personnel to tens of thousands. Some Earthforce-run stations have large civilian populations, and many serve as bases for sizable Ground Forces contingents as well. Almost all Earthforce facilities are actually run by Fleet, though, no matter who uses them. Sometimes Fleet personnel make up all of an outpost's inhabitants, and sometimes they're just a small percentage. So overall, the size of the Fleet presence at a given facility can vary quite a bit, and isn't necessarily related to the overall size of the population.

Like a ship, a Fleet facility command is headed up by a CO and an XO, along with a number of department heads. Most facility commanders are O3 through O6, with XOs typically one rank below that of their commanders. Fighter squadrons assigned to a facility are headed up by their own COs and

XOs, who are commanded by the facility CO but ultimately answer to their wing commanders, which may be based elsewhere if only one or two squadrons are assigned to the facility.

Fighter wings consist of several squadrons—usually six. Every wing has a permanent base—generally a major station—where full-scale command and maintenance facilities are kept. Though the wing is headquartered at this permanent location, squadrons may be indefinitely assigned to far-flung ships and outposts. The wing's CO (typically an O5) is ultimately in charge of these squadrons but operational command lies with the squadron commanders and the commanders of the ships and stations to which they are attached.

The highest unit level in the EA Fleet, and the one that brings all of these elements together, is the Command. Like a Ground Forces division (discussed below), a Command is a complete, largely self-sufficient military unit that contains all the combat, logistics, support and maintenance elements necessary to meet its day-to-day operating requirements. Commands are generally regional, covering perhaps three or four systems, and include all stations, fighter wings, and battle groups based within that area, as well as the local defenses, local law enforcement units, and jumpgates within the Command's jurisdiction. It's not uncommon for one Command to encompass three battle groups, fifteen fighter wings, ten or twelve distinct facilities, and scores of local patrol craft and law enforcement vessels. Command COs rank O6 through O9, based on the importance and size of the given command, which might include up to 200,000 officers and enlisted personnel.

The EA Ground Forces

Informally, they're often called GROPOS, a contraction of the phrase "ground pounders." That term is interchangeable with "marines," which stems—fairly accurately—from the similarity of their military role to that of traditional planetary marines. Neither term is technically correct: they're officially known as the Earth Alliance Ground Forces. GROPOS, marines, Ground Forces,

grunts—whatever the terminology, they're the soldiers and airmen tasked with the hands-on combat of planetary and boarding operations. And despite the primacy always accorded to the Fleet, it's the GROPOS who take and hold ground, who ultimately grasp and defend the Earth Alliance's critical objectives face-to-face and toe-to-toe with the enemies of Humanity.

The Ground Forces are a complete combined arms organization. It includes not just infantry soldiers, but also the transports and breaching pods used to get them into the action, the armor and air forces that fight alongside them, the artillery and support fire units that back them up, and the ground and aquatic transports that maneuver them on the battlefield. In short, the Ground Forces encompass practically every element of a planetary military—and then some.

GROPOS fight in an unending array of environments, and any given unit is trained and equipped for a startling variety of operations. Not only are planetary operations

wildly diverse—varying from airless, icy moons to lush, alien tropical jungles—but marines must also be able to board and take hostile ships and stations, of potentially unknown design and structure, with unpredictable defenses and even low-pressure or poisonous atmospheres. Many GROPOS units specialize in one type of combat condition or another, but all units are capable of some degree of operation in almost any environment.

The smallest operational Ground Forces unit is the platoon—about thirty-five soldiers, along with (usually) a medic, a communications specialist, a Platoon Sergeant (an E6), and a Platoon Leader (an O1). An infantry platoon is broken down into three squads, each of about ten soldiers and headed by a Squad Leader (an E5). In addition, the platoon may have a special weapons section or other special-purpose element attached. As a combat unit, the platoon always acts as a single operational entity—that is, it never splits up into different tasks. Individual squads, however, may handle different parts of a given task individually. For instance, one squad might flank around an enemy position while other squads assault it.

The platoon organization extends to non-infantry units as well, with roughly the same degree of firepower or personnel making up each platoon. For example, an armor platoon consists of four vehicles, each of which is more or less equivalent to a squad of infantry. Air units are organized into flights, which are the equivalent of ground platoons. An air cavalry flight, for instance, consists of four attack craft.

Whatever the unit type, several platoons or flights—usually four—make up a company. Besides its platoons, a company often has several heavy weapons or other special-purpose elements attached. It is headed up by a company commander (an O3, often called, as in the Fleet, the CO), an executive officer (the second in command, an O2, called the XO), and a first sergeant (an E7). It also has a quartermaster section, headed by a supply sergeant (an E5 or E6) assisted by armorers, mechanics, technicians, or other personnel appropriate to the unit type. An infantry company generally totals around 200 soldiers and officers.

Half a dozen companies, give or take, form a battalion. Like a company, a battalion includes separate support elements (generally larger or heavier elements that a company couldn't support), like specialized weapons platoons, medical sections, and supply and repair units. A battalion also includes its own administrative, intelligence, and training personnel, who disseminate information and coordinate programs with higher command. Battalions are headed by COs, XOs, and sergeants major (O5s, O4s, and E8s, respectively), with the typical infantry battalion totaling around 1500 soldiers and officers.

The next step up is the division, which is generally made up of a dozen or so battalions along with many smaller, specialized elements. At the division level, the unit is generally pretty well rounded. A typical infantry division, for example, includes air cav, armor, transportation, engineering, and support fire battalions in addition to its core infantry battalions, along with intel units, military police sections, medical and surgical companies, and a quartermaster network. A division is more-or-less self-sufficient, not relying on any other unit to repair its equipment, arrange for logistics, or provide for other day-to-day needs. Of course, different divisions have their own strengths and weaknesses, and are generally tasked to support each other or even lend units to one another as needed for a particular operation. A typical Ground Forces division is headed by a commanding general (an O7 or O8) and totals 25,000 or 30,000 soldiers and officers, about half of which are actual combatants.

Military Life

Service in Earthforce is a job, a career, and a lifestyle. Few who haven't experienced it really understand what it means to serve in the Force.

Joining Up

Earthforce is an all-volunteer service, meaning that the Earth Alliance doesn't rely on a draft or conscription to fill its ranks. Only during the Minbari war was Earthforce forced to enact a planetary draft to be able to recruit enough troops to keep its growing units up to strength.

New recruits join Earthforce by contacting any of the thousands of recruiting offices located in cities and towns across Earth, and on every sizable colony in Hu-

man space. New enlistees choose their service branch (Fleet or Ground Forces) and their primary "military occupation specialty"—that is, the general field in which they'll be trained and assigned, be it in ship's engineering, transport piloting, combat medicine, etc. They do not generally get to choose their unit, duty station, or other aspects of their eventual assignment. After they complete their induction training, new soldiers are assigned to their posts as Earthforce sees fit. Recruits that meet high educational and testing standards can choose to launch their careers in the officer corps.

The basic Earthforce enlistment period is nine years. Most soldiers don't want to commit to such a lengthy period, though, and choose three- or six-year enlistments

The Rank and File

BAB/COM

Earthforce in the 2250s is composed of a unique blend of personnel–hundreds of thousands of hardened veterans of the Minbari war, along with an equally large influx of starry-eyed new recruits. At the end of the Minbari war, the EA Senate voted to allow any serving member of Earthforce to resign or take indefinite leave from service. It was a controversial decision, as a dramatically depleted Earthforce was desperate for personnel and materiel by the cessation of hostilities. But the Senate felt that it was a fitting reward to those who served, thousands of whom enlisted, or were drafted, in the last, desperate months of the war. It was a popular decision both in Earthforce and among Alliance citizenry at large, and many Earthforce soldiers left service after the war.

In the time since the war ended, Earthforce has aggressively sought to rebuild both its manpower and its materiel. The threat posed by aggressive aliens that might sweep in on Humanity's weakened empire was a central theme in heavy recruitment efforts, along with those of patriotism, adventure, and rebuilding. The efforts were quite successful, with hundreds of thousands of new enlistees, many of whom were too young to participate in the Minbari war, flooding into Earthforce ranks. With almost no middle ground, most Earthforce units are now an almost equal mix of war veterans and newbies, working together to rebuild Earthforce and the Alliance.

instead. Earthforce often offers incentives to recruits who choose the full nine year enlistment, however, such as preferential duty assignments and special educational benefits. Those that do elect a shorter enlistment are placed on an inactive reserve list after they leave service, and can technically be called back to active duty at any time up to nine years after their initial enlistment. Once that nine-year period is up, though, regardless of whether the soldier spent the entire time on active duty, he or she cannot be made to serve again even if the draft is reinstated. Involuntary calls back to active duty are extremely rare.

All soldiers have the option of re-enlisting once their initial commitment is up. Re-enlistment terms are three-year blocks.

Induction Training

The first step in any soldier's career is induction training. For enlisted personnel,

this consists of Basic Training followed by Specialty Training. For officers, it's Officer Candidacy School followed by Pre-Flight School (for Fleet officers) or Ground Combat School (for Ground Forces Officers).

Basic Training is a ten-week course that teaches not only fundamental combat skills, but also instills physical fitness, military discipline, camaraderie, and the strength of character necessary to stand up to the rigors of military life and combat. Recruits from all backgrounds, social strata, and nationalities are thrown together to face weeks of eighteen-hour training days, intense physical challenges, and harrowing levels of mental stress. They learn respect for their superiors, reliance upon one another, and the breadth of their own personal limits.

Upon graduation from Basic, recruits become soldiers. They're still not ready to move on to duty stations, however. Every soldier has a military occupation specialty, in which he or she must be trained at a Specialty Training school. Infantry soldiers move on to more advanced training in weapons, boarding operations, ground tactics, and hostile environment actions. Medics go to the Combat Medic course; support fire crews to the Artillery School; ship technicians to the Electronics or EVA schools. There are dozens of Specialty Training courses, taking anywhere from a few weeks to more than eighteen months to complete, depending on the complexity of the specialty. Once a soldier has completed Specialty Training, his or her career truly kicks off with the first duty station assignment.

The process is more or less the same for officers. After passing through a stiff screening process, enlistees are sent to Officer Candidacy School, a twelve-week program much like a souped-up version of Basic. OCS is generally said to be the toughest course Earthforce imposes on its personnel (with the possible exception of the Special Operation Hostile Environment Survival School) and graduates are well suited for command duties. Those that make it through the program are granted their commission and become officers; those that fall out of OCS are given the option of discharge from Earthforce, or an enlisted career.

A select minority of prospective officers are admitted into the Earthforce Academy for their university education. Some attend other accredited military universities or officer training programs at other colleges. Those that graduate from such programs go on to get their commission without having to attend OCS.

Either way, once commissioned, officers go on to Pre-Flight or Ground Combat School. Unlike enlisted Specialty Training schools, these courses don't cover specific tasks, but instead focus on the rigors of command and the vast but general technical and tactical knowledge required of officers. For their own specialties, officers initially rely on their pre-enlistment education combined with early on-the-job training and experience. Over the course of their first duty assignments, however, many officers attend schools for specialized training.

Life on the Job

A new soldier or officer at his or her first duty station quickly adjusts to the unique lifestyle of Earthforce. There are many differences between life as a civilian and life as a soldier.

The daily routine of most soldiers or officers is not so different from that of a civilian. The work day begins at around 8:00 in the morning, and ends at around 5:00 in the evening. Time is spent maintaining equipment, handling paperwork, training with simulators or in classes, or carrying out whatever duties are part of the soldier's day-to-day responsibilities.

That's not to say that there are no routine differences between military and civilian lives. Many civilians spend an hour every few days at the gym; most Earthforce soldiers must attend strenuous unit Physical Training (PT) workouts four or five times a week. Civilian jobs may or may not entail a dress code; Earthforce personnel go to work every day in uniform. Civilians set their own personal standards; soldiers undergo monthly or quarterly physical fitness tests, regular inspections of quarters, work places, equipment, and person, and frequent performance reviews that scrutinize conduct and bearing as well professional output.

On top of that, military units drill. Ships and battle groups go on cruises, often for months at a time. Ground units conduct exercises, spending weeks in the field. These excursions take the Earthforce soldier away from the daily routine, and away from home, family, and friends outside of the unit. And they're trying—shipboard life is compact and difficult, with few recreational options, while ground exercises take the soldier away from the comforts of civilization, including showers, beds, and hot meals.

Time spent on cruise or exercise can take a soldier away from home for as much as three or four months out of the year. But even home isn't always what a civilian expects. Although Earthforce personnel are welcome to find their own housing at their home station, most live in Earthforce quarters, eat at Earthforce dining halls, shop at Earthforce PXs, and entertain themselves at Earthforce clubs. These facilities have a lot in common with their civilian counterparts, and a lot that set them apart.

Enlisted barracks are a lot like college dormitories. Soldiers live two, sometimes four to a room in relative comfort, with all the typical amenities of home. NCOs generally rate single rooms. Officers' quarters are mostly the same, although a bit more spacious and well appointed. Senior officers rate suites or small apartments. On stations or in colonies, quarters are also provided for both enlisted personnel and officers with families. They vary in size and quality based on the location and the seniority of the personnel for whom they are intended.

Stations, colonies, and even large outposts and ships feature a variety of support facilities, from post offices and PXs to bowling allies, community centers, and Officer, NCO, and Enlisted Clubs.

Pay

Nobody enlists in Earthforce to get rich, but service can provide a decent living. Military personnel are paid monthly, and pay is based on both rank and overall time in service: enlisted pay rates begin about 800 EAcr a month for a new recruit, and run up to about 3,000 EAcr a month for an

E8 with twenty years' under his belt. Officers make a bit more: from 1,200 EAcr per month for a new O1 to over 4,500 EAcr for a crusty old General.

That's just base pay—there are a lot of modifiers. The military provides housing, but those that choose to live off-base are allotted a stipend to help pay the rent or mortgage—100 EAcr to 250 EAcr a month is typical, depending on rank and time in service. Food and uniforms, on the other hand, are not provided for free, and costs of up to 100 EAcr per month are sometimes deducted from paychecks. Soldiers supporting families can draw dependent's pay, which can add up to several hundred EAcr per month, again depending on rank and time of service. And then there's hazardous duty or combat pay, a monthly bonus of around 120 EAcr given to soldiers in certain situations during peacetime.

Roles in Earthforce

Earthforce characters or NPCs can come from an extensive variety of backgrounds, with a wide variety of experience and skills. A handful of typical backgrounds are discussed here, as a basis for Earthforce character ideas and for fleshing out such characters.

Character Rank

Player characters or NPCs in or recently discharged from military service can hold virtually any rank, enlisted or officer (see the sidebar on page 16 for rank levels and titles). The first decision to make when picking a character's rank is, of course, whether the character is (or was, at discharge) enlisted or an officer (non-commissioned officers like sergeants and petty officers are enlisted personnel). This distinction is based on the nature of the character's service: those who command units or major functions on ships or facilities are officers, of course, as are most individuals whose tasks are highly specialized, or incur a great deal of responsibility, like pilots and doctors. Those who carry out their tasks hands-on, whether combat or support personnel, and those who directly supervise them, are generally enlisted personnel. As a rule of thumb, enlisted personnel outnumber officers by around thirty to one in the Ground Forces, and fifteen to one in the Fleet.

The level of rank appropriate to a character depends on time in service and the nature of his or her responsibilities. The average grunt or ship crewman is an E2 (most recruits are promoted out of E1 rank within their first few months of service). A good soldier can look forward to promotion to E3—the first non-commissioned officer rank—after three or four years' service. Some soldiers take five or six years for that promotion, but few take longer; anyone who can't be promoted by that time is probably having so much trouble with military life that they leave the service. Many corporals or petty officers third class are given minor supervisor responsibilities, but most are promoted to E3 because their training has given them special skills that complement tasks of some responsibility. Real supervisory responsibility comes at the rank of E4, which might make a soldier a squad leader in the infantry, or a section shift leader aboard ship. As a skilled and ambitious soldier rises through the ranks as a non-commissioned officer, he or she can expect a promotion every two years or so, with corresponding increases in responsibility. Thus, a character who has served in Earthforce for, say, nine years might be an E5. As is often the case for veterans of the catastrophic Minbari war, experience in a unit that has seen combat can hasten the process a bit.

Some enlisted personnel are "raised through the ranks"—that is, they become officers after serving as enlisted personnel. Most officers, however, began service as officers, and there is no direct career path from enlisted service to the officer corps. Like enlisted personnel, officers begin their careers at the lowest rank and level of responsibility, and are promoted over time as their responsibilities increase. An O1 (ensign or second lieutenant) is as low among officers as an E1 is among the rank and file—a fact not lost on the soldiers they command. O1s come into service as inexperienced as any newbie, but are nevertheless faced with the responsibilities of command over a platoon or section. Within a year or two (longer in the Ground Forces), an O1 is promoted to O2 and responsibility over a larger unit or section, including lesser officers. From that point forward, future promotions are based on close assessment by their commanders, recorded in the "fitness reports" so crucial to any officer's career. A flaw on a fitness report can mean being passed over at the next promotional opportunity. Few officers are passed over more than once—any officer who is not seen as worthy of promotion in two tries is not worthy of further service, and is generally pressured to retire. The further one travels up the ranks, the more competitive the promotional process, and many extremely capable officers leave Earthforce in the middle ranks, not because they were bad officers, but simply because they were not the best. Wartime tempers this effect, of course—casualties create openings in the ranks, and the need for competent leaders keeps any capable officer employed. As a peacetime rule of thumb, a good officer can expect promotion about once every three years.

In choosing a rank for a character or NPC, keep the above guidelines in mind. But also think about what the character was doing over the course of his or her service. A character who is a fighter jock, for example, shouldn't be a Fleet Captain, even with fifteen or eighteen years of service under her harness—fighter pilot Captains are squadron or wing commanders, whose responsibilities generally don't let them fly combat missions any longer. They generally manage to get in barely enough hours to keep their flight pay and no more. If you're determined that the character still be an active combat pilot, you'll have to settle for a rank of O3 or O4. Likewise, an infantry machinegunner won't be an E7, no matter what the time in service, just as a station commander won't be an O2.

GROPOS Characters

If, when you think GROPOS, you think grunt—think again. Infantry soldiers do make up the bulk of the Ground Forces, but there is broad variety in the roles of marines—and even more variety in the many other roles that Ground Forces offers. A few potential character backgrounds are presented here—the possibilities beyond these are endless.

Infantry

The stereotypical role for the GROPOS soldier is the infantry. The truth is that there are many, many different military occupation specialties—but among Ground Forces combat personnel, the most common by far are the "eleven-echoes"—the grunts.

Infantry soldiers are trained in firearm and hand-to-hand combat, squad and platoon tactics for planetary and boarding operations, and hostile environments.

There are quite a few variations on the infantry soldier. Many soldiers are trained in special weapons, breaching or engineering, battlefield communication, support fire (artillery and the like), anti-air, and a myriad of other specialties. Such specialized soldiers make up a good third of ground combat personnel—but the other two thirds are plain old infantry soldiers.

Medics

If the role of the grunt sounds courageous, think of that of the combat medic. Medics go everywhere the GROPOS go, right into the thick of things—unarmed, or with a light pistol at best. More than that, they're the ones who have to reach, treat, and retrieve the wounded often directly under the fire of an alien enemy who may or may not afford medical personnel the amnesty that a human would. In short, the inoffensive combat medic's task is as harrowing as any in the ground forces.

And he or she has the training to match. Combat medics not only have to have all the basic infantry skills of their combat marine counterparts, but must be well trained at trauma medicine and field surgery as well. Many experienced medics (enlisted personnel all) develop skills that would astonish a head surgeon at a civilian hospital—and beyond that, they practice those skills in the most hostile of environments, not just in extremes of weather, but vacuum and poisonous atmospheres as well.

Field doctors (true physicians and surgeons) are always officers or Warrant Officers, as are nurses. Such personnel, however, practice their medicine from evac ships and field hospitals behind the lines. Only the combat medic spends day in and day out with combat units, right on the front lines.

Military Police

From the earliest days of organized human warfare, soldiers have been trouble not only for the enemy but often for their own people as well. Military life is full of rigors, especially in wartime, and soldiers tend to play as hard as they work. Add to that the fact that a typical GROPOS division boasts the population of a small city, and that even in the 2250s many soldiers enter the military as an alternative to rough neighborhoods and unsavory lives, and you can

see how any sizable marine presence must include some force for law and order. Local police are often underequipped for dealing with a visiting Ground Forces division, and don't always understand the issues that affect GROPOS. Hence the military police, or MPs.

Every infantry division has at least a few companies of military police. These personnel not only try to keep the grunts in line when shore leave invades a station or colony, but are also in charge of managing the network of landing sites, supply centers, field hospitals, transit routes, and command posts that quickly springs up behind the lines of any ground operation. Military police are not technically combat personnel, but are trained in basic infantry skills and often operate very close to the combat lines. Given their need to keep the grunts in line, they're often drawn from the toughest of the GROPOS.

Pilots

The image of an Earthforce pilot generally conjures a dashing starfury jock, deftly maneuvering through the starry void head-to-head with the sleek, foreboding craft of some hostile alien. But Ground Forces have nearly as many aerospace units as Fleet—and though less dashing, their jobs are often much tougher.

The cream among the Ground Forces fliers are the air cavalry pilots—the jocks that strap into the sixty-ton flying tanks called assault fliers and guide them into the thickest of enemy fire to support the marines on the ground. Whereas a Fleet fighter pilot might measure his success in kills—one here, another there—the air cav flier's trophies are the shredded stabilizers, the perforated wings, the blasted and bullet-holed fuselages that she brings back from every combat sortie.

Of course, not all GROPOS pilots are air cav—the Ground Forces include the atmospheric fighters that keep enemy air power at bay, the breaching pods that weave through intense defensive fire as they deliver marines boarding enemy ships and stations, and the atmospheric transports that plummet from orbit into landing zones hot with enemy fire as the GROPOS commence planetary invasions. Not every job requires the implacable—some would say insane—nerves of an air cav flier, but there's no job for a Ground Forces pilot that doesn't run into harm's way.

Fleet Characters

The Fleet is the heart of Earthforce—when someone thinks of service in Earthforce, they generally imagine life aboard an EA destroyer, cruising the lanes between the stars. In truth, only a small percentage of all Earthforce personnel crew spaceships; the vast majority man EA stations or outposts, or serve in the Ground Forces. Nevertheless, there are many backgrounds for ship crewmen, a few of which are covered here.

Ship's Complement

The life of a ship crewman is an exciting one. Even in peacetime, up to half the year is spent on cruise, drilling and practicing while traveling the beacon routes of hyperspace and putting in at ports of call in both human and alien systems. Shipboard life is harrowing and claustrophobic, but for those that can take it, it's an adventure not to be missed.

The Fleet crewman can take up any of hundreds of roles, from engineering and maintenance, to weapons and ordnance, to fighter support, communications, medical staff, supply, and on and on. Every task is a skilled, technical role with associated responsibility—there is no grunt-work aboard ship, and there can be no weak links.

Not all Fleet crewmen serve on the huge cruisers and destroyers at the center of the Fleet's battle groups. Every battle group includes support vessels—tenders and transports, for example—and many facilities and systems have small patrol vessels assigned to them that operate locally. The specialties to which crewman are assigned on these ships are about the same sorts of jobs carried out by the crewmen of the major combat vessels.

Flight Officers

Every ship's complement includes officers—the men and women who command the ship and its various functions; who are responsible for the efficiency of the vessel as a combat unit, and for the lives and well-being of the soldiers under their commands. Among the senior officers on every ship is a special class: the CO, the XO, the department heads (usually including the chief engineer, the tactical officer, and the fire control officer), and the bridge officers. These are the ships' flight officers, and their special status is commensurate with their special responsibilities. They are also the ship's decision-makers, the men and women

Captains, Commodores, and Commanding Officers

The title "Captain" often confuses civilians, in that it refers to different ranks in Fleet and Ground Forces. It also has a third use: the common term for a ship's commander. Technically, an EA vessel's commander holds the position of "Commanding Officer," or CO. That's the title given to the commander of any unit, but there are several unofficial or slang terms used specifically for ship commanders: "skipper;" "chief" (for small craft); and "captain" are some of the most common. Calling a ship's CO "captain" isn't likely to get a soldier into trouble, but when used that way the term should never be confused with a rank title. A vessel's CO might in fact be a Fleet Captain (O5 is the common rank for the COs of capital warships)–but he or she might also be a Lieutenant Commander, or even a Major.

Another term often mistaken by civilians for a rank is "commodore." Technically, there is no such title or position, but the term still has meaning in the military. When the CO of one vessel is aboard another, he or she is traditionally called commodore, to recognize his or her position while differentiating from the host ship's CO. Also, the commander of a task force or battle group is sometimes also referred to as commodore when aboard a ship commanded by another officer.

with the highest degree of accountability. The errors of lesser officers lead to inefficiencies and difficulties; a single mistake by a flight officer can end a career at the least, or kill a ship and all aboard if made at the wrong moment. Becoming a flight officer is the pinnacle of many Earthforce careers, superseded only by flag command.

The CO and XO are, as mentioned above, the ship's commanding and executive officers, respectively. Other flight officers typically found on a capital ship include the chief engineer, who is responsible for keeping the ship running and for damage control in combat; the tactical officer, who's job it is to monitor the ship's tactical situation, coordinating with other vessels and recommending courses of action to the CO; and the fire control officer, who manages the ship's weaponry and coordinates fire called for by the captain and tactical officer. The chief medical officer, though not part of the decision-making process during combat, is considered a flight officer,

as is the loadmaster on a tender, transport, or other cargo-carrying vessel. The deck officer, a junior officer who supervises the bridge crew, is included among the counsels of the flight officers even though he or she is technically not counted among them, as are the squadron commanders of any fighter units attached to the ship.

Pilots

The starfury pilot is the most visible and appealing symbol of Earthforce—a dashing and attractive emblem of all that is good, strong, bold, and adventuresome. And with good reason—starfury pilots are the cream of the crop, the most highly trained and capable combat personnel in all of Earthforce. True, Earth's fighters were not much in the face of the Minbari onslaught, but the fact that Earthforce's fighter corps has become one of the most respected among the younger races after only a century in interstellar space cannot be chalked up to technological advances alone.

Station Personnel

Most colonies, stations and outposts are run largely, if not completely, by EA-appointed civilian administrations—but many are not. Those that aren't come under the Earth Alliance's direct governance, and most of them are run by Fleet personnel. But not every station crewmember is necessarily with Fleet—some station functions are carried out by Ground Forces; others by private contractors. Even among Fleet personnel, the roles on a station or colony can be quite different from those aboard ship. Some of the many possible character backgrounds are covered here.

Customs Officers

Among the many civilian duties carried out by Earthforce personnel on stations and colonies, customs is one of the most visible and colorful. Customs officers are in charge of immigration (the coming and going of aliens and other non-Alliance citizens), the flow of restricted or dangerous goods, and the proper taxation of interstellar commerce as it pierces the skin of the Human sphere.

In a large and active galaxy, customs can be a challenging task. Many customs officers don't go a day without seeing some item—or even alien—they've never before encountered, and which aren't anywhere in the records. Deciding appropriate tariffs, quarantine periods, or even whether such a thing should be allowed into Human space, rests solely on the customs officer's judgment.

On most Fleet-run facilities, customs officers are Earthforce—although sometimes private, civilian agencies are employed, and sometimes EarthGov actually assigns real customs agents. The background and training of such personnel varies greatly—more than one Fleet officer has found himself assigned to a customs post without the slightest bit of training or preparation for the job!

Medical Personnel

On Earth, a doctor is just a doctor. On the frontier, a doctor is a pioneer, a discoverer, a scientist. In the hostile environments of space, of foreign planets and bizarre climates, all manner of unknown ailments and traumas demand treatment. And then there are the aliens—some like Humans, others dramatically different; some well known to Human xeno-biology, others a complete mystery. Not every medical professional in Earthforce faces these complex and unique challenges on a daily basis, but on the outskirts of Human space, many do. It takes a special kind of doctor to thrive and succeed under these conditions.

Diplomatic Personnel

EarthGov has an official diplomatic corps, with ambassadors and attaches and representatives well trained for the unique difficulties of dealing with alien governments. Unfortunately, not every facility is blessed with such professionals, and on the more remote outposts, an Earthforce officer is often tasked with the job.

Like customs officers, diplomatic personnel often face new and unique challenges on a day-to-day basis, but many receive little or no training to aid them. Even those who are trained must be versatile, though, as each new diplomatic situation is tricky and requires fast thinking that defies all preparation.

Logistics Personnel

It takes a lot to keep the Earthforce machine running—a lot of weapons, a lot of food, a lot of uniforms, office supplies, fuel, spare parts, medical goods—the list goes on and on and on. Who keeps Earthforce in goods? The quartermaster corps—perhaps the single most important organization in Earthforce.

At any given installation, a sizable chunk of Earthforce personnel are somehow involved in logistics. With the unenviable job of making everyone happy—of seeing to all of their basic needs and many of their, well, less basic ones—Earthforce supply officers are often known for making miracles.

Earthforce Intelligence

A military force, no matter how well equipped and trained, is only as good as the information it relies on. Earthforce Intelligence officers are the masters of that information, gathering, managing, and analyzing thousands of facts and bits of data to put together as complete a picture as possible of the forces and situations that Earthforce might have to face.

Earthforce assigns Intelligence Corps personnel to virtually every Alliance facility, whether run by civilian administrations or Earthforce officers. Intelligence officers keep tabs on the activities of alien vessels and personnel (allied and neutral aliens, as well as known enemies), as well as suspected raiders, insurgents, and organized criminals. Information is gathered through electronic means, such as monitoring open com traffic and jump gate activities, through informants, and through reports from law enforcement officials and other administrators. Some of this data is interpreted locally, but most is send back raw to EarthGov for analysis.

Earthforce Intelligence personnel should not be confused with the intelligence officers that are part of every sizable military unit. The latter are members of those units, tasked with disseminating the information provided by the Intelligence Corps to unit leaders. Conventional military officers, they have no training in the detailed analysis of disparate intelligence findings, nor the resources to gather data beyond their own units' actions and those of enemy forces they sight or engage.

Colonial Forces

Earthforce is Humanity's primary military force, but not its only one. Many of the major colonies maintain their own forces in coordination with Earthforce, for local law enforcement and protection when Earthforce isn't around, and as a reserve that can be drawn upon by Earthforce should another major conflict like the Dilgar or Minbari wars arise. Earthforce coordinates closely with the colonial forces on training and equipment, and though the quality of both can tend to lag a bit (especially ships and equipment—as Earthforce aggressively pursues new acquisitions, the colonial forces inherit many of the leftovers), many colonial forces are respectable military powers.

Colonial forces include both Ground and Fleet components, and are usually organized identically to Earthforce (though some ground units vary in training and organization to better fit their planetary situations). Few of the colonies have more than a single division's worth of troops—most have only a few battalions at most—and none can field an entire battle group of ships. Most do not have any capital ships; only patrol craft and transports. What they lack in numbers, training, and equipment, however, the colonial forces make up for in one key element: they know their turf. Colonial planetary units are invariably well equipped and prepared for, and knowledgeable about, the unique environments that they call home. The same is true throughout the system, though the environment in space is rarely as unique as that on the ground. In the face of alien aggression, Earthforce commanders will often defer to

their local counterparts in preparing for the defense of a system.

Colonial forces characters can come from any of the backgrounds mentioned above for Earthforce characters, with little modification.

Section 2: Special Rules for Earthforce Characters

The Earthforce soldier receives some of the best training available in the Alliance. The rules presented in the remainder of this chapter give players and GMs a resource to recreate some of that training in the game.

While some of these rules are specifically tailored to Earthforce characters, players can choose this type of training for their characters even if they are not members of Earthforce. They can be useful to members of other races' militaries or to highly specialized non-military scientific characters.

Areas of Expertise

When creating a well-conceptualized character, a player often has a specific idea of a character's main field of interest that at first glance may seem to require a specific skill not listed in the base rulebook, or a skill that is an amalgam of the skills listed. In many of these cases, the character requires an Area of Expertise.

Rather than a specific skill, an Area of Expertise is a broad field that consists of several skills, all of which are integral to the understanding of that area. Using the skills given in the base rulebook it is possible to create a much broader spectrum of talents than many players may realize at first glance. These areas can come from education, experience and training, and represent a body of learning rather than just one or two skills. To form an Area of Expertise for a character, break the area down into tasks that the character will often perform, assigning a skill to each task that makes up the area. The loose grouping of skills that result are the Area of Expertise. Areas of Expertise are not rigid skill sets that must be chosen, rather they are a way to organize the skills that a given character might have. They are not represented on the Character Record: simply list the skills that make up the Area of Expertise.

At other times during character creation, a character may be well thought out, but the player may not know what types of skills the character should have learned along the way. This is particularly true of characters with a military background who would have received a lot of specific training that a player might not know. The Areas of Expertise listed in this section are representative of the training Earthforce men and women receive and detail some of the more common areas found in those who serve in the military of any race.

Since an Area of Expertise develops over a lifetime, the list below outlines the character creation process for a character within each area. The types of developments suggested are the most common ways that a character might evolve. If a character's background does not quite fit one of the suggestions, either the player or the GM should alter it to more accurately reflect the way that particular character would have grown.

Command

The ability to command consists of more than just good charisma. It requires years of dedication and study before a character will be able to give orders with the authority to have them followed. A character who has this Area of Expertise will likely have built up a strong sense of personal discipline and will often be able to read people well.

In many cases development of this area starts very early in a character's life—perhaps the character was always the kid in the neighborhood who got the other children together and figured out what game to play. Often these characters develop Leadership as a Characteristic (new Skills, Specialties and Characteristics are explained later) during the Childhood stage of character development, as particularly independent or willful children.

During the Development stage in the character's history he or she might be exposed to the art of handling people in a social situation. Perhaps this is through a class in speech or tutelage at a finishing school, but formal training isn't necessary. Some leaders have always been at the center of the social scene. If the character excels at sports, he or she may have been the captain of the team; in fraternal societies, an officer.

The character might also learn Diplomacy as a Skill (with a Specialty of Direction) at this point. As the character progresses in his or her studies, presumably an interest in command surfaces and the character actively begins to pursue this Area of Expertise. One possible route is to enroll in Officer Candidacy School. While in OCS the character is exposed to the theory and art of warfare, learning any or all of the Tactical and Strategy skills. The character might also become exposed to the psychology of the human mind in an attempt to better understand people. Medical: Psychiatry is another Skill which is very useful to the Command area of expertise.

The last part of Command can only be attained through actual experience. Once the character has started to work with subordinates, he or she starts to learn what does and does not work and learns a unique command style. By learning the best way to deal with the people in their command the character becomes a true commander. At this stage of development, Adulthood, the character would learn Acumen or Savvy, and appropriate Specialties.

Logistics

With more than eighteen colonies in over twenty-four systems spread out across distances greater than thirty light years, the Earth Alliance has a tremendous task maintaining good resource management. It is the job of logistics personnel to keep track of the current amount of resources available, the current and projected demand on those resources, the location of the resources, the distribution of the resources, and the quantity of resources being gathered.

This is obviously not a task which can be handled by someone without the proper training, education, and experience. A character will not start to build the foundation needed to become a successful resource manager until the Developmental stage of life, even though an interest in the field may develop during childhood.

The first real introduction that a character has to logistics is usually either seeing or participating in the management of a business, often as a teenager with his or her first job. The character might learn the Business skill (Specialty of Management). Later on as the character learns more responsibility on the job, he or she might study administration more in depth, learning to apply management to more than just businesses and money. The character might take the Skill Management.

In the Adulthood stage of development, the character might be drafted, or may begin to look for a place of work. Given the size of the military and the number of Earth Alliance colonies, military logistics offers a huge field of work. Characters who enter the military will find a well-organized logistics system that will allow them to advance according to their abilities.

During their employment in the military, logistics personnel need to have at least a basic understanding of fleet and troop movements to know what supplies to send where. As a result of this the character might learn Geography (Specialty of appropriate area). The character might also learn at least one or more of the Strategy and Tactics Skills for the same reason. The final addition to the character's arsenal of skills will be obtained only after endlessly dealing with the people necessary to the completion of the character's job. The character will then have experience with Savvy and Diplomacy with several appropriate Specialties.

Military Doctrine

Advancing past a basic understanding of military doctrine is a long and arduous task. Formal military doctrine will not be learned in the Childhood stage of the character's growth. It will start in the Developmental stage where the character begins to study in depth the areas which interest him or her. Military doctrine is so broad that a well-versed character should spend a great deal of time and effort studying all the areas that apply.

More often than not the time devoted to this pursuit will be during attendance at a military school, where the concepts of moral and physical excellence as well as discipline are taught. It is also conceivable that the character research this area of expertise while at a normal civilian school, where a character particularly intrigued with the workings of the military might take every opportunity to study it. Regardless of the situation, during this time the character will learn several of the following skills: History (Specialty in EA Military), Law (Specialty in EF law), and any of the Tactics or Strategy skills. During later years in which the character is actually putting the knowledge from this area of expertise in practice, it would be likely that he or she receive the skill Savvy with an appropriate Specialty.

Skills

The following is a compilation of skills not included in the base rulebook, but common throughout Earthforce and other military institutions. Characters do not necessarily have to be a part of Earthforce to take these skills, but they are more prevalent in characters with some degree of a military background.

This list includes a general description of each skill, as well the most common Attribute with which the skill is used and some Specialties of that skill, using the same format as the base rulebook.

Engineering, Military: This skill represents the knowledge of the creation, maintenance and tear down of equipment and constructs that are necessary to the operation of the military. It also includes the removal of buildings necessary for an enemy's performance. Tasks requiring this Skill are usually based on Intelligence or Insight.

Specialties: Demolitions, Fortification, Entrenchment, Applications (actual raising and lowering of military structures).

Management: This skill represents the knowledge and application of the principals of large-scale administration. This applies to the management of large groups of people, but does not necessarily have to be related to the fiscal management of a business (which is covered by the skill Business and the specialty of Management). Tasks requiring this Skill are usually based on Intelligence or Insight.

Specialties: Organization, Resources, Coordination

Strategy, Ground: This skill spans the knowledge and application of large-scale troop movement. It includes the utilization of combined-arms forces (including naval forces and air support). It is most useful when planning a military campaign, not in the execution of the specific conflicts (Tactics are more appropriate and useful in individual battles). Tasks requiring this Skill are usually based on Insight or Intelligence.

Specialties: Theater, Global, by military doctrine.

Strategy, Space: This represents the understanding and application of large-scale fleet movement. It is useful when planning a military campaign but not necessarily in the execution of specific conflicts. Tasks requiring this Skill are usually based on Insight or Intelligence.

Specialties: Intrasystem, Intersystem, by military doctrine.

Specialties

This is a list of optional Specialties for Skills already existing in base rulebook that are particularly appropriate for military characters. While any character may have learned these Specialties, they are particularly useful for characters with military backgrounds, and will normally only be taken by such characters. As in the base rulebook, this is in no way an exhaustive list of Specialties.

Combat, Ranged: Rocket Launcher (covers all forms of man-portable rocket-propelled explosives), Semi-Automatic.

Diplomacy: Direction (issuing orders in such a manner as to have them followed without question).

Driving: Armored Vehicles (Tanks, APCs, etc.).

Engineering, Aerospace: Payloads (effects of payloads on atmospheric and space flight).

Engineering, Chemical: Weaponry.

Engineering, Electrical: Military Equipment (usually a higher grade and different design than civilian electrical devices).

Engineering, Mechanical: Military Equipment (usually a higher grade and different design than civilian mechanical devices).

Hiding: Ambush (selecting a spot for oneself which lends itself to an ambush), Camouflaging (making something, including people, blend in with the surroundings), Lurking (actually placing yourself where you can't be seen).

History: EA Military

Medical, Biotech: Weaponry.

Savvy: Military Enlisted, Military Commissioned.

Shiphandling: Orbital Station (using thrusters to correct and maintain orbit).

Tactics, Troop: Offensive, Defensive, Covert.

Tactics, Space Combat: Offensive, Defensive, Covert.

Earthforce Martial Arts

Two types of martial arts training are given to Earthforce personnel. While these are not exclusive to Earthforce, they are usually only gained through military training.

Zero Gravity Combat: Perhaps the newest martial art, zero gravity combat was developed only after extensive exposure to space and zero gravity environments. This is a fast art which makes use of the natural confusion and disorientation created by zero gravity. The practitioner of this art will try to move often and erratically, bouncing off surfaces in unexpected manners. This art is useful both for fleeting attacks while soaring past the opponent, and for close in fighting while grappling. Unlike most martial arts, zero gravity combat can be used both bare handed and with small weapons such as knives and clubs. This practice teaches that on and off the battlefield, keeping the enemy guessing, off balance and confused will bring victory.

Specialties: Grapple/Attack, Strafe, Attack/Flee, Pull off Balance

Commando Training: This is the training that is given to soldiers who are expected to see a good deal of hand to hand combat. Usually these are members of the elite fighting units for the different branches of Earthforce. This form of unarmed combat is quick, efficient, and direct. It has only one purpose and that is to incapacitate the enemy using whatever means are necessary. This martial art may be used with small weapons as well as empty handed.

Specialties: Blind Fighting, Ignore Pain, Block/Hold, Nerve/Vital Strike

New special maneuvers offered by these martial arts are listed below:

Attack/Flee: The use of this maneuver follows a successful attack in a zero gravity fight. If the martial arts task resolution is successful the attacker then pushes off of the defender with all of his or her might. One of two things can be accomplished—either the attacker can simply flee from the fight, or the character can use this attack to force the opponent to move in a certain direction. The greater the success of the initial attack, the faster the two combatants part. As this maneuver specifically exerts as much force as possible to flee the combat, when successful the attack does not suffer the normal half damage penalty for being in zero gravity (see Zero Gravity Combat on page 39).

Grapple/Attack: This maneuver is used after a round of grappling in which the character won with a normal or better success. As this gives the upper hand in a grappling contest the character may then attempt to strike the opponent while holding him or her. Instead of using the normal Unarmed Combat Skill, use the appropriate martial art Skill. The resolution is contested against the opponent's original grappling role. This damage suffers no penalty from zero gravity combat because the attacker uses the grappling adversary for leverage. The Agility modifier for zero gravity is also not applied since the attacker is grappling and has a strong hold on the attacker.

Ignore Pain: The use of this maneuver precedes a conventional combat action. If the martial art task is successful, the combatant reduces his or her immediate impairment by 2 for this action. This takes the place of a martial art maneuver and no other maneuvers may be attempted in the same round. No impairment may be reduced below 0.

Strafe: This specialty may only be used when in a zero gravity environment, and when the combatants are at maneuvering distance. The use of this maneuver follows a successful Agility check to maneuver closer to the opponent. Using the appropriate martial art Skill and this Specialty instead of Unarmed Combat, the character makes an attack against the enemy. Increase the damage of the attack by 1 for a Normal success, 2 for a Significant success, and 4 for a Critical success (after applying the zero gravity penalty gravity as given in Zero Gravity Combat on page 40). Note that unlike typical combat, the use of this maneuver allows a character to close distance to an enemy and attack in the same round. If either the maneuver or the attack fail, the character winds up hurtling off course and possibly damaging him- or herself. Determine the Agility penalty for the attack based off of the starting point and not the actual point of the attack.

Characteristics

This is an optional list of Characteristics that can be used along with those listed in the base rulebook. Like the Skills and Specialties listed above, these Characteristics may apply to any character if the history warrants, but they are most useful and appropriate to characters with a military background. Some of these Characteristics are variants of or overlap with some of those in the base rulebook. They reflect the military experience much more closely. When creating a character with a military background, the Characteristics listed here will usually be more appropriate, so feel free to select whichever best fits the character concept.

Personality Characteristics

Insubordinate: The character has an extreme lack of respect for authority. In this character's eyes, the fact that someone has been around longer or has a higher rank is absolutely no reason to believe them more capable or intelligent than anyone else. He or she has a tremendous dislike for being told what to do with no other justification than the right of authority. Unlike many others, this character will always question authority and never accept a person as an authority figure without sufficient evidence to support that authority.

In a strict environment such as the military this tendency often leads to trouble and most soldiers who are inclined to be insubordinate are either weeded out or broken of the habit. There are, however, a few who are able to squeak by or who are too invaluable to throw out due to minor insubordination. These characters generally get by as long as the acts of insubordination are more of a minor annoyance rather than actually harmful and they remain few and far between.

Pros: Fortune Point award for difficulties or particularly good roleplaying that arises from the character's insubordination. It also serves as a preservation mechanism when the character is ordered to carry out a self-damaging or illegal action.

Cons: Like it or not, the character will have to deal with authority at one time or another. This characteristic can make such exchanges very difficult, especially if the authority figure does not wish to divulge the reasoning behind the task at hand. This may also get the character into a great deal of trouble on a regular basis.

"Interpreting regulations for a senior officer could be considered insubordination."

Leader: For some reason or another this character was a born leader. Usually this is a result of strong charisma and confidence, but it can also stem from particularly clear reasoning or an innate ability to understand and deal with people. Characters with this Characteristic will normally seize any opportunity to take command of a situation whether or not they do so consciously. They do not shy away from power or responsibility, but feel at ease and comfortable with such matters resting on their shoulders, although not every born leader ends up in a position of "official" authority. This kind of person makes a natural NCO or Command level officer in the military. When the common soldier will willingly follow a person based not only on rank but also on this leadership quality, the unit will flourish and be much more productive. Officer Candidacy School, or other equivalent military schools, often seek out such people.

Pros: Any people who work directly under this character will be much more inclined to follow orders and do what he or she wants, without questioning. Higher ups may also recognize the leadership capabilities and yield some leeway in how the character deals with their subordinates.

Cons: In most situations this character is going to be expected to take charge—and will often have no choice in the matter. He or she may be thrust into a leadership role unprepared or without necessary experience, and will be responsible for the consequences regardless.

"We're going to be asking these men and women to do the hardest thing they will ever have to do; one of us needs to go with them."

Militant: The character is a war hawk by definition. According to this character, confrontations or disputes always come down to force in the end. When politics fail, it is the might of the military that holds the peace.

Most people of this mindset are also xenophobes, trusting no one outside of their own circle of friends. They also generally believe that the best way to handle the unknown is with the thunderous firepower of whatever weaponry can be brought to bear. The military should constantly be on a rapid growth program to keep the safety of the union secure.

The first solution that a character with this characteristic will think of is one of violence and destruction. Diplomacy and politics are all fine and good, but when it comes down to the wire, it is the military power that will get things done.

Pros: Fortune Point award for difficulties or particularly good roleplaying when such an instance should arise. People with this mindset will often group together, which might create a set of powerful connections that the character can build from.

Cons: Persuading this character to attempt diplomatic solutions in most situations will be fairly difficult. The character will be an advocate of shooting first and asking questions later, which can be quite a hindrance at times.

"It's like my grandpa used to say, 'Nuke 'em tell they glow, then shoot 'em in the night!'"

Aspect Characteristics

Veteran: The character has been in the service long enough to see action. Studying books, learning theory, and practicing maneuvers are all nothing compared to ac-

tual combat. Some people who were at the top of their classes and the best in combat exercises just freeze up under actual fire. All the rules change when your life is actually on the line. This character has been there, done that, and come back alive.

Most veterans are hardened by the experience, having truly seen what the reality of war is. Combat affects each person differently: some people find it a wake up call to the severity of their profession; others even go so far as to take joy in the combat and slaying of the enemy. Regardless of how they evolve, being a veteran changes a character in his or her own eyes, as well as the eyes of colleagues. Veterans are frequently sought out by newbies in search of words of wisdom or exciting stories.

Pros: Fortune Point awards for difficulties or particularly good roleplaying that arises from this characteristic. Most people, especially enlisted personnel, give a veteran a fair amount of respect. This character will also react with certainty under fire. Having already experienced life or death situations, it is unlikely that the character will freeze up in further similar situations.

Cons: Being under combat situations often brings great psychological stress. Depending upon the intensity of the situations, the character may suffer further repercussions, such as flashbacks. While being a vet imparts respect with most people, it will also create a lack of respect and even loathing from people who are strongly against war.

"I faced death on the Line. Where were you?"

Relational Characteristics

AWOL: The character is, or has been at one time, officially absent without leave. This means that the character either did not show up for duty, left in the middle of duty, or left the grounds of their unit or duty station. There are many different degrees of this offense that can be applied to a character.

When this characteristic is chosen, define the type and severity of the offense. The most inconsequential infractions include not showing up for a routine duty

during peacetime. With generous officers handling the case, this might only result in some extra KP and little more than a blemish on a permanent record.

More extreme cases are when a character is classified as a deserter. This character is AWOL and has no intention of ever returning to duty or to the military. Being a deserter is a most heinous crime in the eyes of Earthforce. In times of war the act of desertion is punishable by death. In peacetime, the punishment is left up to the discretion of a Court Marshal, and is not normally light. At the very least a deserter will be on the run from the military, always running the risk of being caught and punished.

Pros: Fortune Point award for any story situations that arise from this background, or for difficulties or particularly good roleplaying that arise from this crime.

Cons: Depending on the degree of the violation it could make movement around the Alliance difficult if not impossible, and employment will be hard to come by. If a deserter, the military will seek to bring the character to justice.

"We're all dead already, can't you see how badly we're losing this war? I'm not sticking around just to die for them."

Command Rank: This is a specialized version of the Authority Characteristic given in the base rulebook. A character with this Characteristic has a high rank in the military. At the very least he or she is in command of a sizable unit. The character might be a Ground Forces or Battalion commander, or the executive officer of an EA capital ship. Or he or she could be as high ranking as a General, Admiral, or member of the Joint Chiefs of Staff. At that level, decisions that the character makes can drastically effect the entire military as well as the campaign. The character could even be deciding the best way to fight a war, or how to manage the economic burden of the military.

This characteristic goes beyond the power and responsibility of a normal officer, placing the character in the position to have to make crucial decisions. In most campaigns the characters start of as normal people in a fairly low profile position. Instead of giving this to a starting character, it is something added to the character at a later, more fitting time (such as when high level position/promotions are given).

Pros: The character has a great deal of power and influence inside the military. He or she will be able to avoid many of the annoyances that lower ranking officers have to deal with. Characters will also enjoy nearly all the benefits and privileges that the military has to offer. Even people outside of the military institution may recognize and respect the character.

Cons: Along with such great power and position comes an exceptionally great burden of responsibility. The character will always have matters that interrupt things and demand immediate attention. One wrong decision or compromise could cost the lives of thousands of innocent people.

"They've opened fire! Your orders, sir?"

Decorated: The character has, in the course of his or her service, received a medal or commendation for a particular deed. There are many such accolades, most for honor, valor and courage. One of the rarest a living character may possess is the Earth Alliance Medal for Service on the Line, which was awarded to all who fought valiantly in the last dwindling moments of defense for Earth against the Minbari. Most of these medals were posthumous.

Some recipients of medals are heroes who were striving to save lives and uphold their ideals. Others were just in the right place at the right time—or perhaps, according to them, in the wrong place at the wrong time. Regardless of how the medal was obtained, people generally treat the recipient with a certain deal of respect and admiration.

Pros: If they know that the character is decorated, most people lend some more leeway to him or her in everyday life. Being decorated also carries a certain amount of fame with it. People may recognize the character from time to time, especially if they are military savvy.

Cons: Others may expect the character to perform like a hero all the time. The fame that the decoration brings may also be unwanted by the character. Sometimes the character will just want to forget the incident, not glorify it.

"This is the medal for the line. Why didn't you tell me you were on the line?"
"I didn't want to talk about it."

Family in the Service: While this character may or may not actually be enlisted in the military, one or more of the character's immediate family is or was in the service. If it is a father or mother, the character probably moved from base to base a great deal during childhood, and may have lived in a fairly regimented home. A brother or sister has less impact on the home environment. Either way, the character has a contact inside the military. If the family member carries a high rank, the character may even be able to pull strings when necessary.

Pros: Fortune Point award for any story situations that arise from this background or for difficulties or particularly good roleplaying that arise as a result of the characteristic. This may also give the character an inside track in the military whether for information or advancement.

Cons: Often the family will expect the character to follow in the relative's footsteps. Others, such as friends of the family and acquaintances, might also expect this, or might treat the character as if he or she were enlisted. This can cause problems if the character has no wish to join the military, and if the character is in the military, he or she will be expected to match or beat the performance of the relative. If the character was raised in a military home, it is possible that there are feelings of animosity that arise from the strict environment.

"You didn't run a family, you ran a boot camp!"

Optional Combat Rules

Combat is one of the most detailed and deadly sections of play in The Babylon Project, but there are still some specialized circumstances that players may get into that require a little more explanation. These optional rules cover several situations not covered in the base rulebook.

Zero Gravity Combat

Earthforce trains its forces to fight in all manner of environments, many of which

Movement in zero gee is difficult, but walls, objects, or even other people can provide anchors that allow some control. Modifiers for Agility rolls in zero-gee include:

No objects within reach   -12

Free-floating object of substantial mass (another person, a crate, etc.) within reach   -10

Anchored or unmovable object (a wall, a cargo container, a support strut) within reach   -8

Two anchored or unmovable objects (two walls joining, two large crates) within reach   -4

Three or more anchored/unmovable objects (two walls and a ceiling) within reach   -2

Objects with handholds or which are easily gripped get a bonus of +2 (thus, if a character can reach two anchored objects with handholds, the total penalty would only be -2)

---

are hostile to human life. In most cases, this consists of teaching them to fight in suits or breather masks, with various weapons designed for the purpose. But one of the most unusual situations is a gravity free environment. Without gravity, fighting becomes a different art. To prepare its soldiers, Earthforce trains all Ground Forces and many Fleet members in methods of zero gravity combat.

A zero gravity environment makes even simple movement and control difficult: actual combat is worse. The absence of gravity and subsequent loss of constant proper support create a situation in which it becomes troublesome to hit and damage an opponent. Without proper bracing, a blow simply delivers no power. The following rules take effect during hand-to-hand combats in a zero gravity area.

As a result of the minimal amount of force which can be brought to bear on the enemy, all damage dealt in zero gravity Close Combat is reduced by half. Under some circumstances the GM may make this penalty less severe (for example, if one com-

batant is braced against a wall or large object).

It is also much more difficult to maneuver in a zero gravity combat. Any action which is based on Agility (this includes most forms of Close Combat) will suffer penalties due to the weightlessness (see the adjacent table for Difficulty Level guidelines). If a character wishes to maneuver as an action he or she must first succeed at an Agility check (perform a Static Task Resolution with Basic difficulty, 5) which is also subject to the same penalties. A character with Acrobatics may use this skill during these maneuvers. Again, the GM may adjust this penalty, as circumstance require. In some cases, such as a character wearing magnetic boots, this penalty may be ignored all together.

When two people take part in combat in the absence of gravity, the laws of physics play havoc. More often than not, when a character manages to actually connect a blow, it will send the attacker and the defender drifting apart. If a character strikes an opponent and succeeds by a Significant success or better, the attacking character and the defending character will sail away from each other. Remember, however, that the succeeding character will be in a better position from which to maneuver back into combat when they finally stop. The greater the margin of success the quicker the departure. There will be times when both characters have such high penalties that their resolution numbers are negative. The character with the higher result still succeeds, although in the case that neither player rolls higher than a zero, no damage is done by any strike.

Since strikes are so difficult and unpredictable, grappling is the most common form of combat in zero gravity. It is also much easier to succeed in a skirmish when grappling, as attacks are usually based off of Strength and not Agility. Most Martial Arts holds are not really the same as grappling attacks, since they are usually based on Agility or Coordination.

Automatic Fire

Some projectile weapons are designed to fire multiple rounds in rapid succession with a single pull of the trigger. These are considered automatic fire weapons. Any weapon capable of automatic fire has a Burst Rate. This is the number of projectiles that the weapon releases in a round of combat. If the weapon is fired in automatic mode it will fire the entire Burst Rate every combat round, or if the clip does not contain this much it will empty the clip. There are two different ways to fire an automatic weapon: Controlled Burst and Sweeping.

Controlled Burst: When using this method, the attacker attempts to hit the same spot with all of the rounds. The attacker nominates an Aim Point using the same rules as for normal ranged combat. Determine the Difficulty of the shot as before, but increase it by 1 for each round of combat that the attacker continues the automatic fire after the first. As long as the attacker is firing one continuous burst, he or she gains Initiative during all combat rounds but the first.

In each round, the combatant performs task resolution as normal. Unless the shot is a Critical Success, it will deviate from the Aim Point, hitting a Point of Impact determined by the rules for Ranged Combat. Each shot after the first deviates the same amount as the first one, but it deviates from the Point of Impact of the shot before it, and not from the original Aim Point. With a Marginal success each shot deviates 2 hexes on the body map in a random direction each time. The shots deviate 1 hex each for a Normal success. A Significant success means that only every other shot deviates. With a Critical success all shots hit the original Aim Point. The normal damage bonuses (-2 damage for a Marginal success and +2 damage for a Critical success) apply to all shots in the burst.

Sweeping: Using this method, the attacker sweeps the gun across an area, attempting to hit multiple targets. Unlike normal Ranged Combat, the attacker cannot aim before shooting, although he or she may pick an Aim Point other than the Default Aim Point without spending prior rounds aiming the weapon. The attacker nominates the Start and End Points on the body. These points are where he or she

wants to place the first and last bullet respectively. These two points can be spread out across different targets if the combatant chooses map (if two or more people are standing in a group, place two or more copies of the body map next to each other to illustrate the situation adding blank hexes as necessary). The Start Point and the End Point must be at least as many hexes apart as the Burst Rate of the gun being fired. The GM then distributes all of the shots' Aim Points between the Start Point and the End Point as evenly as possible. If the shooter is attempting to sweep from one character to another, or is sweeping in another odd manner, it is not necessary for each shot to be aimed at a hex which has a target in it. This represents the fact that if the bullets spray from one target to the other, some are wasted in the action. Each shot is considered to have its own Aim Point.

The GM determines the Difficulty as normal, adding one for each combat round past the first of continuous automatic fire (again, initiative is automatically given to the attacker when firing one burst over multiple combat rounds). The attacker makes only one attack roll for all of the shots. Depending on the success of the attack roll, the first shot must be checked for deviation. When a shot deviates to its Point of Impact, all further shots have their Aim Points deviated by the same amount in the same direction. Then the second shot must be checked for deviation which effects all further shots in the same manner. This continues until the Point of Impact is determined for all shots. If the success is marginal each shot deviates 2 hexes as per the hit chart. For a normal success each shot moves 1 hex in a random direction. With a significant success every other shot deviates 1 hex. If the success is critical none of the shots deviate. The normal damage bonuses apply to all shots in the burst.

Jonathon's character, an Earthforce enlisted man named McDugal, has been backed into an alley by a street gang. McDugal was patrolling the streets with his EF-issue submachine gun. He figures that the best way to pacify the mob is to take out the leader quickly. He doesn't want to kill the guy so he aims low at the feet. His gun has a Burst Rating of 3 so it fires three bullets per round. Aiming for the feet (see the illustration at the end of this example), he nominates hex 1 as his Start Point, and hex 3 as his End Point. The GM places the third shot in hex 2 which is equidistant from hex 1 and 3. Jonathon's total difficulty number is a 7, and his ability is a 5 (Coordination of 3, Skill in Combat, Ranged of 2). He rolls a +4 for a total of 9. This is a Normal success so each shot will deviate by one hex. For the first shot he rolls a 1, its Point of Impact is in hex 4, which misses. The second and third bullets now have their Aim Points moved the same amount to hexes 5 and 6. He rolls a 6 for the second bullet's deviation so it hits in hex 7 which is zone 10. The last hit's Aim Point is now hex 8. Jonathan rolls a 2 for the last shot's deviation, which puts it in hex 9, a hit to zone 9. The total effect is 14 points of damage to zone 10 and zone 9. The leader is dropped to the ground and the crowd flees seeing that McDugal means business.

Autofire Example

Aim Point

Deviation

Point of Impact

Martial Arts

Listed above (see page 35) are two martial arts styles available through Earthforce training. While this does not mean that they are not available outside of Earthforce, it is uncommon to find non-military personnel with these skills. Most military services have similar skills in which they train their soldiers. These martial arts can easily be used as a basis for similar training received in other such military institutions.

Note that in order to perform a martial art maneuver a character must declare that he or she is attempting the maneuver before any actions are taken. Many of the maneuvers state that they are used after a conventional attack, block, parry, or defensive action. This does not mean that after the initial success is made the player then decides which martial art maneuver to attempt. It means that he or she may only roll for the maneuver if the initial action was successful. If the initial action failed, then the maneuver also fails. Even though the maneuver was never completed it is still considered unsuccessful for the purpose of penalties (for example, jump kick).

Kirsti has been jumped by a mugger on her way home from work. Fortunately she has studied Karate since she was a little girl. The thug however does have the drop on her and gains the initiative. He is going to perform a simple attack. Kirsti decides to try the martial arts maneuver Block/Hold. The assailant's ability is 6 (Agility 4, Unarmed Combat 2). He rolls a Random Modifier of +5, for a total of 11. Kirsti first rolls for her Block as the Block/Hold maneuver says it follows a block of normal or better success. Her ability is 10 (Agility 5, Unarmed Combat 3, Specialty in Block). She rolls a —3 modifier for a total of 7. The thug hits with a significant success, and does 6 points to area 2. Since she failed the Block there is no need for her to roll for the martial art maneuver. Luckily for Kirsti the damage does not produce immediate impairments.

Kirsti's Initiative is higher, so during the next round of combat she gets to act first. She decides that she needs to end this rather quickly so she attempts an Increased Damage Hit. The thug opts to dodge the punch. Kirsti's ability is a 10 again (Agility 5, Unarmed Combat 3, Specialty in Strike) plus her Random Modifier of +2 for a total of 12. The thug rolls a -2 modifier for a total of 4. Kirsti's hit lands with a critical success this increases the damage by 2. Now she attempts the martial art maneuver. She has an ability of 11 (Agility 5, Karate 4, Specialty in Increased Damage Hit). The task has a difficulty number equal to the thug's total, so she needs a 4. She rolls a Random Modifier of -2 for a total of 9. This is a significant success so it raises the damage a further 3 points. Her strength is a 4, +2 from the critical success on the attack, +3 from the Increased Damage and -2 for the thug's Toughness for a total of 7 points to his torso. This causes him to make a stun check at -2, which he does with no problem. It also inflicts an immediate impairment of 2. Kirsti has initiative again but decides to hold her action to see what the attacker will do. The thug realizes that he is hopelessly outclassed and flees into the shadows.

Some martial arts specialties call for you to use the appropriate martial art Skill instead of Unarmed Combat while resolving an attack. This means apply the martial art Skill under which the character has taken the Specialty. The task is then resolved as normal. The only difference is that the character's Ability is derived using the martial art Skill instead of the Unarmed Combat Skill.

Explosive Damage

Damage done to a character by an explosion is more severe than damage done by a single strike or weapon. While one assailant can only hit a character in one body zone at a time, an explosive device can deliver damage to multiple body zones.

Random Location Table

Result ▶ Body Zone Hit

Negative ▼ Die Roll	Positive Die Roll					
	1	2	3	4	5	6
1	10	6	13	4	1	13
2	12	8	15	8	3	11
3	1	7	14	5	2	6
4	7	2	9	11	4	14
5	1	5	15	3	2	4
6	10	9	3	5	12	4

An explosive device delivers one of two forms of damage, Concussive or Fragmentation Damage. Each device has a rating in one or the other type of damage. When an explosive device goes off, resolve the damage according to the type of device.

Concussive Damage is very easy to resolve. Concussive damage is applied to the head. The Concussive rating of the explosive is a single number. This is the Damage Level that a person standing right next to the explosive would take. For each meter away from the device, the Damage Level is reduced by one. So a person with a Toughness of 0 standing next to a device that has a Concussive rating of 7 would receive a Damage Level of 7 to the head, while someone 2 meters away (also with a Toughness of 0) would only take a Damage Level of 5.

Fragmentation Damage is resolved differently. The Fragmentation rating is two numbers expressed in the form X:Y. X represents the number of attacks done by the explosive to someone standing within one meter of the blast, and Y is the Damage Level of each attack. For each meter away from the device, X and Y both decrease by one. So a person standing one meter away from a device with a Fragmentation rating of 4:6 would take three attacks with a Damage Level of 5.

Attacks from Fragmentation damage are allocated to the body at random. The simplest method of doing this is to use the Random Location Table (on page 43). Roll two dice separately. Look up the result of the first die on the horizontal axis and the result of the second die on the vertical axis. The resulting number is the body zone that was hit by the attack. That zone and one adjacent zone (determined randomly by the GM by any fair method) both suffer the damage of the attack.

Rulebook Errata

A few small mistakes were made during the production of the base rulebook. Most were minor typographical errors that don't affect the rules of the game. There are, however, a few errors that misrepresent or even contradict what was intended. The following corrections fix these errors:

Martial Arts Maneuvers

On page 105 the Difficulty for task resolution of a martial art maneuver is stated to be Average Difficulty. Instead, the Difficulty number is the Result of the opponent's task resolution from the attack or defense. Thus the better the opponent does in combat, the harder it is to perform the martial arts maneuver against him or her.

Ranged Combat Aim Point

Page 106 states: "Unlike close combat... the aim point [for ranged combat] is always the Default Aim Point unless the attacker spent one or more rounds aiming." This should read as follows: "The attacker may nominate any aim point on the target just as in hand to hand combat. For every hex away from the Default Aim Point the attacker suffers a -1 penalty to his or her roll. The attacker may pick any aim point with no penalties to the die roll if he or she spends one round aiming."

Equipment Cost

On page 168 the cost of the InTech Poly-9 Forensics Analyzer is listed as 85,000 EAcr. The actual cost is 8,500 EAcr.

Skill Purchasing

In the italicized example on page 118 Dana spends three experience points to give her character the Shiphandling skill. This is not correct; Dana should have to spend four points for the new skill as stated in the rules given on page 117.

Chapter 2: Equipment

Military life is dangerous, and as such, the military protects its people with the most sophisticated equipment available for dangerous situations. This chapter discusses the equipment that Earthforce uses for many different environments and situations. Most equipment is issued to Earthforce members with no cost. Issued equipment must be returned after the person leaves Earthforce. The main exception to this is the personal uniforms and clothing which must be purchased and which is kept after discharge. In the descriptions below, where cost is given for an item normally assigned, it refers to the value of the item, and not to any fees charged to EF personnel.

Personal Equipment

These are small items or groups of items that personnel are rarely without. Most of these items are necessary for everyday operations and it is critical that the Earthforce member carries them.

Identicard: Probably the single most common item used by Humans civilian and military is the identicard. It combines many of the functions that in the past required several different documents. With a holographic picture of its owner, an identicard serves as an item of identification, as well as a vehicle operating license, passport, and access cardkey. In the military, ranks and access privileges are encoded on the card, as well as post and command information. An identicard also contains basic medical information (blood type, allergies, medical conditions, etc.). The identicard can also be linked to an individual's bank account and used as a debit card, but since information on identicards is available to a variety of government officials, most people prefer to use separate credit chits for their financial transactions. Cost: none.

TransCom P2050 Comp Pad: Comp pads are used by technicians and other operations personnel to transfer data from one person or station to another during a duty shift. They are also used to get personal authorization on documents or files from superior officers. Since mundane reports and memos do not often require high-resolution graphical data they do not use specialized display apparatus, and the P2050 is used more commonly than high-capacity storage devices like data crystals on duty.

The screen on the front can be configured to display textual and simple graphical information several ways, depending on

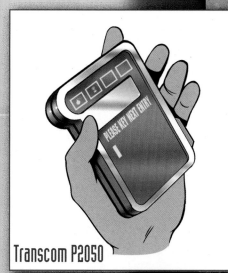

Transcom P2050

the primary need of the user. Information from a user is usually input with a stylus, but a small keyboard can be called up if necessary. Military issue comp pads usually also connect to the local computer system just as handlinks do (see below), so that downloading complete reports or updates is a simple process. Cost: 450 EAcr.

Uniforms: All members of Earthforce must purchase specific uniforms befitting their position when they enter service. There are several different uniforms required for each member of Earthforce. The uniform worn while on duty typically consist of either shoes, socks, pants, shirt, jacket and insignia; or boots, socks, jumpsuit and insignia (depending on rank and duty detail). Officers in the EA Space Fleet wear dark blue jacket and pants while enlisted crew have gray jumpsuits with boots. Space Fleet pilots wear boots and blue jumpsuits while they are not in the full space suit that is necessary to survive in a starfury. EA Ground Forces officers have an olive colored jacket and pants uniform and the enlisted crew wear dark olive-drab jumpsuits with boots. The Ground Forces also have a set of combat fatigues. These fatigues vary from mission to mission but normally have sturdy multi-pocketed pants with a similar jacket and combat boots. Security personnel wear light gray pants and jackets for their uniform. All members have insignia that designate them as members of Earthforce and indicate their rank. Of-

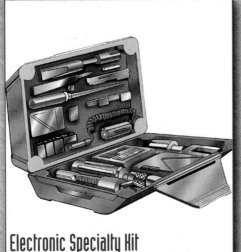

Electronic Specialty Kit

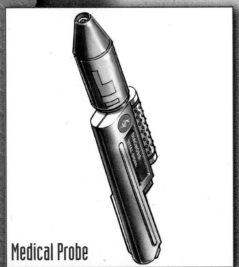

Medical Probe

ficers who can pilot fighters have a small emblem with wings on their right shoulder. Enlisted crew also have their names sewn on the uniforms. Each rank and position also has a full dress uniform. Generally the officers' dress uniforms include coat-length jackets eloquently trimmed with gold, with braid looped around the right shoulder. Enlisted members have a crisp uniform with pants, jackets and shoes which have some trim but not nearly as much as the officers. Along with these dress uniforms personnel also wear all the decorations they have received in their military career. Cost: 300 EAcr.

Specialty Kits: In a highly technological society, there are a number of complex tasks that require specific equipment in order to get the job done. Earthforce has several types of standard kits that are tailored to different fields of work, designed to allow personnel to perform their jobs quickly and efficiently. The standard field specialty kits are: Medical Kit (the first aid kit), Electrical Applications Kit (for working on electronic devices and systems), Mechanical Applications Kit (for working on mechanical devices and systems), Space Applications Kit (designed for basic electrical and mechanical work by personnel in bulky space suits) and the Investigation Kit. Personnel in highly advanced or research positions often build their own Applications Kit that is then assigned to them on a permanent basis.

Medical Kit: MedFirst Trauma Kit, Various bandages, disinfectants, tweezers, painkillers, aspirin, scissors, a laser scalpel, hypodermic needles, common drugs (such as insulin), stims, suture kit, miniature defibrillator, medical scanner. Cost: 3500 EAcr.

Electrical Applications Kit: Multimeter and other measuring tools, logic probe, small screwdriver set, soldering iron, electrical tape, wire cutters/strippers, bread board, assorted pliers, assorted electrical parts. Cost: 350 EAcr.

Mechanical Applications Kit: Assorted pliers, crescent wrench, ratchet set, screwdriver set, duct tape, cutting/drilling laser, hammer, oils, cleaning solvents, soldering torch, several different kinds of solder, earplugs. Cost: 600 EAcr.

Space Applications Kit: Welder, welding visor, various wrenches, ratchet set, wire cutters, grappling arm, magnetic handholds, emergency air tank, emergency magnetic grapple, magnetic storage board (for loose metal pieces). Cost: 2300 EAcr.

Investigation Kit: Fingerprint duster, tape measure, plastic sample baggies, MegaLan ML30 ImageCorder, diagnostic computer, magnifying lenses of assorted intensities, latex rubber gloves, InTech Poly-9 Forensics Analyzer. Cost: 10,000 EAcr.

Communication Devices

In order to coordinate the astonishing number of people in Earthforce, it is imperative that they all be able to stay in constant contact. The military uses the most sophisticated communications equipment available to achieve this goal. Each member of Earthforce has some form of communications device issued when necessary. This is particularly true during combat maneuvers when coordination must be fluid and as close to immediate as possible. During non-combat situations it is not such a pressing matter and only personnel stationed on permanent posts or personnel whose job require it have constant communication.

Corpsman Signal Devices Inc. Handlink Transceiver: The handlink is the piece of equipment most commonly issued to Earthforce personnel. The link is a small communications device that attaches to the back of the hand by a process called molecular bonding, causing it to adhere to the skin safely and securely until it is pulled off painlessly. The bonding surface does not adhere to other surfaces, and does not rub off, so the same surface can be used for months at a time without worry. Links are powered by a highly efficient battery that can last for up to a month and can be flash-charged in a matter of seconds. Chargers for links are built into the military computer systems that use them.

Most often used solely for its communications functions, the handlink is actually a small computer terminal easily programmable to perform a number of func-

tions. Handlinks operate on a reserved range of coded frequencies, and have two operating modes. In normal operating mode, they are merely remote terminals for the computer system of a military base, colony, ship, or station. The link provides direct access to the computer's voice command system and to the communications system. Through this access (or through a terminal), an individual can program the handlink's control studs to perform any number of simple tasks, such as marking the time, opening a door, or activating a video screen.

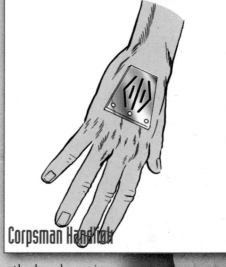
Corpsman Handlink

Normally, the wearer activates the link by pressing one of the control studs, raising the hand wearing the link and identifying the originator and the recipient of the transmission. After the computer verifies via voiceprint analysis that the user is authorized to use the link, it calls the appropriate destination. The signal is terminated either by pressing the control stud again or by dropping the hand to the person's side, thus inverting the link.

When there is no central computer nearby for a handlink to communicate with, it is usable in its standalone mode as a simple audio communicator, using its frequency channels to broadcast to and receive from other handlinks in the area, much like a walkie-talkie. The effective range of a handlink's broadcast is about one kilometer with no interference. Cost: 40 EAcr.

FujamiLink DRS-28B Communications Headset: For

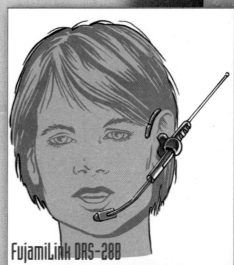
FujamiLink DRS-28B

personnel at duty stations that require frequent or private communication, a communications headset can be assigned. This provides the wearer a hands-free device that interfaces with the computer system just like a handlink. The primary use for these devices is for operations technicians for stations or colonies, or for personnel who operate communications links. Each headset is sized so that the usual operator can comfortably wear it.

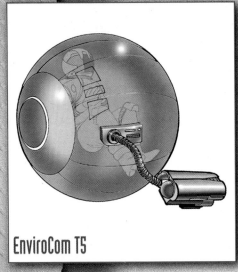

EnviroCom T5

Normally, the keyboard for the computer station at which the technician works has a toggle switch that allows the operator to activate and deactivate the headset. He or she can also usually type in a destination on the keyboard to activate it.

The headset is also assigned to personnel during combat conditions in non-hostile atmospheres. Just like a handlink, it can be used with or without a central system to allow troop coordination. Its hands-free operation allows combat personnel to concentrate on the task at hand rather than requiring the user to hold one hand to his or her face. Combat headsets are a bit more sophisticated than handlinks, however, and communicate on scrambled channels for privacy. They also have extra frequency channels to allow separate units to communicate independently.

EnviroCom 2603

Usually in combat situations, the headset is activated and deactivated from the commanding officer's station, conveying only those instructions that the soldier needs to hear and filtering out any confusing chatter.

The soldier can also activate and deactivate it with a short push on the earpiece to make reports or check in. Individual squads or platoons can also pick a common frequency to use as a free-form tactical link, allowing unit members to stay in constant communication during an action. In this case pressing the earpiece switches to one of the command frequencies. Cost: 25 EAcr.

Hostile Environment Equipment

With the exception of Earth itself, many duty stations require military personnel to work in or near environments that are unsuitable for Human life, such as the harsh winds and low pressure of colony worlds like Mars, the caustic atmosphere of colony worlds like Dakota, or even the void of space itself. Earthforce issues several types of equipment to personnel who work in these environments.

EnviroCom T5 Life Pod: Even though spaceship redundancies can handle a wide variety of punishment and accidents, there are times when a ship becomes uninhabitable. For this reason, most ships are equipped with life pods. Life pods maintain an environment safe from the dangers of space long enough (hopefully) for rescue, but are generally not capable of much travel. The many life pod models that EnviroCom makes that can hold and support different numbers of people. The T5 is a one-person inflatable life pod used mainly on small ships with crews no larger than five people, or as emergency backups on larger ships. The translucent outer shell gives the T5 and similar models their "life bubble" nickname. Inside the bubble is a forty-hour air supply, a bit of food and water, a thermal blanket and a signal transmitter to facilitate location and rescue. Cost: 3000 EAcr.

EnviroCom 2603 Half-Mask Respirator: There are two varieties of breather masks used in Earthforce today. The first is the simple respiratory mask (pictured here). The breather attaches around the nose and mouth using elastic straps around the head to create an airtight seal. This mask contains a small rebreather system much like those used in underwater diving that filters out the harmful gasses in an atmosphere and stores the breathable ones in the small tanks on the mask. These half-masks can provide sufficient oxygen for nearly two hours at a time possibly more, depending on the atmosphere. Most areas where respirators are used on a regular basis have convenient recharging stations, which will refresh the masks in several hours. EnviroCom implements this convenient recharge routine in all of their respirators, making them very popular. This mask is the most commonly used right now, but is being replaced by the newer facial mask. Cost: 140 EAcr.

EnviroCom 3270/A Full-Mask Respirator: The newer masks are more efficient versions of the rebreathers above, and incorporate a full faceplate. By sealing around the forehead and sides of the face, they protect the eyes of the wearer from the irritation reported by some people after long-term exposure to methane and other non-earth atmospheres. The 3270/As have a much larger storage capacity then their predecessors the 2603 Half-Mask Respirator. The Full-Masks are able to maintain oxygen levels for up to four hours. They also use the same easy recharge feature that all EnviroCom breathers do. They are not very common, but they are just entering mass production and are predicted to completely replace the older masks by the end of 2257. Cost: 300 EAcr.

EnviroCom FBL-42/JR Space Suit: The void of space is the most hostile of environments, and working in space requires the utmost care. The space suit is essential, allowing a Human to survive in a zero-pressure environment. It also protects the wearer from the harsh radiation from nearby suns. EnviroCom has created an excellent safety mechanism in the FBL-42/JR. In the event of a tear, the suit is compartmentalized and the area can be sealed off until the tear is repaired. These suits are equipped with magnetic boots that allow the wearer to walk along the outer hull of

space structures instead of floating completely free. They also contain a hands free communications device in the helmet so the person in the suit can communicate with others. Personnel assigned to work in space suits are trained in emergency procedures including suit repair and pressure loss. They are also given training in zero-gravity maneuvering.

Envirocom FBL-42/JR

Space suits have an air supply designed to last approximately eight hours. Extra air supply can increase this time. They also have built-in communicators that allow the wearer to keep in contact with the base. Cost: 2500 EAcr.

EnviroCom GN-339 Biological Anti-contamination Suit: Ever since Humans first began to understand the nature of viruses and disease, some form of anti-contamination suit has been in use. This suit protects the wearer from harmful agents that can be transmitted to a Human by touch or through the air. Since a breather might not filter out unknown dangerous contaminants, this suit contains a separate air supply designed to last eight hours and is completely sealed from the outside environment. The GN-339 may also be hooked up to an umbilical airline that feeds from outside the hostile environment. Using this method instead of an internal air supply, the wearer can work for an unlimited time inside the lab without having to worry about oxygen levels. It is also resistant to accidental cuts or punctures in the laboratory. It is light and flexible, designed to accommodate a full

EnviroCom GN-339

work shift. However, it is not a space suit and useless in depressurized environments. Cost: 1500 EAcr.

EnviroCom RE-698 Radiation Suit: While short-term exposure to most forms of radiation isn't too harmful, those who must work with it on a regular basis use the EnviroCom RE-698, the most commonly used protective suit. Like the biological suit, it is not pressurized. The most common model of the suit uses an EnviroCom 2603 or 3270/A breather filter (exactly like that from a breather mask) to provide an air supply while the suit is being worn. The suit has a protective cowl that goes on over the breather to protect the head from harmful radiation. Breathers are capable of adapting most atmospheres, but in those few circumstances where they are ineffective, a more expensive model of the radiation suit, the EnviroCom RE-698/S, with its own eight-hour air supply, is available. Cost: 1700 EAcr.

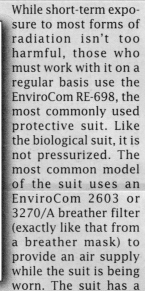
EnviroCom RE-698

EnviroCom Survival Kit: All operations in space or other hostile environments are conducted with great care; from station operations to shipboard travels to base operations on colony worlds. Wherever a support mechanism is required to keep Humans alive and healthy, plans are drawn up to cover as many contingencies as possible. Accidents that put personnel in jeopardy aren't common, but they do happen. In order to pre

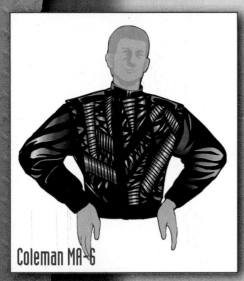
Coleman MA-6

serve life in these circumstances, all hostile environment postings have survival equipment in an easily accessible location, and all personnel assigned to these stations must have training in the proper emergency procedures. Depending on the environment, the survival kits consist of different items. There are several items that are standard to any survival kit: EnviroCom 2603 or 3270/A Respirator, air-tight sealable sleeping bag, small heater, rations, water filtration system, flare gun, first aid kit, chronometer, HoraComm OneNet locator device, twine, and matches. Other items that might be included in a kit include painkillers, antidote for toxic atmospheres and other useful items specific to certain situations. Cost: 1100 EAcr (typical; varies depending on kit contents).

Combat Issue Equipment

In combat situations, specialized equipment is issued to Earthforce personnel who will be involved in hostilities. This type of equipment may be issued in addition to any normal equipment the soldier may already have.

Protective Equipment

The safety of personnel in Earthforce is a primary concern. As such, Earthforce has contracted Coleman to produce a line of protective gear. This gear is issued to members of Earthforce when the situation requires it.

Coleman Protective Gear: During heavy combat situations, EF personnel wear armor designed to protect their lives. Since the most common weapons faced by EF Soldiers are bladed weapons for close combat and PPG weapons for ranged combat, the Coleman manufactured armor is designed to protect the wearer from these hazards. EF combat personnel are issued Coleman MA-6 Body Armor while those facing civilian altercations wear Coleman CG-9 Riot Gear.

Coleman MA-6 Body Armor: Body armor consists of a jacket and pants. In hand to hand situations, the body armor provides a tough surface that is difficult to penetrate with a knife. In ranged combat, the armor can mostly shield the wearer from the effects of the PPG blast, but must be discarded immediately to prevent the burning material from damaging the wearer. After five rounds, the wearer suffers one additional level of damage from plasma burns (PP type damage) for each round that the armor remains in place. Cost: 850 EAcr.

CG-9 riot gear: consists of a Coleman EF Riot Helmet, Coleman EF Riot Shield, and Coleman EF Riot Jacket. The Riot Helmet and Riot Shield are much more resistant to damage than the more flexible body armor and do not need to be removed after taking a PPG hit, but they are often unwieldy (the shield in particular interferes w/ use of longarm weapons), so they are normally only used in crowd control actions. Cost: 1090 EAcr.

KR-4/BX Hostile Environment Armor: Not all theaters that GROPOS must operate in are friendly to Human physiology. Sometimes a Human will be seriously injured or even killed through exposure to a planet's atmosphere. Yet even in such harsh conditions GROPOS fight on, protected by the KR-4/BX. For this state of the art system, Coleman and EnviroCom worked together in a joint operation. This full-enclosed suit of armor is designed to withstand an enormous amount of abuse without compromising the integrity of the seal. Not only does the suit not yield to breaches; it also protects the soldiers from physical damage. The completely self-contained system has the ability to provide the wearer with nearly 12 hours of oxygen. The suit has two layers; the internal layer is designed by EnviroCom and serves to keep the wearer shielded from the outer atmosphere, while the outer layer is armored plating. The armor plates are designed to be easily removable in the event of a direct PPG or other burning weapon hit. The armor is segmented and the plates covering each of the 15 body zones can be jettisoned at any time. Any section that sustains a direct hit from a PPG must be taken off within six turns.

Every turn after the sixth the soldier receives one extra level of PP damage if he or she does not take that part of the armor off. The only exception to this is for area 1, which is the helmet. Just like the Coleman EF Riot Helmet this does not need to be removed after taking a PPG hit. In fact removing the helmet of the KR-4/BX is a decidedly bad move that will almost certainly result in serious injure or death. Cost: 4600 EAcr.

Wesson Enforcer

Weapons

There are a variety of items that Earthforce uses to disable, injure or kill the enemy. These weapons range greatly in form and function. The following weapons are the most common and typical weapons found in use in both the EA Space Fleet and the EA Ground Forces.

Projectile weapons offer the ability to deal a great amount of damage over an extended range. There are many different forms of projectile weapons and certain models are used to achieve particular goals. Which weapon is best used often depends on the situation.

Slug Projectile Weapons

Although Earthforce uses PPG weapons as its standard issue, there are some circumstances where they are not desirable. In desert environments, static charges in the air can disrupt the magnetic field around the plasma. In very moist environments, the field deteriorates

Wesson Sportsman

quickly. And in warfare, sometimes the goal is to destroy as many of the enemy's buildings and vehicles as possible.

In these cases, Earthforce will issue a slug weapon. These cases are very rare, and except for combat conditions, restricted to Earth-bound personnel only.

Coleman Magnum

With the introduction of the PPG, manufacture of these slug throwers has slowed down but by no means stopped. Smith & Wesson still primarily manufacture these weapons, as does Coleman, while Westlake & Grumman almost solely produces PPGs. Even with the decline in production these guns are easily available anywhere on Earth though in space-borne installations it is next to impossible to obtain slug throwing weapons due to the great risk this brings to these structures.

Browning EF-492: When the military needs a heavy machine gun, they call on Browning. The Browning EF-492 is a fearsome belt-fed machine gun. It is light enough to be carried by one man and is designed to be operated without the assistance of another soldier even though it is belt fed. The ammunition is carefully laid down in a box that hangs off to the side of the chamber. This ammo box feeds the chained ammunition into the gun and eliminates the need for a second person to feed the gun's ammo. Though it can be fired from a carrying position, it has a built in bipod that creates a much more stable platform to fire from. The

Auricon EF-PR

best firing position with the EF-492 is lying prone or dug into a fortified position. This gun is restricted to Earthforce personal and is not legal for civilian ownership. Cost: 2500 EAcr.

Browning EF-G26: The EF-G26 is a hand held grenade launcher. Each grenade has not only an explosive section but also a large area that is propellant. In this respect a self-propelled grenade is much like a very large bullet with an explosive head. The large size of each round makes it impractical to have any sort of ammunition clip. The EF-G26 only houses one round and must be reloaded after each shot. Using a grenade launcher increases the range and accuracy with which grenades can be delivered. This model can utilize a variety of different grenades but is most commonly used with a D-21 or S-30. Cost: 500 EAcr.

Coleman Magnum: The Coleman Magnum is a very popular civilian slug-throwing pistol. It is extremely reliable and easy to maintain. When not in a situation where damage to structures is a concern, the Magnum is the preferred weapon of security forces. Cost: 200 EAcr.

Wesson Enforcer: Larger than the Wesson Sportsman, this rifle is not meant for hunting. The Wesson Enforcer is often times used to provide support or sniper fire. Its long range capabilities and heavy firepower make it an excellent surgical weapon. Typically the Enforcer is used with a 10x or 5x optical sight. Cost: 550 EAcr.

Wesson Rattler: The Wesson Rattler is the most popular submachine gun around. In the rare occasion that Earthforce issues a SMG, the Rattler is it. Light weight and compact, with a folding stock it is easy to carry and conceals relatively well. It fires 9mm bullets at a respectable rate. While not capable of doing major destructive damage, it is more than adequate to stop several assailants without pause. Cost: 300 EAcr.

Westlake & Grumman EF-52: Usually when soldiers enter combat, they are equipped with PPG rifles. In some situations it is more advantageous to give the GROPOS ballistic assault rifles. Westlake & Grumman make the EF-52, the standard Earthforce issue assault rifle. This is one of the few ballistic products of W&G, though the standard of quality that they hold their PPGs too is still present. The EF-52 is rugged and durable. It has no trouble being a piece of well-used field equipment and fires just as well when wet or caked with mud. These are Earthforce-only weapons and not legally obtainable outside of the military. Cost: 1500 EAcr.

PPG Weapons

The most versatile and most common weapon in use today is the Phased Plasma Gun, or PPG. Firing a superheated blast of helium within a magnetic field, the PPG can incapacitate or kill an enemy without risking damage to inanimate structures around. In space, or in domed colonies, this is very important, as structural damage could injure or kill civilians, or even the person firing the gun. Since a PPG will also work in normal atmospheres, it is the standard Earthforce issue sidearm. All officers are issued a sidearm (whether or not they choose to wear it), as well as those enlisted personnel whose duties require it.

As mentioned in the base rulebook, PPGs can be set to inflict less damage and extend capacity by turning the cap down to do 2 fewer damage levels for 1 extra shot. Once used this way, the cap cannot be re-adjusted to its original damage level without being recharged.

Besides turning the cap down, PPG weapons can also be overcharged by turning their caps up. Overcharging a PPG pushes it beyond safe operating levels, doubling its firing rate and increasing the damage level by 2 for one continuous barrage. While overcharged, the PPG is considered to have a Burst Rate of 2. However, once the PPG has been overcharged the cap will fuse to the gun, rendering the gun useless without extensive repair. The gun will also overheat, doing 2 damage levels to the hand of the person holding it. Like a normal PPG shot, an overloaded shot will not cause structural damage even though they are much more powerful. These shots do have an increased chance to catch things on fire,

which is not normally a problem inside installations since most of the materials are flame-retardant. The military frowns on the practice, often censuring and/or docking the pay of EF personnel who overcharge their weapons except in the most dire of emergencies.

Auricon EF-7 and EF-PR: Auricon is the military supplier of PPGs. The EF-7 is the PPG pistol currently is issued to Earthforce personal. In the case that a rifle is needed, Earthforce issues the EF-PR. The Auricon weapons are lighter and more accurate than civilian models. The caps that the Auricon EF-7 and EF-PR use are designed to hold three times more helium than most civilian magazines. These are not legal for civilian use and are only obtainable through Earthforce. Cost: EF-7: 450 EAcr; EF-PR: 550 EAcr.

Auricon EF-749/ AC: PPG pistols are not Auricon's only products. They also produce the EF-PR, which is a PPG rifle that the

Typical PPG Caps

military uses. This is however not the largest PPG made by Auricon. They are the manufacturers of the awe-inspiring Auricon EF-749/AC "Harbinger." The most massive and deadly man-portable PPG in production, the "Harbinger" is capable firing coconut-sized balls of phased plasma at a horrendous rate. Nearly one fourth of the entire weapon is a coolant system. The "Harbinger" is already stretched to its maximum limits and as such cannot be put on overcharge. Too large and cumbersome to wield normally, the EF-749/AC is carried with a strap around the person's shoulder. Due to their bulk, these weapons were originally produced solely for defensive detail. The "Harbinger" is not suitable for highly mobile operations that require the soldiers to be constantly on the move. As a result, there are not many EF-749/ACs in the field. Only the luckiest and most well equipped squads have a "Harbinger" with them. These squads are happy to have a "Harbinger" in their midst even though its bulk slows them down. Cost: 9500 EAcr.

There are a wide variety of non-military PPGs available to the public. Much like handguns of the twentieth century, several different companies manufacture a fairly large number of PPGs. They have become much more popular than slug throwing handguns due to the lack of damage they inflict on structures. This makes the gun much safer to have around than one that fires slugs. With the proper papers any civilian of legal age and with no criminal record can obtain a PPG with little trouble if he or she goes through the correct channels. The most prominent and popular manufacturers are Westlake & Grumman, Smith & Wesson, and Coleman. Most of the current manufacturers were originally makers of slug throwers. When the PPG was created, they realized that there was going to be a large market in it and either switched entirely to PPG production or added the PPG to their production lines.

Grenades

A grenade is a small explosive device meant to be primed and thrown by a solider or fired from a grenade launcher. Grenades are not as accurate as a gun but have the potential to eliminate or incapacitate several threats at one time.

There are two main types of handheld explosives used in combat situations. The first is the standard fragmentation grenade, which is used only in open areas and not on stations or ships. The second type is the concussion grenade, which relies on the sheer force of the explosion to do damage. Unlike a fragmentation grenade, it does not have an outer shell that breaks apart into projectiles when the grenade explodes. Certain types of concussion grenades are designed only to incapacitate. This kind of grenade does some form of sensory damage that can render an opponent unconscious without damaging the surrounding area. Concussion grenades are more common on colonies. Usually, it is a "flash-bang" grenade, which generates a lot of noise and an intensely bright flash of light, blinding and deafening anyone who is nearby and not protecting themselves for anywhere from ten to thirty seconds. Grenades and other explosive devices can be highly dangerous on ships and stations. The extremely close quarters provided by these tight environments increase the risk of collateral damage or damage to friendly forces, and are thus not normally used in these situations.

D-21: This grenade uses an internal explosion to send shards of shrapnel in all directions. Earthforce may issue D-21 fragmentation grenades to troops entering

Auricon EF-7

Typical Grenades

battles where they can be used without significant risk. The D-21 is a handheld grenade though another version is available as ammunition for a grenade launcher. Cost: 90 EAcr.

S-30: The S-30 is a very potent and reliable flash-bang grenade that also uses a non-lethal but potent concussive force. These are very handy when dealing with hostage situations, where using a D-21 would kill both the abductor and the hostages. An S-30 will incapacitate and probably knock everyone in the room unconscious but do no lasting damage. This is a handheld grenade and is also available in a self-propelled form to be used with a grenade launcher. Cost: 70 EAcr.

Hand to Hand Weapons

Not all combat is done at a range that is appropriate for projectile weaponry. Especially given that PPGs actually "splash" when they hit their target, making them risky to use at close range. In such circumstances it is better to use weapons meant for hand to hand combat.

Combat Knives: Useful as both a tool and a weapon, combat blades are still a valued piece of equipment in the military. Any member of the Earth Alliance Ground Forces is issued a K-Bar knife as part of their gear. Even in this era of modern warfare, it is sometimes necessary to use a knife in combat. As well as a weapon for use in combat, these knives usually have multiple functions. They can normally be used as wire cutters, a saw, a screw driver, a hammer, etc. This form of weapon is preferred by GROPOS more often than pilots, and by those stationed on colonies rather than those on space stations, where heavier restrictions are in place. Cost: 100 EAcr.

Universal Tech Scorpion Stun Baton: Since some of Earthforce's functions on colonies and outposts are police duties, security forces can be issued stun batons as part of their duty equipment. These batons are much like the old nightsticks used by police of the past, but instead of relying on the force of the blow, they deliver an electrical charge to the target. They are often more effective than nightsticks because they require less strength to use effectively and they do less lasting damage than a heavy club does. Cost: 120 EAcr.

Weapon Accessories

Earthforce members are not always given just a bare weapon to use. Often times the weapons are outfitted with items which enhance their capabilities. With weapons that have been augmented by extra items, a solider is better able to execute his or her objective.

Typical Combat Knife

InTech Night Vision Gear: Night vision gear helps soldiers and others operate in near or complete darkness. InTech makes several different models of night vision devices, most of which (like the commonly-issued EN-PNV4) amplify existing light thousands of times, so that even deepest of nighttime gloom can be seen through. More high-end devices (like the EN-11) also see into the near end of the infrared spectrum to augment the picture, and can be used with IR illuminators (like flashlights, but shining light invisible to the naked eye) where there are not even the faintest traces of ambient light. InTech also makes the EN-BNC5 binocular, which combines night-vision capacity with 10x magnification. Cost: EN-PNV4: 400EAcr; EN-11: 1400EAcr; EN-BNC5: 3200EAcr.

InTech EN-PNV4

Optical sights: Optical sights are used to make a projectile weapon more accurate.

They are available in several different forms. Optical sights may be purchased with Infra Red and night vision capabilities. Each sight has a power rating, usually from 2x to 10x. This determines how much the sight magnifies objects in its field of vision. To determine the Difficulty of a shot from a gun with a sight on it, simply divide the range by the power of the sight. So a longarm with a 2x sight on it making a 120 meter shot (normally Difficult) would be considered to be making a 60 meter shot (Tricky) instead. These sights can be mounted on most longarms. Using a sight properly takes a fair amount of time, as a result only one shot may be made per turn when firing with the aid of a sight. Some typical sights are a 2x, 6x, 10x and 4x - 8x zoom. Cost: 2x: 250 EAcr; 6x: 480 EAcr; 10x: 1200 EAcr; 4x - 8x zoom: 1350 EAcr.

Common Issue

What each particular person receives as Earthforce-issue equipment varies from position to position. Medics for example often receive equipment that is quite different from that of an *Omega*-class destroyer's chief engineer. All required equipment is not always free either. Several items must be paid for out of the person's own pocket. For instance uniforms are sold and not given to the soldiers along with a few other items. This list gives several examples of what would be issued or required equipment for several different posts.

Ground Forces Field Medic: Identicard, Uniform, Medical Kit, FujamiLink DRS-28B (during combat), Coleman MA-6 Body Armor, Auricon EF-7, EnviroCom 2603 Half-Mask Respirator (depending on environment), EnviroCom Survival Kit.

Ground Forces Infantry: Identicard, Uniform, FujamiLink DRS-28B (during combat), Coleman MA-6 Body Armor, Auricon EF-7, EF-PR (in rare circumstance an EF-749/AC), Combat Knife, D-21 or S-30 if conditions are correct, EnviroCom Survival Kit.

Ground Forces Engineer: Identicard, Uniform, FujamiLink DRS-28B (during combat), TransCom P2050 Comp Pad, Coleman MA-6 Body Armor, Auricon EF-7, Combat Knife, Explosive Charges, Mechanical Applications Kit, EnviroCom Survival Kit.

Space Fleet Officer: Identicard, Uniform, Handlink, Auricon EF-7, EnviroCom FBL-42/JR Space Suit (if checked out to fly a starfury).

Space Fleet Pilot: Identicard, Uniform, Auricon EF-7, EnviroCom FBL-42/JR Space Suit

Space Fleet Engineer: Identicard, Uniform, Auricon EF-7, TransCom 2050 Comp Pad, Electrical Applications Kit or Mechanical Applications Kit or Space Applications Kit.

Chapter 3: Ships

The Alliance learned early on that the absence of gravity and atmosphere makes the vacuum of space a demanding environment to traverse. Early accidents in the space program stalled Earth's efforts for decades, and even after Humans had begun to colonize other planets, a certain loss of life and property was thought inevitable. Spaceship designs are not hindered by the constraints of aerodynamics that dictate the design of a race's first aircraft, but there are other restraints that are just as confining. The ships must be airtight and provide an inner atmosphere for their crews' survival. The structure of the ships must be arranged to contain the pressure of that atmosphere without allowing any to escape, and they must withstand a drastic pressure difference to keep the hull from exploding.

And perhaps most importantly, the ship must be able to hold its own under the stress that hyperspace travel or combat can put upon it. Combat is an unfortunate fact of life, but all spacefaring races have to deal with it at some point. Most races build large fleets to protect their interests. Others, such

as the League of Non-Aligned Worlds, band together to make their smaller fleets larger. And yet others hire fleets from other races to protect their interests in return for money, goods or services.

The first section of this chapter details many of the ships that Earthforce uses to protect the EA's interests. From the smaller ships that support military operations to the mighty warships that make up its backbone, the EA Fleet makes use of a number of different types of craft.

The second section of this chapter details how these mighty warships fight. It is an optional set of rules that allow GMs and players to actually act out ship combat in much more detail.

Section 1: Earthforce Ships

It is difficult to build any craft that is spaceworthy, let alone one that is designed for combat. Most Earthforce ships are designed with several redundant systems and many sealed, air tight rooms. Ships built in this way are able to take several damaging shots to different areas before the ship becomes disabled. Some ships are built so well that the entire outer hull can be compromised, leaving the ship still functional.

Although Earth Alliance is one of the newest races among the stars, they are by no means the weakest. Once aware of the danger that other civilizations among the stars pose, Earth started rapid development of space combat vessels. It was not long before EA engineers had created ships that could compete with the warships of the other races. The four most recent and effective of these capital ships are the *Nova*-class dreadnought, the *Olympus*-class corvette, the *Hyperion*-class heavy cruiser, and the *Omega*-class destroyer. The SA-23 Aurora and the SA-25 Badger are the current Starfury models that support fleet actions. The CS-244 "Porcupine" is the most used starfury transport, and Boeing's CAS-958

"Condor" is the most common troop transport. The *Cotten*-class long-range tender is the best non-tactical support vessel used (game statistics for these ships are found in Section 2 of this chapter).

Nova-Class Dreadnought

Of the three most common ships in the EA Fleet, the *Nova* is the oldest and most antiquated. Earth Alliance wanted a ship that could stand its ground against alien forces. This ship was designed as not much more than a mobile weapons platform. With a total of 18 dual-barreled heavy pulse cannons and an interceptor grid, the Nova wields a great deal of firepower. Instead of engaging separate targets, the weapon guidance systems of these cannons link together and split the fire between very few targets. While this means that the *Nova* cannot engage very many ships at one time, the concentrated fire of its cannons will cripple enemy ships rapidly.

These guns consume an enormous amount of power to operate, which the *Nova* isn't always able to supply. With the insatiable energy requirements, the dreadnought is not able to put all of its power towards the engines and the guns at the same time. This created an inability to maneuver and fire in combat at the same time. The top tactic used by *Nova* COs is to get into an advantageous position, remain stationary and pour fire into the combat. This lack of mobility creates a weakness in the ship's defenses. To compensate for this, each dreadnought is fitted with four fighter squadrons. The fighters and the launch bay are located in the fore of the ship. The purpose of these fighters is to make up for the immobility of the *Nova* by harrying and harassing the enemy ships, counteracting flanking and escaping maneuvers.

With a crew complement of three hundred, living conditions are very cramped on the *Nova*. The ship has no gravity so each bunking area has sleeping bags attached to all of the walls as well as the ceiling and the floor. The ships are crowded with oversized engineering equipment. This, coupled with the zero-g environment, has the side effect of creating a feeling of claustrophobia and disorientation.

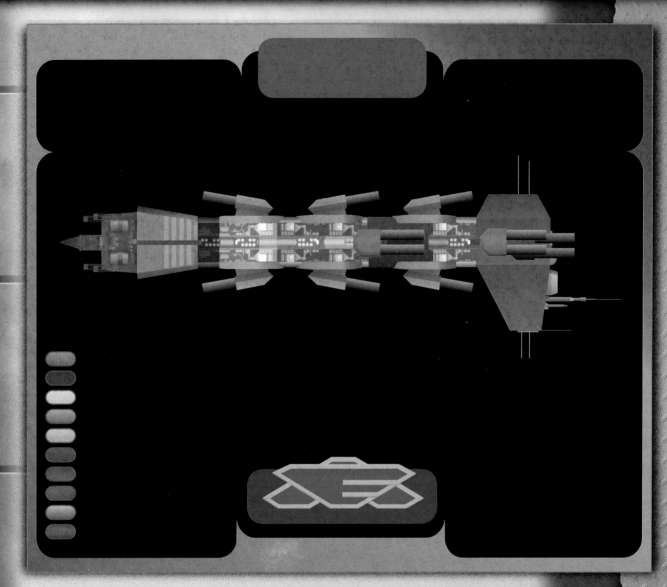

Olympus-Class Corvette

Light, fast and deadly, the *Olympus* is the most aggressive ship for its size. A minimal amount of space is devoted to the complement of 75 men and women who crew the ship. The rest of the *Olympus* is crammed tightly with massive engines and powerful weaponry. It is the fastest capital ship in the Earth Alliance Space Fleet.

Not heavy enough to stand toe-to-toe with most warships, the *Olympus* relies on speed and guerilla tactics to stay alive. Several of these corvettes are excellent addi-tions to any task force. While the larger capital ships pair off and trade shots the corvettes remain free to attack the enemy lines at high speeds.

The amount of firepower that the *Olympus* carries compared to its size is staggering. The *Olympus* is the first EA Fleet vessel that carries a powerful laser battery as its main weapon. Instead of being fairly well armed all around like most EA ships, the *Olympus* faces the majority of its offensive capability directly to the fore. With its maneuverability the *Olympus* can usually bring these weapons to train on the enemy. This gives the *Olympus* concentrated firepower

At one time military vessels carried armaments of horrific destructive power known as mass drivers. These weapons are large rail guns that operate by accelerating pieces of metal using electromagnetic force. The result is a massive projectile traveling at high speed. Mass drivers generate so much force that any ship hit by even one projectile is ripped apart. They can also be used in orbital bombardment to literally level cities. The damage that these weapons can inflict is so cataclysmic that all spacefaring races signed treaties agreeing not to use them. Instead, ships mount energy-based weapons, normally lasers or pulse batteries. As a result, ship survivability has increased dramatically.

comparable to larger ships even though its total weapons payload is lower.

The main weakness of the *Olympus* is that the only anti-fighter capability it has is a moderately sized defense grid. It lacks a hanger bay and fighters. Instead the *Olympus* must rely on fighter squadrons from other EA ships to protect it. This means that the *Olympus* has a very hard time operating without other ships to assist it but could not be more suited to assist other ships in combat.

Hyperion-Class Heavy Cruiser

The *Hyperion* was a revolutionary ship for its time. Unlike the *Nova*-class dreadnought, the *Hyperion* has an efficient power grid, more compact equipment and a stronger overall structure. The end product is a lighter, more durable and more maneuverable warship.

The smaller, sleeker chassis has less room for weaponry than its predecessor. This is not as problematic as it seems at first glance. It was discovered that the *Novas* had an excessive amount of firepower.

The *Hyperion* class has only eight turret mounted pulse cannons, one fore bearing pulse battery, a fore bearing laser system and an interceptor grid. Though these units are much smaller than the *Novas'* cannons and in fewer numbers, coupled with a laser system they still pack the punch necessary to incapacitate enemy ships. The middle portion of the ship carries two fighter squadrons, which launch from port and starboard bays.

The main crew quarters are toward the middle and stacked on top of each other in a tower formation. This creates a spacious environment for the 250 crewmembers on board. With this much space, it was possible to lay the ship out as if it did have gravity, thus serving aboard a *Hyperion* is much less disorienting. On the top of the crew tower protrudes the semicircular bridge section. Being at the top of the ship with a true view to augment the battle schematics gives the commander of the ship an excellent vantage point from which to direct the battle. Having the bridge so visible is a risky proposition as it can easily be damaged during the fight. For that reason, the *Hyperion* has a secondary bridge in the middle of the forward section. This bridge is built for redundancy, and is heavily shielded.

With its mobility and moderate firepower, this vessel makes a perfect counterpart for the *Nova*. With *Hyperions* on the field, less maneuverable dreadnoughts can stay in one spot and give supporting fire while the *Hyperions* roam the battlefield in an attempt to control the chaotic action.

Omega-Class Destroyer

After the Earth Minbari war, the Alliance realized that it needed to rebuild and upgrade the military might of the Fleet. The *Novas* and *Hyperions* were both good ships, but they had weaknesses. It was only natural that EA shipbuilders take the new and improved technology of the *Hyperions* and mesh them with the chassis and power of the *Novas*.

Not only did the EA take the best of their previous warships, but by adapting the body of the *Nova* class, they took the design one step further and added a rotating

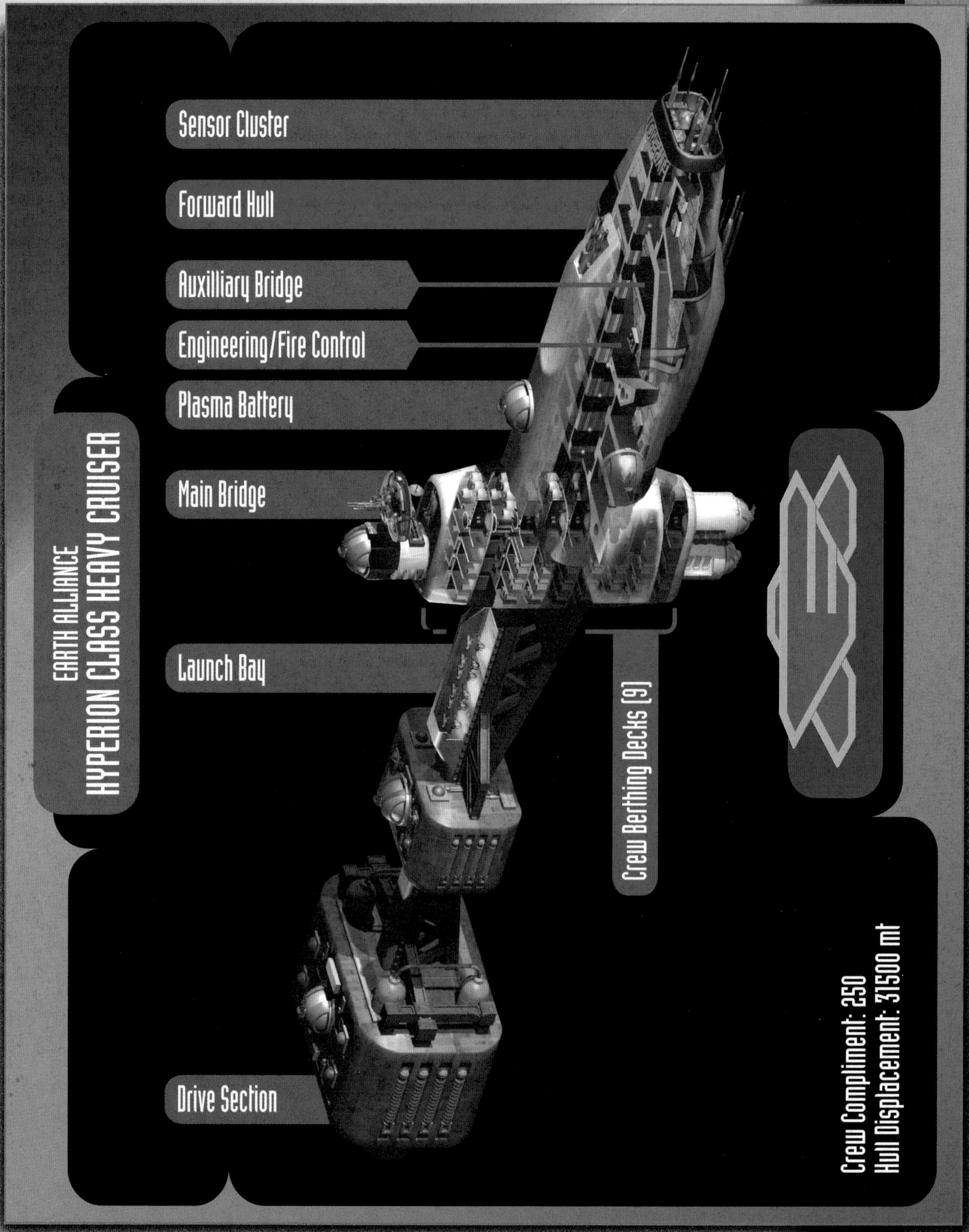

Sensor Cluster

Forward Hull

Auxilliary Bridge

Engineering/Fire Control

Plasma Battery

Main Bridge

Launch Bay

EARTH ALLIANCE
HYPERION CLASS HEAVY CRUISER

Crew Berthing Decks (9)

Drive Section

Crew Compliment: 250
Hull Displacement: 31500 mt

section to create gravity, which enables the crew to function much more efficiently. The rotating area houses the crew quarters, most of the duty stations, the main bridge, and one of the two redundant bridges. This massive section easily accommodates the entire crew complement of 550 people.

Though the rotation makes an environment that is comfortable to the crew and increases their abilities, it creates several problems. When an *Omega* takes a jarring hit to the rotating section, not only does the ship move but the rotational velocity of the section changes which makes the direction and strength of the simulated gravity change. The crew, relying on grav-

ity instead of straps to keep them at their posts, can go flying. This is especially true of green crews who have never been under actual fire. If one side of this section takes more damage than the other side, it will create an imbalance. When this happens the crew of the ship must lock down the rotating section and go zero-g or the ship will be rent asunder by the stress. Aside from the problems created by the rotation of the section is the problem that its size alone creates. It is positioned in the middle of the ship, and as a result the large pulse cannons that the *Novas* carry cannot be mounted on an *Omega* class. This does not mean that it is unarmed—in fact far from it.

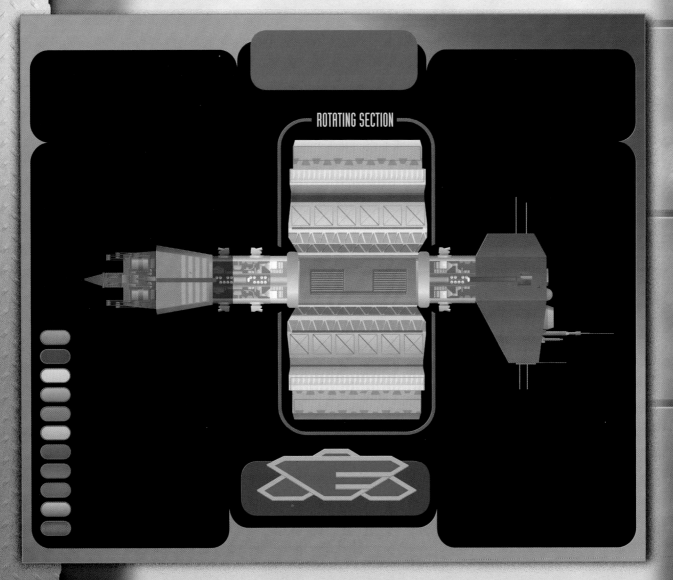

ROTATING SECTION

An *Omega* carries 12 turret mounted pulse cannons, 6 fixed mount pulse cannons, and an interceptor grid. Its main weapons are two high power laser beams mounted on the fore and aft of the ship. These weapons are integrated with the best tracking system that the Alliance has to offer. In addition to this firepower the *Omega* carries a launch bay with four fighter squadrons.

When all of these components are assembled, the *Omega*-class destroyer takes shape. It is the most deadly ship in the fleet. The Earth Alliance has mass-produced these vessels in an attempt to fill the holes in the fleet and expand the size of it as well. There are many military minds that feel that if we had *Omegas* in our fleets during the war the result would have been different. In fact, the very name of the project, the "Omega", supports this philosophy.

Starfury SA-23E "Aurora"

The Aurora is the current top of the line starfury produced by Mitchell-Hyundyne. Starfury fighters are much more agile and versatile than larger capital ships but they cannot carry anywhere near the payload of the capital vessels and are much more limited by fuel and range.

The role of fighters varies from situation to situation. Most commonly they intercept enemy fighters to protect the larger ships which cannot maneuver quickly enough to keep small fighters off of their flanks. If given the opportunity, fighters can flank larger ships, attacking from the least protected and most unexpected angle. A single fighter cannot do much damage to a capital ship, so they usually fly in squadrons of four or more. This creates a swarm effect, which is hard to defend against due to the sheer number of targets to track and fire on. When several squadrons attack at the same time, the concentrated firepower is enough to cause significant damage to a ship. Fighters are so light that they rely entirely on speed and maneuverability to survive in combat. Even a glancing hit from the smallest weapon is usually enough to disable or even destroy the fighter.

The starfury is one of the only fighters capable of unlimited three-dimensional movement. In earlier fighters the durability of the pilot was a great limit to the craft's ability to turn. If a turn that a ship made created more gees than the pilot could handle the pilot would pass out. To reduce this problem in the starfury, the pilot's cockpit is placed as close to the center of gravity as possible and the pilot is in a standing position. This allows the pilot to execute very quick turns and pivots while reducing the amount of physical stress on him or her.

Under the cockpit, the 'fury carries a dual pulse cannon which is fix-mounted. As this is its only weaponry, it is limited to engaging targets directly in front of it. Quite often a starfury pilot uses a "spin and fire" tactic. Instead of chasing the target, the 'fury pilot plots an intercept course. As the starfury travels closer to the target, the pilot spins to orient the guns on the enemy ship. The fury can track and fire on the target no matter how the target maneuvers, without diverging from the intercept course. This is also a common tactic used to dispose of enemies who get behind a starfury, mistaking it for a safe spot.

SA-25 "Badger"

This two-person starfury is larger and heavier than the SA-23 "Aurora." Much more self-sufficient, the Badger is designed as a long-range heavy fighter. Well armored and designed for long missions, the Badger is much more flexible than the Aurora.

Even with the added person, the Badger has life support and propellant-fuel capacity that almost doubles that of an Aurora. With this addition the SA-25 can patrol deeper and longer, eliminating the need to constantly refresh the starfuries on patrol or in a mission. Most bases and ships that have SA-25s keep several squadrons constantly in flight, unlike those outfitted with Auroras, which don't support enough flight time to have a squadron continually in use.

Each flight crew of a Badger consists of two people, the pilot and the RIO. The RIO or Radar Intercept Officer does not actually control the movement of the starfury except in an emergency, when the pilot is unable to fly the ship. The RIO handles most of the fighter's electronics. The target acquisition and identification systems, the communications, the detailed ship status and damage systems are all handled mainly by the RIO. With the RIO dealing with most of the in-depth and time-consuming operations of the fighter, the pilot is free to devote all of his or her attention to the actual maneuvering of the craft. It is also the pilot and not the RIO who fires the weaponry, the RIO just assists as an extra pair of eyes and to keep track of the enemy on the radar.

Despite the superiority of the craft there are several problems with the Badger. It is more costly and bulky than a single person fighter so there are more logistics problems with the ship. It must be stored in special docking bays, which reduces the ability to dock in strange and emergency situations, as not all ships are equipped with these systems. It also requires not one but two fully trained and highly specialized pilots to make the craft effective. Even with all of the tactical and strategic advantages of the Badger, the logistical problems are large enough to keep it from being widely used. The upcoming Thunderbolt design may solve some of these problems.

Hyundyne CS-244 "Porcupine"/CAS-320 "Shepherd"

Starfuries have two very limiting factors. First of all, they are not capable of at-

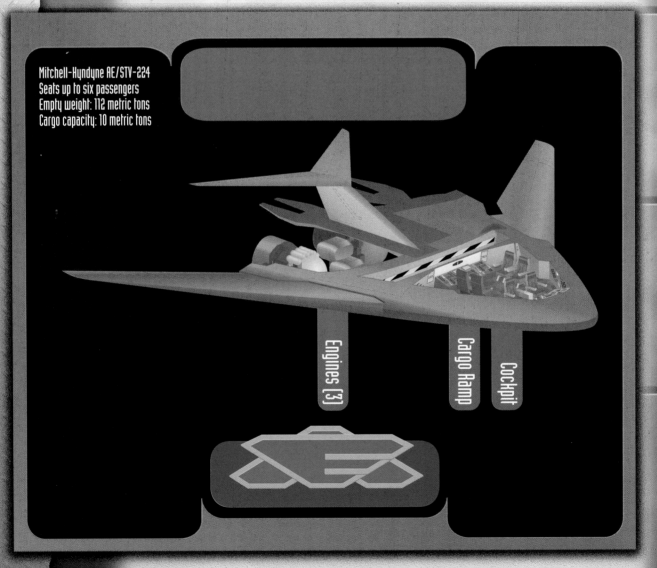

Mitchell-Hyndyne AE/STV-224
Seats up to six passengers
Empty weight: 112 metric tons
Cargo capacity: 10 metric tons

Engines [3]

Cargo Ramp

Cockpit

mospheric travel. Secondly, they have a very limited range. These two ships were designed to help overcome these problems.

These craft are small shuttles with minimal armament. By themselves, they are not very impressive or threatening. The danger lies in the exposed cargo bay on board. It is here that these ships carry a deadly payload of starfuries. Up to a full squadron of fighters can be carried by either variant. Assuming that their engines are heated, fighters can break off from these transports and form up for battle in less than 4 seconds.

Hyundyne designed these ships for two similar purposes. The CS-244 "Porcupine" can be used as a fighter carrier of sorts. In this role the starfuries are attached to the bottom of the craft and remain there, inactive, while the "Porcupine" transports them from location to location. While the ship is not large enough to carry jump engines; it still drastically increases the range of the fighters. As it was designed specifically for this job, the CS-244 is non-atmospheric capable.

The second duty belongs to the CAS-320 "Shepherd." Unlike its relative, this shuttle is atmospheric capable. Not all colonies and outposts have orbital space stations to protect them. This means that starfuries cannot patrol the area unaided. When starfuries need to get onto or off of a planet or colony it is the CAS-320 that delivers them. Instead of being loaded on the underbelly like the "Porcupine," starfuries are placed on the back of the CAS-320. This allows the "Shepherd" to protect the starfuries from the intense heat during re-entry. When the "Shepherd" is filling this role starfuries can be docked and serviced on the ground and then taken back into space for patrols, which they could not do on their own. Both of these shuttles give starfuries more options and expand their already astounding versatility.

Boeing CAS-958 "Condor"

The CAS-958 "Condor" is the ship that carries the oft-forgotten ground forces into a region once the Fleet has finished its job. These massive, heavily armored shuttles must drop down through a planet's atmo-
sphere into hostile territory, land and disgorge their complement of GROPOs. The ship is designed to be able to absorb several direct hits from ground. The CAS-958 "Condor" can remain flying with only one of its engines, half its tail and most of one wing missing. The entire front section of the ship is hinged and opens to allow easy access to the cargo area.

These giants can carry upwards of 450 GROPOs with equipment or a dozen armored units. A ramp extends from the interior to the ground below when the ship prepares to unload. This allows for a quick dispersal time, letting the GROPOs run off of the ship and the vehicles actually drive off. They are also equipped with a decent amount of air to ground weaponry so that they can clear the landing sight of enemy presence. It is common practice for a CAS-958 to enter atmosphere, circle the landing sight while unleashing its weaponry and then land to allow the troops to disembark. After unloading, the ships will leave the planet's atmosphere and stay in a low-line orbit awaiting the troops' signal for recall. These vessels make it possible to quickly deploy a strong ground force even when confronted with hostile conditions.

Cotten-Class Long-range Tender

No ship in the EA Fleet is self-sufficient. At one time or another they all need to be refueled and refitted. Typically this means a long sojourn back to a station or outpost. The *Cotten*-class helps minimize the frequency which these trips are needed.

The *Cotten*-class long-range tender is a fairly large ship by itself. Unlike most ships in the fleet, it is a dedicated supply vessel not meant to participate in combat at all. Slightly larger than a *Nova* class and with a crew of only 35 it can store a great deal of food and life support with a small amount of fuel for the reactors. Along with the raw materials the *Cotten* also totes replacement parts and repair tools. In fact, the *Cotten* itself is able to act as a pseudo dry dock, using its length as a framework from which to repair other ships.

However, carrying all of these materials is quite dangerous, as many of them are not stable. Even though the *Cotten* has sev-

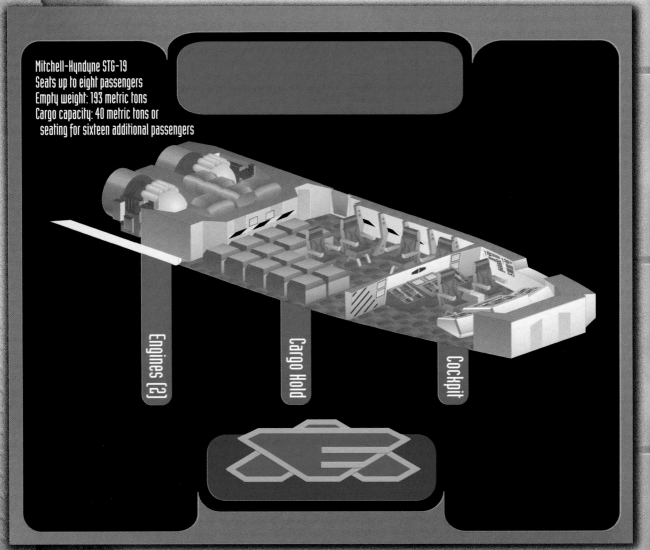

Mitchell-Hyndyne STG-19
Seats up to eight passengers
Empty weight: 193 metric tons
Cargo capacity: 40 metric tons or
    seating for sixteen additional passengers

Engines (2)

Cargo Hold

Cockpit

eral pulse cannons and an interceptor grid it is very vulnerable. If one hit punctures the hull of the ship and strikes the internal stores, secondary explosions are almost inevitable.

Except for difficult or extensive repairs, the *Cotten* can refurbish a ship in less than one hour. It carries enough supplies to be able to bring twenty-four ships that are completely expended up to full status. This means that ships do not have to leave their deep patrols or the combat lines in order to be replenished. When being cared for by a *Cotten* class, ships may spend a much greater amount of time in field duty and

Earth Alliance can use each ship to its fullest capabilities and beyond.

With nearly infinite supplies for its minuscule crew and a jump engine, the *Cotten* can go virtually anywhere it is needed. Without expending its stores on other ships the *Cotten* can travel for several years with no need to restock. Of course, since it is a microgravity ship, the crew would need rotation regularly. Normally it moves from task force to task force topping off their supply reserves, so it doesn't stay in space long before returning to a base to refill.

Section 2: Space Combat

In most scenarios, player characters play out the story through direct interaction with other characters or through narrative with the GM. When their characters come into conflict with NPCs the conflict is handled by using the Task Resolution or Combat rules in the main rulebook. Ship combat is normally resolved through standard Contested Task Resolution. In some cases, however, the players and GM may wish to tell the whole story of the combat by playing it out rather than just performing one or two contested task rolls and summarizing the results. This might be particularly important when player characters are directly involved in the combat or are on a ship that could be dangerously affected by the combat. An exciting blow-by-blow of the combat in these cases will often raise the dramatic tension of the story and draw the players in on a different level.

The tactical space combat rules presented in this chapter allow two or more players to detail encounters between starships, fighters and other craft in a traditional miniatures wargame using either model starships or counters on a table-top. A space battle may be fought as a stand-alone game, but these rules allow it to best be played as part of an ongoing roleplaying session; in the former case these rules can be used without a GM, but normally the GM oversees the battle game and adjudicates on any special events, especially ones that have a direct impact on the PCs or the plot of the story.

When played as part of an ongoing story arc, the GM guides the battle with special events that refine it without spoiling the fun of the miniatures game too much. The GM also usually plays the "opposing" force in the battle, just as he or she regulates the NPCs in a roleplaying session; each of the players in the group can then be allocated a ship or ships to control in the battle, whether or not their characters actually fight. PCs who have appropriate skills may be called upon to fly a fighter or man the guns (see Player Characters in Ship Combat on page 92), or they might help keep vital ship systems running.

The outcome of the miniatures battle can drastically change the upcoming series of events, depending on how well the players fought the battle. For example, if the characters are part of an Earthforce naval task group on a mission to relieve a besieged colony and are ambushed enroute by an enemy force, the GM may have to bend the tactical rules just a little to ensure that the player characters win the engagement and that most of their vital ships and assets are not destroyed—but if the

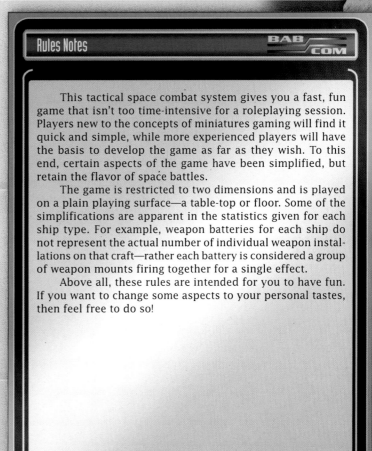

Rules Notes

This tactical space combat system gives you a fast, fun game that isn't too time-intensive for a roleplaying session. Players new to the concepts of miniatures gaming will find it quick and simple, while more experienced players will have the basis to develop the game as far as they wish. To this end, certain aspects of the game have been simplified, but retain the flavor of space battles.

The game is restricted to two dimensions and is played on a plain playing surface—a table-top or floor. Some of the simplifications are apparent in the statistics given for each ship type. For example, weapon batteries for each ship do not represent the actual number of individual weapon installations on that craft—rather each battery is considered a group of weapon mounts firing together for a single effect.

Above all, these rules are intended for you to have fun. If you want to change some aspects to your personal tastes, then feel free to do so!

Ship Naming

Earthforce has had various conventions for naming ships. Prior to the Earth-Minbari war conventional wisdom indicated that naming ships after historic Earth locations, or great leaders or military minds was appropriate. Around the time of the war this shifted towards a more generic and politically neutral system of using names from ancient Greek history and mythology. Not everyone was happy with this system, and occasional exceptions would be made, and individual EA Presidents would periodically reverse this pattern for new ships.

Hyperion Class: The class vessel, the Hyperion itself, is an example of the Greek naming tradition. However many vessels in this series have not continued that pattern. Ships include the EAS Amundsen, Clarkstown, Coeus, Cronus, Cygnus, De Gaulle, Deimos, Hermes, Hyperion, Iapetus, Phobos, Rhea, Roosevelt, Themis, Uranus, and Zeus.

Olympus Class: The Olympus class is interesting to note, because its class ship was destroyed during the war, and subsequently honored by being reused in the new Omega class. Ships include the EAS Acheron, Aegis, Alecto, Archimides, Argus, Athens, Cerberus, Erinyes, Megarea, Perseus, Thebes, and Tisiphone.

Nova Class: Most Nova class vessels did get named after Greek characters, creating the impression in many people that "all the good names were gone," and increasing the impetus to change the existing naming scheme. A few did get different names, often to satisfy some prominent senator. Ships in the class include the EAS Ares, Athena, Atreus, Caesar, Daedalus, Hades, Harpies, Hecate, Lexington, Maenads, Nereus, Nova, Pandora, Pegasus, Prometheus, Sibyl, Sophocles, Styx, Sun Tsu, Thanatos, Titan, Triton, and Zalmoxis.

Omega Class: The Omega class is unique in that the class name has never been used to name a ship. Originally the code name for the "Advanced Tactical Destroyer" project, it reflects the prevailing opinion of many in the military that it was the ultimate ship design, and would be the "last" ship Earthforce ever needed. The first ship off the line was actually the Achilles, and for the early part of the project ships were actually named in alphabetical order from a pre-selected list, due to the huge numbers being built. Later ships have had names breaking the Greek pattern assigned. Many Omega ships were named in honor of fallen ships of previous lines. Current names in use, or scheduled to be used include the EAS Achilles, Agamemnon, Agrippa, Alexander, Apollo, Cadmus, Churchill, Charon, Charybdis, Damocles, Delphi, Furies, Gorgons, Hamato, Heracles, Hydra, Juno, Midway, Nemesis, Nimrod, Odysseus, Olympus, Orion, Pollux, Pournelle, Roanoke, Vesta, Yeager, and Zethus.

Cotten Class: The Cotten Class is alone amongst the current ships for being older than the Greek naming scheme. Later ships in the series began getting Greek names for a while, although most ships are named after various military references, support ships of older Earth navies, or population centers. Ship names include the EAS Auckland, Berlin, Blue Ridge, Cotten, Eisenhower, Gaia, Geneva, London, Nepal, Nimitz, Patton, Persephone, Powell, and Sydney.

---

battle goes badly and the players lose most of their escort ships then they are going to have a much harder time of it when they finally reach their destination....

Space combat is always dangerous and is never without consequence. Lives are almost always lost in combat, and thousands (if not hundreds of thousands) of credits of damage are done to ships. It is especially risky for player characters, as they may well have no control over whether they live or die. Avoiding any sort of combat if at all possible, is always the safer for the characters' well being.

There will be times, however, where characters are forced or choose to participate in the space battle, either as combatants or as bystanders (such as passengers on a transport that comes under enemy attack). With this kind of situation, there is obviously a significant chance that a ship carrying PCs will be damaged or destroyed in the battle. If this occurs, then it is up the GM to adjudicate what happens to the characters. Space ships have several emergency survival systems, from survival pods on transport ships or cruisers to ejection systems in fighters. Characters can usually escape immediate death in most cases, although their circumstances might be very precarious. Lost battles can, however, enhance the plot of the adventure, as the players now have more problems to solve—if they are floating helplessly in an escape pod, how do they get picked up safely, and what happens if the bad guys find them first?

Overview of Ship Combat

These ship-to-ship combat rules are designed to be easy to understand, quick to read and fun to play. They also reflect the danger and brutality of combat in space. The object of any ship-to-ship engagement is to outthink the enemy and accomplish the mission objective (anything from disabling the enemy to protecting a merchant convoy) while taking a minimal amount of damage.

During combat, ships maneuver around each other trying to get a good line of fire while at the same time trying to make the opponent's line of fire inferior. When they open fire on one another, each attempts to damage the enemy ships enough so that they have no choice but to disengage or die. Each ship is capable of absorbing a certain amount of damage; once it has received that damage, it is destroyed.

Ships can move using two different methods. Each race uses one of these two methods. The first is a Reaction Drive system. Most of the younger races utilize these drive systems. Ships using Reaction Drives operate with engines and thrusters, which they use to push their ships through space. Once traveling in one direction the ship must exert effort to overcome its momentum if it wishes to travel in another direction. Races that have more technology use the second method of movement, a Gravimetric Drive. Grav systems make use of artificial gravity to decrease the strain on crewmembers inside and propel the ships. Unlike a Reaction Drive, a ship with a Grav Drive is able to transfer its momentum when it turns. This creates a system of movement best likened to flying in atmosphere.

In order for ships to move in the game, the players controlling them must decide what orders to have them execute. Before any of the ships move all of the players involved must put the movement orders their ships will execute in written form. Each side must anticipate the maneuvers the other will make and write orders such that their ships end in superior firing positions.

Once a ship is in a good position it opens fire on the opponent. Each ship has systems onboard which allow them to target and fire on one or more enemy vessel. There are several different types of weapons that ships use to try to damage their adversaries. If the ships are lucky they will be victorious over their foe and still be operational after the battle.

Large capital ships and their weapons are not the only factor in these life or death scenarios. Brave men and women who risk their lives in single pilot fighters attempt to keep the ships and crew on their side of the battle alive. Fighter Groups can attack enemy ships, helping to facilitate their demise. They can also set up defensive screens around the ships they wish to protect, forming a layer that other fighters must penetrate before they can attack the ship.

Fighters and capital ships cannot operate without their crews. The better the crew is, the more effective and efficient a ship will be in battle. As such if the crew of a fighter or capital ship contains player characters it can be expected to do exceptionally well. If these rules are being used to supplement roleplaying and PCs are aboard one or more of the vessels amazing things can happen. PCs may attempt to execute tasks that are more spectacular than the normal actions performed by everyday crewmembers in battle. As a result, ships that PCs are controlling to some extent can execute difficult maneuvers, which greatly increase those ships' potential in battle.

As ships continually clash, struggling for a victory, the game proceeds in a turn-based fashion. During each turn several phases occur which detail the order of events. The game continues turn after turn until one side has defeated the other. If the game was taking place as part of an ongoing roleplaying campaign, the tabletop game ends and the PCs must deal with the aftermath of the battle. The type of scenario the GM has created and the degree of success or failure of the players in combat will guide events that happen in the roleplaying game afterwards.

Setting up the Game

To play out a battle under these rules, you will need a few extra items beyond those used in regular roleplaying. In addition to paper and pencil, you will need a ruler marked in inches or centimeters (depending on your choice of scale) and copies of the Ship Control Sheet and Ship Order Sheet (in the Appendix) for each ship involved in the combat. You will also need several six-sided dice (it is helpful to have a few more than usual), some counters like those included in this book (also in the Appendix) to represent ships, and a playing surface. Some players will also prefer to use small models (also called miniatures) to represent their ships, as well.

The playing surface for your battles may be as simple as a plain tabletop or floor, as the game does not require a hex-grid or any other markings on the playing area. For best visual effect you may want to cover the playing surface with a black cloth or mat (several decorated with starfields are available through game and hobby stores). Place any fixed items, such as stations, jumpgates and asteroids in appropriate places on the table. Make sure you've got counters to represent each player's forces. Each counter represents one sizable ship in the battle or one group of six fighters. Each Fighter Group may be accompanied on the table by a small die that indicates how many of the original fighters in the group are still operational as the group takes losses in combat.

During a game session, the EAS Charon and the EAS Achilles are on border patrol and receive a distress call from a merchant caravan being attacked by Centauri ships. The three merchant ships are the center of the action so the GM places them on the board before the Charon and Achilles. The merchants were in a one-day long transit between jumpgates so there isn't anything else on the table. If the merchants had just left hyperspace or were just about to enter it, the GM would place the jumpgate and any other appropriate permanent structures on the playing field. Surrounding the merchants, the GM places two Centauri Battle Cruisers and a Light Cruiser. In this case the GM decides that the two EA destroyers will not enter the table until the second round.

Basic Concepts

Here are a few basic concepts that are used to define the method by which ships operate.

Ranges and Distances

Throughout the tactical combat rules that follow, all distances (whether for movement or weapons range) are quoted in Movement Units (usually abbreviated "MU"). One MU can be anything that the players agree it to be, depending on the size of playing area they have available, the number of ships in the battle, size of miniatures or counters in use and so on. For most games, 1 MU is taken to be one inch (or 25mm), as this scale gives a good battle on any area larger than about three feet by four. If space is restricted, it is quite acceptable to use a scale as small as 1 MU = 1 centimeter.

The Ship Control Sheet

Each large ship in the game is represented on the table by a single counter. The information about the ship that is required for play is recorded on a Ship Control Sheet; this sheet shows (among other things) all the systems installed on the ship in the form of small icons (for example, the drive or propulsion units, offensive and defensive weapons and so on). The chart also shows a number of small boxes that form the Damage Track of the ship. Each box represents one damage point, and the boxes are filled in as the ship takes damage from enemy fire. Finally, at the bottom of the chart are Order Boxes in which the player writes the Movement Orders (and any other notes) for that ship in each game turn.

Vector Movement

Most movement in space is not limited by factors such as air friction or constant gravity. As a result, once a ship begins to move in one direction it will continue to move in that direction without expending energy. If enough force is applied in the correct direction the ship will either stop or change course. To reflect this a vector-based movement system is utilized. The direction and speed a ship travels depends not only on the thrusts and pushes it applies in each turn, but also on its movement in previous turns.

Courses and Directions

This system doesn't use a printed grid to regulate movement and directions. Instead, it uses a "clockface" method—imagine a clock superimposed over the ship, so that the front of the ship points to 12 o'clock. The ship model turns in increments of 30 degrees at a time, so that a right turn will make its Heading 1 o'clock, 2 o'clock etc. If it turns right around through 180 degrees it will face 6 o'clock. Each 30 degree increment is called a Course Point, so if a ship currently facing 12 o'clock is turned three points to starboard (fore is the front of a ship, port is the left side, starboard is the right side and aft is the back of the ship) it will end up facing 3 o'clock, having turned 90 degrees.

Counters

The counters included with this book are twelve-sided just like this clockface. By turning the counter for a ship exactly one face for every Course Point that the ship turns (it's easy to do this accurately by placing a ruler against one edge of the counter), you can quickly turn your ships without worrying about the angles. Each counter has a small dot in its center. These dots are used to determine all distances. Any time the distance between two objects is required measure from dot to dot.

The Turn Sequence

Space combat is carried out in turns. During each turn the players perform a number of Phases in order. These are: the Order Phase, the Ship Movement Phase, the Fighter Movement Phase and the Combat Phase. After the Combat Phase, the next turn begins with its Order Phase, and so on.

Phase 1: Order Phase

During this phase, all players note the Movement Orders (see Movement on page 74) for each of their ships on their Ship Control Sheets. These orders indicate whether the ship will make any changes to its Course and/or Velocity during the present turn—a ship with no Movement Orders will simply move in the same direction as it did the previous turn, at the same speed. Ships equipped with multi-role systems (such as Interceptors, which can be used against incoming pulse fire or against fighters, but not both in the same turn) should note in their orders which mode the system will be using for the duration of that turn. Written orders are not required for Fighter Groups.

Written orders remain secret until the Ship Movement Phase, although any player may ask another about the Velocity of a ship.

If any ships are recharging in this turn (see page 81) roll for additional charge and note the new charge level in the Order Box ready for the Combat Phase of the turn.

Phase 2: Ship Movement Phase

Certain special weapons systems, such as Energy Mines, are launched at the begin-ning of this phase of the turn, before anything moves or orders are revealed. Also, any ship launching fighters does so before movement begins.

All players now reveal their ships' Movement Orders and move each of their ships according to those orders, in any sequence (all movement is considered simultaneous for game purposes). Fighter Groups screening other ships are moved along with the ship they protect.

Once a ship has been moved, note its new Velocity in the Order Box for the next turn and rotate its Direction Arrow counter to a new facing if necessary (see Movement).

Phase 3: Fighter Movement Phase

In this phase, all players may move any or all Fighter Groups that they have in play up to the maximum distances allowed under the Fighter Movement Rules (see p. 84).

If more than one player has fighters in use, each alternates moving a group, starting with the player with the most groups in play. The only Fighter Groups that are not moved in this phase are those presently providing Fighter Screens (see Screening, page 85) for other ships—such groups are moved at the same time as the ships they escort.

After fighters have finished their movement, Energy Mine detonation is resolved. Following Energy Mine detonation, any ships may fire their Anti-Fighter Batteries if they have valid targets.

At the end of this phase Fighter Groups choose and engage the targets that they will be firing on during this turn.

Phase 4: Combat Phase

This is often the longest and most interesting phase of the turn. Each ship may now fire any weapon systems it wishes, provided of course that the systems are in range of and can be brought to bear on a suitable target (counters are marked with Fire Arcs to determine this). The Combat Phase consists of two sub-phases: Ship Selection and Weapons Fire. Players decide randomly by rolling a die which side gets to go first, and then take turns executing

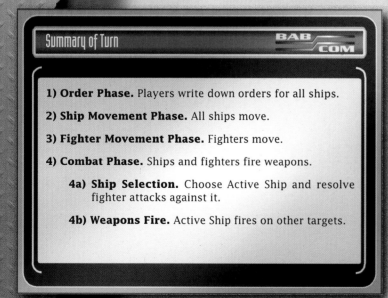

Summary of Turn

BAB COM

1) **Order Phase.** Players write down orders for all ships.

2) **Ship Movement Phase.** All ships move.

3) **Fighter Movement Phase.** Fighters move.

4) **Combat Phase.** Ships and fighters fire weapons.

   4a) **Ship Selection.** Choose Active Ship and resolve fighter attacks against it.

   4b) **Weapons Fire.** Active Ship fires on other targets.

these sub-phases until there are no more ships left that can fire their weapons. If one side has more ships than another does, the player controlling the smaller force will run out of ships first. The player with the larger force may keep firing until he or she runs out of ships.

Weapons Fire is not considered simultaneous. All damage inflicted takes effect immediately, so a ship sufficiently damaged (or destroyed) by enemy fire might not be able to return fire on its attacker.

4A: Ship Selection

Choose a ship that has not yet fired this turn. This becomes the Active Ship.

If several Fighter Groups are engaged with each other and none of them are screening or firing on ships, the entire dogfight may be selected as the Active Ship. Any player with Fighter Groups involved in the dogfight may select it.

If a PC is in a Fighter Group, that group may be selected as the Active Ship regardless of its target. This means that the Fighter Group may be able to fire on a ship before that ship becomes the Active Ship. This is the only instance in which a Fighter Group may fire before the ship it is attacking becomes the Active Ship.

If the Active Ship is under attack by enemy Fighter Groups, resolve these attacks. If a Fighter Screen is defending the ship, start by resolving all combats between Fighter Groups (see Dogfights on page 86). Finally, any Fighter Groups that have survived get their chance to attack the ship (see Fighter Attacks on page 87).

4B: Weapons Fire

Now the Active Ship selects its target or targets, according to the range and Fire Arc for each (see Weapons Systems on page 80). Resolve the Weapons Fire for each target.

If a dogfight was selected as the Active Ship, resolve the combat as per the rules for dogfighting (see page 86). Once the dogfight has been resolved it may not be selected as the Active Ship again in the same round.

Movement Orders

MD (X): Main Drive (X) moves the ship X MU along its Heading.

RP (X): Rotate Port (X) rotates the ship X Course Points to port.

RS (X): Rotate Starboard (X) rotates the ship X Course Points to starboard.

PP (X): Push Port (X) moves the ship X MU directly to port.

PS (X): Push Starboard (X) moves the ship X MU directly to starboard.

PA (X): Push Aft (X) moves the ship X MU directly to the aft.

LFG (X): Launch Fighter Groups (X) launches X Fighter Groups (X cannot exceed the maximum number of Fighter Groups the ship can launch per turn).

LEM (X): Launch Energy Mine (X) launches X Energy Mines.

R: Ram indicates an intentional attempt to ram another ship.

JP: Jump Point begins the jump point formation process (this will keep guns offline for two rounds and the point will not open until the beginning of the next round).

AP: Anti-Pulse sets the ship's Interceptors to anti-pulse mode.

AF: Anti-Fighters sets the ship's Interceptors to anti-fighter mode.

The Active Ship is now finished with its actions for the turn, and cannot become an Active Ship again until next turn.

Since becoming an Active Ship not only allows a vessel to fire weapons, but also allows Fighter Groups to attack it, every ship in combat must become an Active Ship each phase—even if it takes no offensive action. The phase does not end until all eligible ships have been selected as the Active Ship once.

If a ship has fired any weapons or systems that require Recharging before further use, then a note of their remaining charge level (if any) is made in the Order Box ready for the next turn.

push to its original movement. The faster a ship is moving, the less a given amount of thrust will change its Course.

Grav Drives allow ships to ignore at least some of the normal laws of physics—a ship under Grav Drive can slide along lines of gravitational force, allowing it to maneuver much more easily than the more primitive Reaction Drive ships. Grav Drive movement rules are considered optional and are given in the Systems section under Gravimetric Drives on page 106. The normal rules given here are those used by Reaction Drives, as they are the most common system in use.

Course and Heading

A ship under Reaction Drive does not have to be moving in the direction the ship counter is facing, and indeed most of the time it will not be—it will usually need to have its main drives (at the stern) facing in a different direction in order to apply thrust to maneuver. Reaction Drive ships are therefore always marked with a small Direction Arrow counter placed by the ship counter; this marker always points along the actual Course (the direction that the ship is moving) irrespective of the orientation (facing) of the model or ship counter. The actual facing of the ship model or counter at any given time is called its Heading—thus a ship that is currently facing "backwards" (using its main drives to reduce its Velocity) might have a Course of 12, but a Heading of 6.

Velocity

One of the key concepts that players must remember is a ship's Velocity. At the beginning of a scenario or battle, all ships have a Velocity determined by the GM or by the guidelines for that scenario. During the game, a ship's movements will add to or subtract from the magnitude of its Velocity. At the end of each turn, the ship's Velocity is calculated and then written into the Order Box for the next turn.

The faster a ship is going, the harder it will be to maneuver, and if players are not careful ships will end up traveling so fast that they will fly off the table before they

Movement

There are two different movement systems in these rules, to reflect the technological differences between the ships of the various races. Most of the "younger" races—the Narn, Earth Alliance and most of the non-aligned worlds—use Reaction Drives to propel their ships; the Centauri use a weak gravimetric drive that operates under most of the rules for a Reaction Drive the full rules are detailed under the Systems section under Centauri Drive Systems on page 105. Those races of superior technologies—the Minbari, Vorlons and other "older" races—use a Grav Drive instead.

Reaction Drive ships move using vector movement. If a ship is traveling in one direction, and is pushed in another direction by using its drives, its resultant path is a new vector given by adding the new can stop. If this does happen, you may either "scroll" the play area (by moving all of the other ships on the table over a few inches) or you may declare that the ship is "turning around" and that it will return to play soon (roll a die: the ship will return to play where it left that number of turns later with a Velocity of 0).

Drive Units

Each Reaction Drive icon on the Ship Control Sheet represents a main propulsion unit with a thrust rating of 2—so a ship capable of thrust 4 will have two drive units. Each drive unit is treated as a separate system when checking for damage at Threshold Points (see Recording Damage, page 82). The loss of one drive unit reduces the total thrust available by 2, so if a ship with thrust 6 loses one drive unit it will be reduced to thrust 4; loss of a second unit will reduce it to thrust 2; and loss of all three will mean it can apply no thrust at all.

A ship's drive system consists of two components: its main drive (which moves it forward) and its thrusters (which steer it and allow non-sophisticated maneuvers). A ship's main drive capacity is equal to its thrust; its thruster capacity is equal to half its thrust. Thus a ship with thrust 6 (three drive units) can in a single turn apply up to six points of main drive and three points to thrusters.

Main Drives

The main drive of a ship is the primary engine. This engine is normally very powerful and capable of producing a large amount of force. The main drive is usually mounted in the aft of a ship and only propels the ship in the direction it is facing.

The primary engine's size allows it to change the Course of a ship more quickly and efficiently than thrusters by themselves. A common maneuver is to use the thrusters to point the main drive in the proper direction. Then with one powerful main drive burn, change the Course radically compared to what maneuvering thrusters can do.

To indicate use of main drive in ship orders, write orders as "MD [amount of thrust]" (for example, MD4 would be a burn of thrust 4 with the Main Drives, moving the ship 4 MU in whatever direction it is currently facing).

Thrusters

Thrusters can be used in several ways, depending on how they are to maneuver or steer the ship. These methods and notations for ship orders are discussed here.

Rotation

In order to use its main drives to change Course, a ship under Reaction Drive must be rotated so that its drives point in the direction that the thrust is to be applied. Rotation can also be used when no thrust is required, to change the Heading of the ship in order to bring weapons to bear. Rotation is accomplished by the ship's thrusters—each point of thruster power used for rotation turns the ship by one Course Point

Summary of Reaction Drive movement

1) **Move ship** according to final vector from previous turn (direction as indicated by Direction Arrow, distance as recorded Velocity).

2) **Apply any ship maneuvers** (main drive, rotations and pushes in the order written).

3) **Measure distance** from Direction Arrow to new ship position, note this as new Velocity.

4) **Turn and move Direction Arrow** up to ship to show new Course.

(30 degrees or one side of a Counter), so a ship on Heading 12 that applies three points of thruster power to starboard rotation will turn through 90 degrees to face Heading 3.

Thruster rotation orders should be noted as RP (for Rotate Port) or RS (Rotate Starboard), plus the amount of thrust applied—so RS3 would be a starboard rotation of 3 points as in the example above.

Pushes

A ship making a thruster push uses its maneuvering thrusters to alter the Course and/or Velocity of the ship without affecting its actual Heading—so that the ship ends the maneuver pointing the same way it started. Pushes may be made to port, starboard or aft (using the forward thrusters to slow the ship down without having to spin it around and use the main drive).

Push orders should be written as PP (Push to Port), PS (Push to Starboard) or PA (Push Aft), again followed by the number of thrust points applied—so PA3 would indicate 3 thruster points from the retros to push the ship 3 units "backwards" relative to its current Heading.

Pushes may only be applied directly to port, starboard or aft relative to the ship's Heading at that moment. No push movement can change the Heading of a ship.

Combining Maneuvers

If desired, a ship may combine several different uses of its maneuvering thrusters in a single game turn, provided the total of thruster points expended does not exceed the total available. It is quite acceptable for a ship with three thruster points available to make a 2-point rotation before applying a main drive burn, then a further 1-point rotation afterwards (probably to bring weaponry to bear on its desired target); alternatively it could, for example, make the 2-point rotation and then use the remaining thruster point for a 1 MU thruster push to port, starboard or aft as desired.

The actual sequence in which thruster and main drive burns are applied in a single turn makes a difference to the final Course and Velocity of the ship. Thus, the Move-

ment Orders are applied to the ship strictly in the order that they appear in the Order Box. If the player writes "RP2, MD6", the ship will first be moved according to its starting vector (as always), then rotated 2 points to port (RP2) and moved 6 units along its new Heading (MD6). If, on the other hand, the order is written "MD6, RP2" (thus applying the main drive burn before rotating the ship to its new Heading) then the result will be very different in terms of the ship's final vector and position.

Atmospheric Capability

Some space vessels are designed in such a way that they are able to travel through atmosphere. Not only must these craft be able to handle the rigors of space travel, but they must also survive planetary re-entry and fly in a wide variety of atmospheres.

Ships with atmospheric capabilities are indicated with an icon on the Ship Control Sheet. Unlike other icons this does not represent an actual system on the ship. Instead it represents the overall structural and aerodynamic integrity of the ship. If the ship takes enough damage it is possible that the hull could be battered into a shape which will make the craft burn up on re-entry or be unable to maintain altitude in atmosphere. If a ship loses all of its Atmospheric Capability icons it is no longer able to function in atmosphere and will not survive an attempt to do so.

Moving the Counters

Movement under Reaction Drives is performed in a number of steps. First, move the ship along the Course it was on at the end of its previous turn (the direction indicated by the arrow on its Direction Arrow marker) a distance equal to its Velocity as noted at the end of the previous turn. This movement is always made exactly as per the end of the last turn, regardless of whatever Movement Orders have been written for the ship for this turn. The ship's Direction Arrow counter is left in its starting position at this stage, and is not moved with the ship.

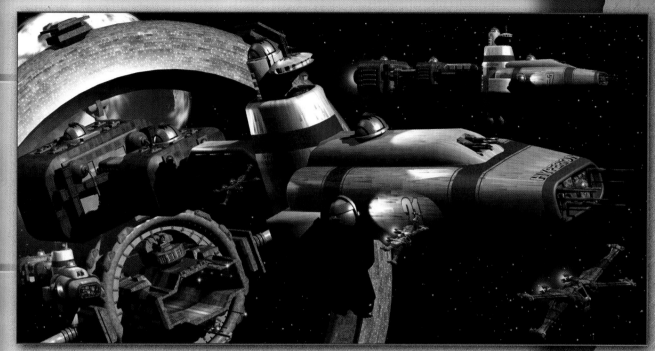

Now apply any Movement Orders written for the ship in the Order Box. These can be burns with the main drive, rotations from the thrusters, and pushes from the thrusters. Apply these moves in the order they are written.

After the ship has finished executing its orders, lay a ruler or tape measure between the ship's new position and the Direction Arrow counter (which was left at the starting point), and measure the distance between the two. Round this to the nearest full MU and record this as the new Velocity for the turn end. Finally, with the ruler or tape still in position, move the Direction Arrow up to the ship again, pointing it parallel to the ruler line. Carefully lift the ship up and place the Direction Arrow underneath of the ship so that the dots on the center of each counter line up, then place the Ship Counter back on top of the Direction Arrow. The Direction Arrow now indicates the ship's new Course at the beginning of the next turn.

The Charon enters the board with a Velocity of 8 and a Course coinciding with 12. Rob is controlling the Charon during the game because his character Captain Erik Weisshaupt is in command.

The battle area is still quite a ways off and to the starboard side of the ship. As there is not much time to get there, Capt. Weisshaupt decides to step up the speed of the Charon. Rob tells Jeff, the player controlling Lieutenant Commander Hiroshige Tanaka who is on helm, to write the following orders: RS2 MD4. When it is time to move the ship, Jeff first picks up the Ship Counter and moves it 8 MU along its Course, but leaves the Direction Arrow where it was. Now he turns the ship 2 Course Points to the starboard. Then the ship is moved 4 MU straightforward as the ship's main engines kick in. Jeff measures from the Direction Arrow to the Ship Counter and rounds to the closest full MU to determine the new Velocity, which is 10. The Direction Arrow is then pointed at the dot in the center of the Ship Counter (parallel to the ruler or tape measure). This gives the new Course of the Charon. This new Course is just shy of the Course Point 1. The Direction Arrow is then placed underneath the Ship Counter, keeping the Direction Arrow pointing along the Course, the Ship Counter pointing along the Heading and both dots centered.

At their current speed, the EAS Charon will arrive at the battle just before the EAS Achilles. Satisfied with this, Capt. Weisshaupt orders his crew to correct their Course to line up with the battle. To do this quickly Hiroshige turns the ship further away from the battle and uses the main engine of the ship. Jeff writes RS1 MD3 PS1 as the orders for the ship. The ship moves its Velocity of 10 along its Course before the orders are applied. Then it turns one more Course Point, which puts it on a Heading of 3. The Charon's Main Drive pushes it 3 MU along its Heading. Then it is moved 1 MU to the starboard. Jeff measures from the dot on the Direction Arrow to the dot on the Ship Counter. The Velocity is still 10. When he aligns the Direction Arrow the Course is somewhere between the Course Points of 1 and 2, pointing almost directly toward the combat. At the end of the turn the ship is on a Heading of 3, but moving on the new Course indicated by its Direction Arrow at the Velocity of 10 MU per turn.

Maximum Speed

There is no maximum limit to Velocity in this game—in theory a ship can continue to accelerate each turn until it reaches an enormous speed. In practice, however, because meetings between ships most often occur in relatively small areas of space—around planets, stations and jumpgates—the relative velocities tend to be reasonably low. Jump point entry and exit must be made within certain narrow Velocity limits for safety, and as soon as ships start to move fast they become very difficult to maneuver. Of course, this does not stop a ship from doing a "fast pass" attack across the playing area. The major races do not normally practice such tactics as it is hard to control and at that speed the path of a ship becomes predictable. Indeed, many battles are fought with the capital ships virtually stationary in order to allow them to pivot on the spot to aim their limited-arc main weaponry more effectively, with only the fighters zipping around for highly mobile attacks.

Weapon Systems and Combat

Weapon systems are complex mechanisms that require lots of manpower and equipment to work properly. Most weapons can be used only offensively (to score damage on opposing forces) or defensively (to intercept incoming fire or fighters), although some weapons can be used for both purposes.

Ship weapons are defined by several key elements. The first is the Fire Arc. This is the direction in which the weapon can fire, based on how it is mounted on the ship. The second element of a weapon is the ships' Fire Control system. Fire Control encompasses the targeting and other electronic systems that make the weapon fire, and determine what targets the ship may engage. Finally, there is the Weapon Battery. This is not just the actual turret of guns, but also the power source and associated mechanisms. The type of weapon in the battery determines the range and effect of the weapon when it hits the target.

Fire Arc

Each ship has four Fire Arcs through which its various weapons and systems may operate; they are the forward, port, starboard and aft arcs. The forward and aft arcs are each 60 degrees wide, while the port and starboard arcs are each 120 degrees. Fire Arcs are marked on the provided counters.

Most shipboard weapons systems (and some defenses as well) may only bear through one Fire Arc—thus a weapon mounted to fire forward may be used against targets in the ship's forward arc, but may not fire at targets in the side or aft arcs. The Fire Arcs are also relevant to incoming fire against the ship, as the arc where the incoming fire originates determines which defensive systems are able to function against it (if a ship takes fire from an enemy vessel that is in its port arc, only the ship's port-mounted Interceptor systems can protect against the incoming fire).

To determine the relevant arc for either outgoing or incoming fire, lay your measuring tape or ruler between the two ships and look at which side of the counter it intersects—this will show which is the correct Fire Arc. If the bearing to the target ship falls exactly on the dividing line between two arcs (or closely enough to cause dispute), simply roll a d6 to decide, with an even result indicating one arc and an odd result the other. No target may ever occupy two Fire Arcs at the same time.

Fire Control Systems

Each ship type has one or more Fire Control systems for its anti-ship weaponry. All ships have at least one Fire Control, with larger warships having two or even three. Each Fire Control system on a ship allows it to obtain a firing solution on any one target per turn, which may then be attacked with any combination of weapons that the firing ship can bring to bear on it. Thus a ship with two Fire Control systems may engage two different targets in the same game turn, dividing its available weaponry in any way desired between the two targets. Each weapon system may fire only once per turn, of course, regardless of the number of Fire Control systems on the ship.

As the battle begins, the Centauri ships surround the Charon in an attempt to cripple it quickly. The main gunner on board, Lieutenant Jose Guerrero, must decide how to split the fire. A Centauri Battle Cruiser and Light Cruiser are in the fore arc and another Battle Cruiser is in the port arc. The Charon has three Fire Control systems so it can fire on up to three ships at the same time. As there are three Fire Controls and only one ship to port, Jose will obviously fire the port bearing weapon batteries at the Battle Cruiser in that arc. In addition to that, Jose can either shoot all the fore bearing weapons at one ship or split the fire between the two. Instead of concentrating his firepower to destroy the Battle Cruiser, Jose splits his fire. He shoots the Battle Cruiser with a small blast from the laser cannon, and fires the fore mounted pulse cannons at the

Light Cruiser. Jose hopes these shots coupled with the fire on the Battle Cruiser in the port arc, will deter the Centauri from further battle and save them from having to combat the Centauri ships.

If a Fire Control system is lost due to damage, the ship's targeting ability is reduced accordingly—if it was the only (or last remaining) Fire Control then the ship is now unable to fire ranged weapons. Interceptors, Anti-Fighter Batteries and similar defensive systems do not require the use of a Fire Control (they are assumed to have their own integral short-range targeting systems). Weapons that do not require Fire Control systems note this in their definitions.

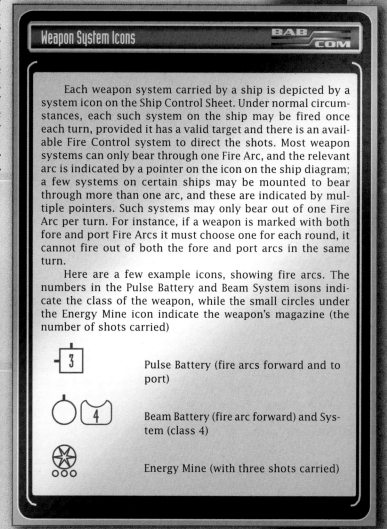

Weapon System Icons

Each weapon system carried by a ship is depicted by a system icon on the Ship Control Sheet. Under normal circumstances, each such system on the ship may be fired once each turn, provided it has a valid target and there is an available Fire Control system to direct the shots. Most weapon systems can only bear through one Fire Arc, and the relevant arc is indicated by a pointer on the icon on the ship diagram; a few systems on certain ships may be mounted to bear through more than one arc, and these are indicated by multiple pointers. Such systems may only bear out of one Fire Arc per turn. For instance, if a weapon is marked with both fore and port Fire Arcs it must choose one for each round, it cannot fire out of both the fore and port arcs in the same turn.

Here are a few example icons, showing fire arcs. The numbers in the Pulse Battery and Beam System isons indicate the class of the weapon, while the small circles under the Energy Mine icon indicate the weapon's magazine (the number of shots carried)

Pulse Battery (fire arcs forward and to port)

Beam Battery (fire arc forward) and System (class 4)

Energy Mine (with three shots carried)

Offensive Weapon Systems

There are two main types of offensive weapon systems carried by Earth Alliance ships and those races of similar technology levels: Pulse Batteries and Beam Batteries. Pulse Batteries are multiple guns that work much like giant PPGs, firing rapid volleys of plasma pulses which (although very fast) travel at sublight speeds and can therefore be intercepted by similar systems used in a defensive role (see Interceptors, page 83).

Beam Batteries are projectors for very powerful continuous-beam energy weapons. Each beam travels at the speed of light and is therefore impossible to intercept. But beam weapons require enormous energy input compared to that of the pulse weapons—the firing system for a ship's Beam Batteries must recharge between shots, so the weapons are not always able to fire at full power in every turn of the game.

Pulse Batteries

There are four different classes of Pulse Batteries; each battery may fire once per turn, at any target that is in range and within its Fire Arc. Pulse systems do not require any recharging period—they may fire every turn if desired. Each Pulse Battery has a class rating. From 0 to 10 MU the battery rolls a number of dice equal to its class rating. For each 10 MU past that the battery rolls one die less. For instance a class 2 Pulse Battery would roll 2 dice between 0 and 10 MU and 1 die between 10 and 20 MU.

For each die rolled during Pulse Weapons fire, count the results as follows:

Scores of 1, 2 or 3 = No Effect (either the shot misses altogether, or hits but with negligible damage).

Scores of 4 or 5 = One damage point is inflicted on the target.

Score of 6 = Two damage points inflicted, PLUS the firer gets to reroll the die and thus may inflict further damage (treat the reroll as if it were a normal roll so a 4 or 5 is one point and a 6 is 2 with yet another reroll).

The Centauri Battle Cruiser to the port of the EAS Charon is at 16 MU. This is in the 10-20 MU range for the class 2 Pulse Batteries on that side of the Charon. Mark, who is playing Jose, rolls two dice (one for each battery). He scores a 6 and a 4. He inflicts one point of dam-

age for the 4 and two points for the 6. He also gets to reroll the 6, scoring a 4, which gives him an additional one damage point. The final total of damage inflicted on the target from this attack is 4 points.

Beam Batteries

A Beam Battery consists of two (or more) separate elements: a Beam Power System (BPS) and one or more Projectors (each of which is considered a separate system for the purposes of damage rolls at Threshold Points). The BPS is a generator and power storage facility which produces the energy required for firing the beams, holding it in capacitor banks until it is discharged through the Projector(s). The BPS may store a number of Energy Points equal to the Class of the BPS—thus a Class 6 beam system could store up to 6 Energy Points in its capacitor banks at any one time. Each Energy Point stored allows one die to be rolled when a beam is fired. In a given turn, a BPS may discharge as many Energy Points as it has stored at that moment, through as many different Projectors as the player wishes (subject to usual targeting limitations and available Fire Control systems). It does not have to use all its stored energy at one time, though it may if desired.

Seeing the attack on the EAS Charon, the captain of the EAS Achilles, Captain Gustav Hunbecker, orders his ship to move in closer to assist Capt. Weisshaupt and his crew. The Achilles forcefully barrels its way into the middle of the fray displaying the tactical style that gives Capt. Hunbecker his nickname of Gustav the Hun. The Achilles, an Omega class destroyer, has a Class 6 Beam System and four Projectors. The Projectors are mounted as 2 each fore and aft. Lieutenant Commander Fazil Mahmood, the main gunner on the Achilles, could use the three Fire Control systems to split the beam shot. He can divide the energy he discharges any way he wants. He may decide to fire a 4-dice beam shot at a ship in the fore arc and use the aft Projectors for a 2-dice shot to the ship behind them. Fazil could also fire a smaller

shot, which is less powerful than a full 6-dice shot but would leave Energy Points in the BPS for next round. Fazil can fire out of as many Projectors as he wishes but he has a maximum of 6 Energy Points to divide between them.

Resolving Beam Weapon Fire

Fire from Beam Batteries is resolved differently from that of Pulse Batteries. First, measure the range to the target ship. The effectiveness of the beam diminishes with range—for every full 6 MU between firer and target, subtract 1 from the score of each die rolled. The resulting total score of all the dice in the shot, after deducting this range modifier from each die, is the total amount of damage done by the beam shot. Any die that rolls a 6 before range modifiers are deducted allows a reroll, and any rerolled damage is counted for full value, without any range deductions.

Fazil decides to shoot a single blast at the Centauri Battle Cruiser in the fore arc. He only expends 3 Energy Points, saving some in the BPS to make sure he has a full charge when he gets a better shot. The shot is fired at a range of 15 MU. There are two full multiples of 6 MU in the range, so 2 will be subtracted from each die rolled to account for the lessened effect over distance. Bill, the player controlling Fazil, rolls his three dice and scores 3,1 and 6. Subtracting the 2 from each die means that the roll of 1 scores nothing, the 3 is reduced to 1 and the 6 to 4. Thus the final total damage scored is 5 points (4 plus 1). However, one of the rolls was a 6, which allows a reroll (even though it was later modified down to just 4). This reroll scores 3, this is not modified for range, and results in a final damage total of 8 points.

Recharging

At the start of each turn, during the Order Phase, roll 1 die for the Beam Power System on each ship equipped with Beam Batteries. On a 1 or 2 the result is 2 Energy Points, a 3 or 4 is 3 Energy Points and a 5 or

6 is 4 Energy Points. These points are added to the remaining state of charge from the previous turn. If the roll (or the power total) exceeds the Class rating of the system, any surplus Energy Points are wasted—no BPS may store more Energy Points than its Class allows.

Bill, rolls a die to recharge the BPS at the beginning of the next turn and scores 1. This increases the charge by 2. Adding this to the stored Energy Points gives a total of 5 that can be used, if desired, in the new turn. Had Bill rolled 5 with his recharge die, this would have received 4 Energy Points giving a total of 7—more than the system can store, so it would be considered fully charged at 6 Energy Points and the surplus point would be ignored.

Damage to Beam Weapons

When performing a Threshold Check on a Beam Battery (see Recording Damage below), roll separately for the Beam Power System and for each Projector. Projectors that suffer a critical hit from a Threshold Check are simply knocked out as with any other system. If the BPS is hit, immediately roll the die again: on a roll of 1 or 2 the system simply loses any stored power—it may begin to recharge again next turn as normal, and is otherwise undamaged. On a 3, 4 or 5 the system loses all stored power and its storage capacity is permanently halved—it may not be charged to more than half its original capacity (rounded up) for the rest of the game. On a roll of 6, the power system is completely knocked-out—the ship may not fire beam weapons from any Projector for the rest of the game—and the ship suffers a number of additional damage points equal to the amount of stored Energy Points currently in the system (thus if a Class 6 BPS were hit while fully charged it would do 6 points of damage to its own ship as well as being rendered useless for the remainder of the game).

Recording Damage

Damage is recorded by filling in the boxes on the Damage Track on the ship diagram, starting on the top row and filling successive boxes from left to right. Whenever you reach the right-hand end of a row of damage boxes, you have reached a Threshold Point where the accumulated damage is sufficient that it may cause some of the ship's systems (weapons, drives etc.) to fail. At this point a Threshold Check is made against all the systems on the ship, to see if any are damaged and rendered inoperative.

To make a Threshold Check, roll one die for each operational system on the ship—every symbol on the ship diagram. If the result is equal to or higher than the Threshold Number (the number at the end of the row of damage boxes) the particular system that is being rolled for is knocked out for the remainder of the game. Roll for all systems on the ship at each Threshold Check, regardless of their location on the ship or the direction from which the damage was taken. The final row of damage boxes has no Threshold Number, because when a ship has had its Damage Track filled the ship is destroyed.

Most systems on ships are knocked out the first time they fail a Threshold Check. There are a few exceptions to this rule (such as Jump Engines or Beam Batteries), as explained in the rules for those systems.

The Centauri open fire on the Charon. In one round they score 14 points of damage. This is the entire first row of damage plus 10 more boxes on the second row (The Charon had already taken 8 points of damage from the previous round). As one full line of damage boxes has now been filled, Rob must make a Threshold Check on each of the systems on the ship, to see if any have been knocked out by the accumulated damage.

Catastrophic Damage and Chain Reactions

Most of the time damage to ships is progressive—each attack will knock a few more damage boxes off until eventually the ship is reduced to a drifting hulk. There are occasions, however, where a ship will suffer such massive damage in a short space of time that a chain-reaction starts in the ship's structure, with damage building upon damage until the entire craft explodes or breaks up.

If a ship takes enough damage in one game turn to require it to make two or more Threshold Checks, then there is the danger of a Chain-Reaction destroying the ship completely. The damage does not have to be caused in one single attack—several ships can fire on one target in order to cause this effect—what matters is that the total amount of damage suffered by the ship during all the fire combat of one turn is enough to require two or more Threshold Checks that turn. At the point that more than one Threshold Check is required, in addition to rolling for each system on the ship, first the player must make one extra roll. If this die scores over the number required for the most recent Threshold Check, then the entire next row of damage boxes is immediately filled in—thus requiring another Threshold Check, and another of the special Chain-Reaction rolls. If this progression results in the last row of damage boxes being filled, then the ship is totally destroyed.

The next round of combat, the Achilles and the Charon both line up on the same target. Capt. Weisshaupt and Capt. Hunbecker concentrate their firepower on one of the Battle Cruisers, which has only taken 4 points of damage so far. Both EA Destroyers fire all of their fore bearing weaponry at the target and do 25 points of damage. The Centauri Battle Cruiser has five rows of 10 damage boxes. This damage fills the top two rows and 9 of the damage boxes on the third row (the ship already had 4 points of damage). Before a Threshold Check is made for the first row (at 6 to knock out systems), and for the second row (a 5 or 6 required to knock out systems). The GM must make the Chain-Reaction roll—the GM is unlucky, and rolls 5. Bits of the ship blow up in all directions as the damage spreads, wiping out all the last damage box of the third row and forcing another Threshold Check (this time with a 4,5 or 6 knocking out systems). Again, before the Threshold Check, the Chain-Reaction roll is made and again luck is not with the cruiser, as the GM rolls a 6 this time—losing the fourth damage row. This results in another check (this time at 3,4,5 or 6)—by now the damage is virtually unstoppable, and with only one row of damage boxes left the GM rolls a 4. The last row of damage boxes is filled in on the Damage Track. With a huge and soundless blast the Battle Cruiser becomes an expanding cloud of debris.

Defensive Weapon Systems: Interceptors

Most warships carry defensive batteries of small pulse-firing cannon known as Interceptors, to protect them against incoming fire from some weapons systems. Interceptors can target incoming fire from Pulse Batteries and Fighter Groups that fire pulse weapons, reducing their effectiveness. They are not, however, of any use against Beam Batteries. In anti-pulse mode the Interceptors are actively shooting weapons fire directed at them. While they cannot shoot Fighter Groups in this mode, they can still target the fire that Fighter Groups use as long as it is a pulse weapon. The Narn, Centauri, Earthforce and Raider Fighter Groups all use some form of pulse weaponry. The Minbari Fighter Groups use a beam system. Each Interceptor Battery can cover only one arc of a ship, so for all-round protection a separate Interceptor system must be mounted in each of the four Fire Arcs. Very large ships may sometimes carry two Interceptor systems in some or all arcs. Each Interceptor may only protect against fire that is directed through its arc of coverage.

If there is one active Interceptor system covering an arc in which enemy pulse weapons are firing, then only rolls of 5 or 6 will damage the ship. Any rolls of 5 or 6 still inflict their usual damage, including rerolls for scores of 6. Note that since damage rolls of 6 do more damage and allow rerolls, just subtracting one from the attack die will not work.

If two active Interceptors protect the relevant arc of the ship, then only pulse weapon attack rolls of 6 damage the ship. These get through the Interceptor barrage and cause normal damage (including rerolls). Note that because a roll of 6 will inflict two points of damage and result in a reroll, subtracting two from each attack die rolled will not achieve the same effect.

More than two Interceptors in one arc have no additional protective effect, though there is no reason that a very large ship might not carry additional systems for backup in case of damage. Interceptor systems may also function as anti-fighter weapons against any Fighter Groups that are within 6 MU the ship (see below). In any given turn of the game, however, a single Interceptor Battery on a particular ship may be fired only once. If it is used against a Fighter Group, it may not be used to intercept incoming fire on the same turn. All Interceptor Batteries on one ship must be dedicated to either Anti-Fighter or Anti-Pulse fire in the ship's orders at the start of the turn—if the orders do not specify, the Interceptors remain at the same setting as they were in the previous turn. Interceptors begin the game configured for Anti-Pulse fire. An Interceptor system that is currently dedicated for use against one threat cannot be used against the other until it is reconfigured at the start of the next turn.

Anti-Fighter Batteries

Anti-Fighter Batteries are a simplified version of Interceptor Batteries, which may be used against attacking Fighter Groups only—they lack the capability to intercept incoming pulse Weapons Fire. Ships that are equipped with Anti-Fighter Batteries may use them as defense against Fighter Groups. An Anti-Fighter Battery may shoot at one Fighter Group that is within its specific arc of fire, and is within 6 MU. The Fighter Group does not have to actually be making an attack on the ship. If the ship has two or more AFBs covering the same arc, each can fire at a different Fighter Group or their fire may be combined against one group. All Anti-Fighter fire takes place at the end of ship movement. To fire an AFB roll one die. The number rolled on the die minus 2 is the number of fighters killed in the target Fighter Group. Note that this means that an Interceptor shot will not always take out fighters.

Fighters

Small one- or two-pilot fighters often make the difference between victory and defeat in a battle. Fast and maneuverable, they are able to do significant damage if they are not destroyed or engaged by other fighters. All races use some form of fighter craft in their space fleets.

Fighters move and attack in groups, known as squadrons. For the purposes of this game, each squadron is a Fighter Group of six fighters, represented by one Counter on the table. Next to each Fighter Group is also a die that represents how many individual fighters remain in the group. As fighters are killed from the group, the face of the die is turned to reflect how many survive. When there are no fighters left in the group, the Counter and die are removed from the table.

Fighter Group Movement

Fighter Groups move differently than other larger ships in game terms. In relation to large warships and transports, fighters are incredibly maneuverable and able to react to the movement of the larger vessels—they can quite literally fly rings round them. For this reason each Fighter Group does not require any written orders, but may simply be moved in any desired direction during the Fighter Movement Phase, up to a maximum distance according to the type of fighter. Fighter Maximum Movement is 20 MU for Raider, Narn and Centauri Fighters and 30 MU for EA Starfuries and Minbari Fighters.

Launching and Recovering Fighters

Ships that carry Fighter Groups have sufficient launching capability to handle half their total fighter complement each turn. A ship carrying four Fighter Groups could launch two of those groups in one turn, but one carrying only two Fighter Group could launch only one group per turn. Fighter Groups land back on the carrier ship at the same rate. However, the total number of Fighter Groups launched and recovered in one turn cannot exceed half the fighter complement, so a ship with four groups embarked could launch two Fighter Groups, recover two Fighter Groups, or launch one and recover another in the same turn.

To launch Fighter Groups, write a Launch order into the ship's Movement Orders at the start of the turn. The Fighter Groups are launched at the start of the Ship Movement Phase. When launched, a Fighter Group moves directly away from the front of the ship along a Course of the ship's current Heading 6 MU, and then moves along the ship's current Course for a distance equal to its Velocity. So if the carrier ship is traveling at 8 MU on Course 3 and Heading 6 at the time of launch, the fighters will move on Course 6 for a distance of 6 MU and then along Course 3 for 8 MU.

That launch is the Fighter Group's movement for the turn. A Fighter Group may not make attacks the turn it launches, but may defend itself if attacked by other Fighter Groups. On the following turn the fighters may move freely as per the normal Fighter Movement rules.

Ships may recover Fighter Groups during a turn without the need for written orders to that effect. To recover a Fighter Group, they must be moved so that they are within 6 MU of their carrier at the end of the Ship Movement Phase. If neither the Fighter Groups nor the carrier come under attack by enemy fighters during the Combat Phase the Fighter Groups are recovered, safely landing aboard the carrier, and their counters are removed from the table. If attacked by enemy Fighter Groups, they may either break to engage or attempt to land regardless. If they do not break to engage, the enemy Fighter Groups make their at-tack as normal with no danger of the landing fighters returning fire. If any of the landing fighters survive the attack they succeed in their landing attempt.

Scrambling Fighters

In an emergency situation, a player may wish to launch Fighter Groups to react to an attack by enemy Fighter Groups even though there are no Launch orders for Fighter Groups that turn. Scrambling fighters may only be attempted immediately after the Ship Movement Phase, and only if two criteria are met: the ship must have enemy Fighter Groups able to attack it (within 6 MU); and it must have no Fighter Screens. To attempt to scramble a Fighter Group, roll a die. On a score of 1-3, no Fighter Groups scramble. On a 4 or 5 one Fighter Group may scramble to meet the attackers. On a 6 the ship successfully Scrambles as many Fighter Groups as it may normally launch in a turn. Fighter Groups that are Scrambled are not moved away from the carrying ship as they are during normal launches, but instead immediately take up position to Screen the ship from the attacking Fighter Groups (see Fighter Screens below). Unlike normal fighter launches, Scrambled groups may attack the same turn they launch.

Fighter Screens

Fighter Groups may closely escort larger ships specifically to ward off enemy fighter attacks on that ship. When used in this role, a Fighter Group acts as a Fighter Screen for the ship it is escorting.

At the beginning of any Ship Movement Phase, any Fighter Groups within 3 MU of a ship may be declared a Fighter Screen for that ship.

When acting as a Fighter Screen, Fighter Groups remain within 3 MU of the ship they are escorting at all times. A Fighter Screen (which may be a single Fighter Group or several) does not move in the Fighter Movement Phase, instead it moves at the same time as the ship it is screening, during the Ship Movement Phase. If a Fighter Group chooses to move during the Fighter Move-

ment Phase, it must break off of the Fighter Screen before the ship moves, and is once again on its own.

Whenever a ship with a Fighter Screen comes under attack from enemy Fighter Groups, the attacking Fighter Groups must engage the Fighter Screen using the Dogfighting rules before they may fire on the escorted ship. Each Fighter Group in the Fighter Screen must be engaged by at least one attacking Fighter Group. Once this condition has been satisfied, any further uncommitted attacking groups may fire on the escorted ship.

During the entire battle, the Achilles and Charon each have their four Fighter Groups in Fighter Screens. Five Centauri Fighter Groups move to attack the Achilles. Four of them must pair off against the four Fighter Groups in the Fighter Screen and engage them in Dogfights while the fifth is free to attack the destroyer directly. If the GM prefers, he or she could instead allocate all five Fighter Groups against the Fighter Screen (two Fighter Groups onto one, and one each onto the other three) in an attempt to destroy as many starfuries

as possible, hopefully leaving the destroyer without a Fighter Screen.

Dogfights

Whenever two or more Fighter Groups end the Fighter Movement Phase within 6 MU of each other, one may engage the other in a dogfight. This represents the individual fighters attacking and trying to destroy the craft in the opposing group. Since a single counter represents each Fighter Group the action is resolved abstractly. Move both/all Fighter Groups so that they are directly facing each other (simply to indicate that they are engaged in a dogfight). Each player rolls a number of dice equal to the number of fighters they have remaining in his or her Fighter Group. The table opposite gives the score required to kill one fighter from the opposing Fighter Group, depending on the types of craft involved. EA starfuries are better in combat than fighters from the Narn, Centauri or Raiders are, but poorer than the Minbari fighters due to the latter's advanced stealth technology.

In certain cases (indicated by a red 6 on the table), a score of 6 on any die kills two fighters from the opposing Fighter Group, and allows a reroll of that die as well. Where there is no red 6, a 6 is counted as just one fighter killed, with no reroll permitted. All fighter-to-fighter combat is simultaneous. Both players roll their dice at the same time, and no losses are noted until all Fighter Groups' hits have been determined.

Multiple Group Dogfights ("Furballs")

There will be times, especially when Fighter Groups are acting as a Fighter Screen for larger ships, where multiple Fighter Groups will be close enough to engage in a Dogfight. In such combats, all groups engaged in the Dogfight may fight only once per turn, firing on any one group of their choosing. The choice of whom to attack alternates between groups at the end of the Fighter Movement Phase starting with the player who moved the first Fighter Group. One Fighter Group may be attacked more than once, but all results and losses are still adjudicated simultaneously—that is, no fighters are counted as lost until all have had a chance to attack.

Fighter Attacks

A Fighter Group may attack any ship within 6 MU during the Combat Phase. The position of the Fighter Group relative to the ship will show which arc of the ship is under attack, and hence which Defensive Weapon Systems (if any) may be used against the attacking fighters. It is not necessary for the Fighter Groups to have ended their movement pointed at the ship they are attacking—merely being within the 6 MU range

limit is sufficient, as fighters are agile enough to spin in flight and fire in any direction. As noted in the Combat Phase rules, any defensive fire by the ship under attack occurs at the end of the Fighter Movement Phase. Any losses to the Fighter Group from defensive fire are applied immediately and lost fighters will not get a chance to attack the ship.

A Fighter Group will fire on the ship it is attacking when that ship is chosen as the Active Ship (as described on page 73). The

only exception to this is if the Fighter Group has a player character in it. In this case it is possible to select that particular Fighter Group as the Active Ship which means that it does not need to wait for the ship to fire before it can attack.

For each individual fighter attacking, roll a die and count the results exactly as for Pulse Battery fire (rolls of 1-3 have no effect, 4 or 5 give 1 point of damage to the target, and a 6 gives two damage points plus a reroll).

The fifth Centauri Fighter Group, which engaged the Achilles directly, has all six of its original craft remaining. When it attacks the Achilles, it rolls six dice (one per fighter). The GM rolls and scores 1,3,6,5,3,2—he inflicts three damage points (one for the 5, two for the 6) and rerolls for the six, which scores a 4. Since the Achilles has an active Interceptor Battery in that Fire Arc in anti-pulse mode, the roll of a 4 is considered to have done no damage. The final total is three points of damage. Fred crosses off three damage boxes on the Achilles' Damage Track.

Fighter Pilot Aces

Most fighter pilots are assumed to be reasonably good at their job. However, there

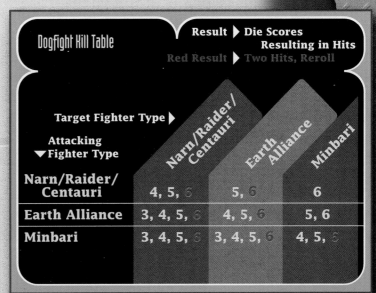

Dogfight Kill Table		Result ▶ Die Scores Resulting in Hits Red Result ▶ Two Hits, Reroll		
Target Fighter Type ▶ Attacking ▼ Fighter Type		Narn/Raider/ Centauri	Earth Alliance	Minbari
Narn/Raider/ Centauri		4, 5, 6	5, 6	6
Earth Alliance		3, 4, 5, 6	4, 5, 6	5, 6
Minbari		3, 4, 5, 6	3, 4, 5, 6	4, 5, 6

are a few that are significantly better than others—these are considered Aces. If a player-character has good fighter pilot skills and is involved in a tactical combat, then he or she might be considered an Ace for the purposes of these rules—even if he or she hasn't been recognized as such in the game (see Player Characters in Ship Combat, page 92). Additionally, the GM may choose to allow players to randomly allocate a few Aces among their Fighter Groups by any agreed method (a good method is to roll one die for each group at the start of the game. Any groups that score a 6 have one Ace pilot with them). A Fighter Group with an Ace gains a bonus in normal attacks and Dogfighting, and may also attempt certain special actions. When a group containing an Ace takes losses, the Ace is the last fighter to be destroyed—after all, he or she is the best pilot in the Fighter Group.

Attacking Aces

If an attacking Fighter Group contains an Ace, that pilot may be used in one of two ways. First, he or she may attack normally with the rest of the group. When attacking normally, an Ace adds an extra die to the number of dice the Fighter Group would otherwise roll. So an undamaged Fighter Group with six fighters and an Ace among them will roll seven dice rather than the usual six.

Alternatively, the Ace can choose to attack a specific system on the target ship (such as a Weapon Battery, a Fire Control system or the ship's Main Drives). When attacking a system the Ace rolls one die. If a 6 is scored then the targeted system is knocked out. Any other result scores no damage. If an Ace attempts specific targeting, the rest of the group makes a normal attack at the same time, with normal damage results.

Aces in Dogfighting

If a Fighter Group contains an Ace, that Fighter Group rolls an extra die in dogfight situations. Thus an undamaged Fighter Group of six fighters including an Ace pilot

would get to roll seven dice rather than the usual six. The result of this extra die is counted normally.

If both Fighter Groups involved in a dogfight have an Ace, then either player may choose to have his or her Ace seek out the opposing Ace and engage that fighter directly while the rest of the dogfight is going on around them. In this case, each of the Aces rolls just one die and consults the dogfight kill table for the results. If both roll sufficient scores, they can both be destroyed at the same time. While this single combat is going on, the remaining fighters in each Fighter Group roll for their normal dogfight attacks as usual.

SA-25 "Badger"

Both heavier and longer ranged than normal starfuries, Badgers have certain advantages. With their extended capabilities Badgers can stay on patrol more often than other fighters. If a ship has a compliment of Badgers on board it may have up to half of the SA-25s screening it at the beginning of combat. They are also more sturdy and heavy than most fighters. As a result, ignore the first score resulting in a kill on a Fighter Group of Badgers from each attacking Fighter Group or form of anti-fighter weapon every time the group is attacked.

Shuttles and Other Small Craft

A small craft is any spacecraft that is larger than a fighter, but too small to be worth representing in the game as a full ship design. Typical examples include the small shuttles used to ferry personnel and cargo between space stations and major ships. Each such small craft is represented by its own counter or model, but does not require a Ship Control Sheet. It moves during the Fighter Movement Phase and follows the same movement guidelines as fighters with the following exceptions: first, small craft may only move up to 12 MU per turn; second, small craft may not change Course by more than 3 Course Points in one game turn.

Each small craft has two damage points. It has no Threshold Points—it is simply damaged (but still functional) after it receives one point of damage, and destroyed after two. Damage to small craft can either be indicated with a marker or noted by the players.

Small craft may or may not be armed, at the players' or GM's discretion. An armed small craft can fire as if it were one fighter (with all-round fire, it rolls a single die to attack any target within a range of 6 MU. Results of 1-3 = no effect, 4-5 = 1 hit, 6 = 2 hits + reroll). An armed small craft that is damaged (i.e.: takes one hit) loses the use of its weapon system.

Collisions and Ramming

Space is very big and the chances of an accidental collision between ships are negligible, so for the sake of simplicity there are no rules for unintentional collisions. If two counters end up close enough that they touch or overlap, simply move each slightly to accommodate them on the table with the minimum changes of position. The counters do not represent the actual size of ships at scale anyway, so their touching does not indicate collision.

Deliberate ramming of one ship by another is possible in space combat, but is thankfully rare. It will usually occur only as a last act of desperation, sacrificing a ship and its crew so that others can survive. Ships' Captains are obviously very reluctant to use such tactics unless the situation is otherwise hopeless, and even then it takes a very brave and honorable commander to carry it through. The following ramming rules are meant to be used only with a stand-alone tabletop game. If a situation occurs during a campaign where PCs who are controlling a ship wish to ram, use the rules below in the Ramming with Player Characters section.

In order to attempt a ram, the ramming player must write Movement Orders so that the ship is within 3 MU of the target ship at the end of the Ship Movement Phase and specify that he or she intends to ram. The ramming ship must have at least one functioning Main Drive unit at this point.

It is a difficult task to decide to ram an enemy and even more difficult to convince the crew that it is the necessary and right thing to do. To reflect this (and to prevent players using ramming as a tactic of choice with no regard for their crews), any ship which wishes to attempt a ram must first roll a die during the Movement Phase on the chart below:

If the Ramming ship rolls the score listed or better, then it may attempt to ram. At the discretion of the referee or the agreement of the other players, modifiers to the die roll may be allowed in special circumstances. For example a Narn warship trying to stop a Centauri attack on a Narn refugee ship could well be given a +1 or even +2 on its die roll.

Provided the roll is successful, each player involved rolls one die, and adds to that roll the current Drive Rating remaining on the ship (any undamaged drives). If the ramming ship scores highest, it manages to ram the target. If the scores are equal or the target ship scores highest, it evades successfully. If the ramming attempt is successful, both ships suffer an amount of damage equal to the total original damage points of the smaller ship. The smaller

Ramming Table			Result ▶ Die Roll Needed to Ram	
Target Ship ▶ **▼Ramming Ship**	Human	Narn	Centauri	Minbari
Human	6	6	5	5
Narn	5	6	4	5
Centauri	5	5	6	5
Minbari	5	5	5	6

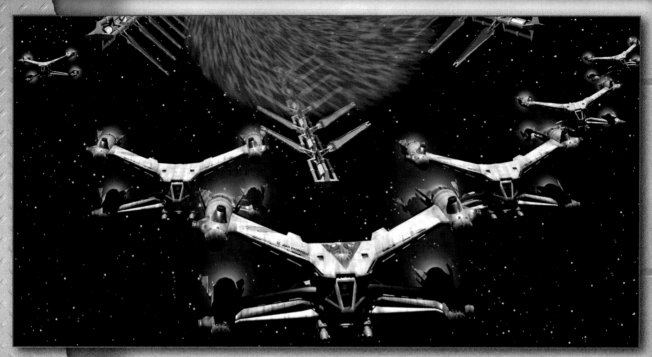

ship will always be destroyed, and the larger probably crippled.

Ramming by Fighters

Fighter Groups may attempt to ram ships or other Fighter Groups in desperate circumstances, using the same rules and chart as for larger ships, with the following special conditions: all surviving fighters in a given Fighter Group must attempt to Ram or none may; and one morale roll is made for the entire Fighter Group.

If a ramming Fighter Group is dogfighting with another Fighter Group, each one rolls one die per fighter to see which make contact and which are evaded. Any fighters that Ram successfully destroy both the other fighter and themselves.

If the Fighter Group attempts to ram a capital ship, they will always be successful—larger ships have no opportunity to evade (although the fighters must have rolled on the ramming chart first to make sure that they will go through with it). Each fighter in the group will cause an automatic two points of damage to the target ship, destroying itself in the process.

Ramming with Player Characters

The above ramming rules should only be used in a stand-alone tabletop game. If the ramming ship is in the control of PCs, the decision is left to the players. The ramifications of ramming a vessel in a campaign are much more severe than when just playing a single game without PCs involved. If the players deem the situation dire enough to elicit ramming the enemy ship then they may attempt with no moral role.

If a capital ship is in the control of PCs and they wish to ram these rules are used instead of the ones listed above. First the player who is writing the orders for the ship must note the attempt to ram in the orders, and the ship must be 3 MU from the target vessel at the end of the Ship Movement Phase. If this occurs than the character who is actually steering the ship must make a static task resolution. It is not considered contested with the helmsman on the target ship because it is more of a matter of plotting the correct Course instead of outmaneuvering the enemy. The base difficulty is Tricky and 2 is added to the difficulty for each drive unit the enemy ship has above the amount on the PCs ship.

Ramming Damage

Damage caused by ramming an enemy ship is extremely brutal. It is very unlikely that that either ship will survive the ram. For this reason, Fortune Points may not be used to keep a ramming ship from being destroyed. It is also very unlikely that a character on board a ramming ship will be able to make it to a life pod before the ship is destroyed. It is rare that a player character survives if on the ramming ship.

Any character that is piloting a fighter may attempt to ram either a capital ship or an enemy fighter. No roll is made if the character wishes to ram into a capital ship. Fighters have such an agility advantage over these cumbersome ships that there is no way for them to evade the incoming fighter. If the character wants to ram an enemy fighter, he or she must beat the enemy fighter in a contested task resolution. If the character succeeds both fighters are destroyed. In both cases the pilot may not eject before impact. Constant course adjustments must be made to ensure hitting the target until the very last moment and ejecting would alter the path. There is no possibility of a pilot surviving an intentional ram.

Jump Points and Jumpgates

Ships may enter or leave the battle area via hyperspace through a jump point created either by a permanent jumpgate or one generated by a ship's Jump Engines. jumpgates must be placed on the table before the game (see the Counters), and remain in a fixed position.

Any player may activate an unsecured jumpgate at the start of any game turn. A player may only open a secured jumpgate if their side owns the gate; any non-friendly ships must enter through jump points of their own making. Obviously, the GM must decide the security status of any jumpgates before the scenario begins. To open the gate, a player designates one ship as the requesting ship, which is the ship that sends the signal to the gate.

When a jump point or jumpgate is activated, place a jump point counter on the table at the beginning of the turn. The gate will remain open until the requesting or creating ship either passes through the gate, moves more than 12 MU away from the gate, or is destroyed, to a maximum of five turns.

A jump point formed by a ship's Jump Engines may be formed anywhere within 12 MU of that ship. Normally ships open jump points for themselves and any escorting craft, and thus form the point directly ahead of themselves in order to fly straight into it or behind them in order to protect their escorts; however there is nothing to stop a ship forming the jump point in any other direction in order to allow other craft to use it while the generating ship remains in normal space. In all cases, the point will collapse at the end of the turn when the ship forming the point has gone through, moved more than 12 MU away, or closes the point, to a maximum of four turns from the turn the point formed.

Ships equipped with Jump Engines require an enormous amount of power in order to use those engines. In order to open a jump point using Jump Engines, a ship must write an activate Jump Engines order into its Movement Orders (written "JP") on one turn. The ship may then open the jump point on the following turn. During these two turns, that ship may not fire any weapons: the power is diverted to the Jump Engines.

Once used, Jump Engines must recharge before they can open another point. Ships that arrive on-table through a jump point of their own making or that open a jump point on the table but do not go through may not open another jump point until six full game turns have elapsed. They may, of course, use a jump point created by another ship or a jumpgate at any time.

Successful jump point entry requires certain criteria to be met:

1) The ship's Course must take it into the point within the safe arc of the jump point counter (the front two faces of the counter) and the ship's current Course and heading must be within 1 Course Point of the Heading of the jump point—if the jump

point counter is aligned on Course 12, then a ship must be traveling on Course 11, 12 or 1 in order to enter the jump point safely. A ship that intersects with the jump point counter at an incorrect angle will be destroyed.

2) The ship's Velocity must be at least 6 MU, but not more than 12 MU—any ship traveling at velocities outside these limits will suffer one complete row of damage on its Damage Track automatically on trying to enter the jump point. A ship can accelerate or decelerate on the turn it enters the point in order to be within the Velocity limits, provided it has the required thrust power available from its drives.

3) A jump order must be in the Movement Orders for that ship that turn, along with any Course change and/or thrust necessary to line it up with the jump point.

Collapsing Jump Points

All ships transiting a jump point during a turn that it is active will make the jump with no problems (provided they follow the successful jump point entry criteria). However, traveling through a collapsing jump point can prove fatal. A jump point collapses when it is terminated (either the ship which created it decides to collapse it, or the ship that created it has traversed the point). It starts to collapse at the beginning of the turn after it is terminated. It remains collapsing for one entire turn. At the beginning of the turn after collapsing it is gone and the counter is removed from the table.

A ship may make an attempt to transit a collapsing jump point. This is a significant risk, though—if caught in the "backwash" of the collapsing point the ship will be destroyed. Any ship attempting to use a collapsing jump point must roll a die. On a roll of 5 or 6 it makes a successful jump, following any others that may have gone through the point, but on a 4 or less it is completely destroyed in the attempt.

Feedback from Jump Points

Jump points take an enormous amount of power and effort to keep open. Without this constant attention they quickly become unstable. If a ship is damaged while going through a jump point, the energy discharge disturbs the forces keeping the point open and creates feedback through the Jump Engine of the ship that created the point. This feedback can damage and even destroy the Jump Engine, as well as the ship. If a jump point deals damage to a ship traversing the point, additionally it deals half of that damage (rounded up) to the ship holding the point open. If a ship is destroyed within the point use the amount of damage boxes it had left before being destroyed to calculate how much damage the feedback does.

If a ship with an undamaged Jump Engine takes feedback in this manner, roll a die. On a score of 5 or 6 the engine is damaged and the rules for a damaged Jump Engine take effect immediately, causing the point to collapse.

Damage to Jump Engines

Jump Engines, like any ship systems, may be damaged or destroyed during a Threshold Check. The first time the Jump Engines fail a Threshold Check, they are considered damaged. After failing a second Threshold Check, the Jump Engines are assumed to be disabled and unable to open a jump point at all.

Any time a damaged Jump Engine attempts to open a jump point, it is immediately considered to be collapsing. This point is considered to have been collapsing from the beginning of the current turn and will only stay on the table the round it was created.

If the Jump Engine forming the jump point is damaged while the point is open, the point is considered to be terminated and will begin to collapse at the beginning of the next turn.

Player Characters in Ship Combat

Combat between starships is deadly, using weapons of massive destructive power. More often than not battles will result in expensive ships being gutted or destroyed, with the loss of many (if not all) crew members. Players who are involved are at incredible risk.

Sometimes a space battle may occur as a backdrop to a game scenario, with the player-characters simply observing the battle from relative safety and then being influenced by its outcome. For example, the characters might be on a world or a large station while a battle rages in near space for the control of the area—the battle itself will not necessarily endanger the characters directly, but its outcome will have a significant effect on their immediate futures.

At other times, however, the characters may be directly involved in a battle. When this is the case they might be pilots or crew of a ship, and their skills will directly affect the outcome of the battle.

When a character has a skill directly applicable to a battle, he or she may contribute to the fight. There are many different skills that have a direct influence on combat, listed below. Under each job type a set of tasks are listed with difficulty numbers. These are tasks are above and beyond normal combat procedures.

Any character with the correct skill that is at an appropriate post may attempt these tasks. A normal static task resolution is performed to see what the result of the effort is. If the PC succeeds then a particular operation will be augmented. In the case of a Marginal or Normal failure the bonus is not received but no penalties are incurred and the operation resolves just as it would have had the character not attempted to enhance it. In the event of a Significant Failure or worse something detrimental happens as a result.

It is possible for two characters to use the teamwork rules when working on a given task. In order for them to be able to do this, they must both be on a console that allows proper access to the system and they must both be able to talk to one another. Usually this means they need to be in the same room as ships are sealed tightly in combat situations to minimize depressurization during hull breaches. They could also be speaking over a communications device such as a hand link or head set. The

fact that two characters are using the teamwork rules must be declared before task resolution, as usual.

These tasks are performed under the stress of combat. They are complex and difficult to carry out in the very limited time that battle allows. Coordinating work between people in such a chaotic time frame is difficult to say the least. As a result more than two people may not be working together on any one of these tasks.

A character may take as many actions in one round as they want. However for each action after the first a cumulative penalty of four is added to the difficulty number. So it is a plus four on the second task; a plus eight for the third and so on.

Communications

Communications work deals with incoming and out going transmissions. Without communications it would be impossible to have several units working together in a battle. People who work in communications don't just send and receive friendly signals, often they are trying to intercept enemy transmissions, or jam enemy equipment. Consoles that allow access to these types of tasks are usually on the bridge of a starship.

Coordinate Fire (Miraculous): The character attempts to coordinate the firepower of two ships down to the split second. In the heat of battle it is an extremely arduous feat to organize the offensive capabilities of more than one ship so precisely. The character must attempt this when the first of the two ships he or she is coordinating is selected as the Active Ship. If it is successful, the Active Ship and the second ship both fire their weapons simultaneously in the Weapons Fire phase. This does not make the second ship the Active Ship, so the second ship must be selected at a later time (although it may not actually fire again). These ships must share at least one target. If the result is a Significant Failure or worse, the Active Ship does not fire now. Instead when the second ship is selected as the Active Ship they both fire. This is normally used with the System Operations skill.

During the next turn of combat, Rob and Fred have won initiative. Normally this means that they get to select the first Active Ship and fire its weapons. The Achilles is selected as the Active Ship. However, they decide it would be best to attempt to coordinate their fire and be able to hit the Centauri Battle Cruiser with both the Achilles' and the Charon's weaponry before it can fire. This is a Miraculous task so the difficulty number is a 25. The communications officer of the Achilles, Lieutenant Otto Unger, and the communications officer of the Charon, Lieutenant Gina Tomasetti, begin to coordinate the attempt and use the teamwork rules to do so. The player controlling Otto, Josh, rolls and scores a positive 1. Otto's Ability is an 11 (Wits of 5 plus System Operations skill of 4 with a specialty in Communications) so his total is a 12. Sarah, who is controlling Gina, rolls a minus 4 modifier. Gina's Ability is a 12 (Wits of 6 plus System Operations skill of 4 with a specialty in Communications) which makes her total an 8. Gina's 8 plus Otto's 12 is only a 20 which means it is a Significant Failure. Instead of both ships firing during phase 4B while the Achilles is the Active Ship, they must wait until the Charon is the Active Ship. In the mean time the GM selects the Battle Cruiser as the Active Ship and fires on the Achilles dealing 11 points of damage. Unfortunately the hit causes Fred to make a Threshold Check and the Achilles loses its primary weapon system, the class 6 Beam Power System. Then the Charon becomes active and both EA destroyers fire their weapons doing much less damage then they had originally hoped as a result of the Achilles' missing laser.

Intercept Enemy Transmissions (Next to Impossible): The character attempts to intercept and decipher the enemy communications of a single ship. This task must be attempted after the opponent has written the orders for his or her ships but before the ship the character is on has its orders written. If successful, the character receives the written orders for that particular ship. If the task resolution results in a Significant Failure or worse, instead of obtaining the correct orders, the character messes up the deciphering and the opponent may tell the character any orders they choose (the orders do not have to reflect the actual written orders of that ship). This is normally used with the System Operations skill.

Jam Fire Control (Next to Impossible): Through the use of interference, the character tries to disrupt the enemy's ability to achieve a weapons lock on the ship. This task must be attempted after a ship has declared its targets but before it has fired. If the character succeeds the particular Fire Control system will fail to lock on and any weapons using that Fire Control to target will be unable to fire. Any Fire Control system that is jammed in considered to have already fired and cannot be used again on the same turn. If the result is a Significant Failure or worse, the character has managed to produce enough electronic noise that instead of jamming they have made their ship a glowing beacon and no other ships must expend a Fire Control to fire on it. This is normally used with the System Operations skill.

Increase Initiative (Difficult): The character tries to increase the speed that their side's ships react at. This task must be attempted before the die roll to determine who fires first is made in Phase 4. If done successfully a +1 is added to the die roll to see who fires first in Phase 4. On a Significant Failure or worse the character has only served to bog down the firing orders of the ships and their side suffers a -1 to the die roll. This is normally used with the System Operations skill.

Engineering

Engineering is one of the most broad-ranged job descriptions on board a starship. Engineers do everything from keeping a ship running to upgrading systems to repairing damage done to the ship. There are literally hundreds of conduits and engineering consoles around a ship from which an engineer can work.

Increase Laser Recharge Rate (Next to Impossible): The character attempts to redirect more energy to the Beam Power System to recharge it more quickly. This must be resolved at the beginning of the turn before the die is rolled to determine how much energy the beam system recharges. If successful add one to the result of the recharge roll (it will then recharge between 3 and 5). If the result is a Significant Failure or worse, the Beam Power System is over loaded: subtract one from the result of the recharge roll (between 1 and 3). In addition, this task runs the risk of damaging the Beam Power System. Roll a die: on a 5 or 6 the system is considered damaged (refer to the rules on Beam Systems for results). This is normally used with the Engineering, Electrical skill.

Increase Main Drive Output (Difficult): The character puts the reactor above normal safe output ranges and tries to provide the ship with a little extra power. This must be attempted before orders are written for that turn. If successful the main drive output of the drive unit the engineer was working on is increased by 1. A Significant Failure or worse indicates that the engine may burn itself out. Roll a die and on a 5 or 6 the engine is lost. This is normally used with the Engineering, Aerospace skill.

Repair System (Variable): When a system is destroyed during a Threshold Check it may still be possible to repair or replace it. An engineering character must attempt to repair a system at the beginning of the turn. The difficulty number depends on the amount of time the character wishes to spend repairing the system. The longer the character takes the easier it is to repair. For a single turn repair the Difficulty is Next to Impossible. If successful this system will be functioning at the beginning of next turn. For a two-turn repair the Difficulty is Very Difficult. If successful this system will be functioning at the beginning of the turn two turns from now. For a three turn repair the Difficulty is Difficult. If successful this system will be functioning at the beginning of the turn three turns from now. If the attempt is successful, treat the system as if it had not been destroyed at all. This means that if a system has several levels of damage, such as a Beam Power System or a Jump Engine, and is repaired it functions normally no matter what level of damage it was at before. If the character fails he or she must still spend the allotted amount of time

attempting to fix the system. If the result is a Significant Failure or worse the system has been more severely damaged by the attempt and must be repaired back in dry dock. This is normally used with the Engineering, Mechanical skill.

After the hit to the Achilles' laser system Capt. Hunbecker radios down to engineering and demands that the laser be made operational as of 2 minutes ago. Fortunately Lieutenant Commander Teresa Walters is the chief engineer on the ship and is quite remarkable. Her ability is a 14 (Insight of 7 and a skill in Engineering, Electrical of 5 with a specialty in Systems Design). The task of repairing a system in one round is Next to Impossible so the difficulty number is a 17. Jennifer, who plays Teresa, rolls a +1 for a Random Modifier. This makes her total a 15, which would not be enough. Given Capt. Hunbecker's reputation and the severity of the situation, Jennifer decides it would be beneficial to her character's future to spend a Fortune Point. She rolls the extra die and gets a 3. This added to the 15 is a total of 18 so she is successful. This means that at the start of the next turn the Beam System will be fully operational.

Gunnery

Stationed throughout the ship are many gunnery consoles. There is normally one main console in the bridge, backed up by several redundant modules in various positions throughout the ship. From these areas characters can access the targeting systems and give orders to unleash offensive capabilities.

Rapid Fire (Miraculous): The character attempts to fire weaponry at a faster rate. This task is resolved before the character rolls for damage from the weapons groups by a Fire Control, but after the target is selected. If successful all Pulse Batteries under that Fire Control double the normal number of dice they roll. If the result is a Significant Failure or worse the guns overload and shut down, not firing at all and there is also a chance that the guns have been rendered inoperable in the process; roll a die, on a 5 or 6 the pulse guns are considered destroyed. This is normally used with the Weapons System skill.

Critical Hit (Next to Impossible): While firing, the character tries to locate a weak spot in the structure of the ship and exploit it, in an attempt to inflict more damage. This can be used when a shot from the gunner forces a ship to make a Threshold Check. If successful it decreases the Threshold number that the ship must use by one. On a Significant Failure or worse, the character has hit the exact wrong spot and the Threshold number is raised by one (never higher than 6). This is normally used with the Weapons System skill.

Blind Fire (Very Difficult): The character tries to approximate where the target is based only on visual information and fire on it without the assistance of a Fire Control. This must be done at the same time other weapons are fired. The character must nominate the target and may fire one weapon without the use of a Fire Control (even if the ship has no undamaged Fire Controls). If successful the character has hit the target and that weapon rolls for damage as normal. A Significant Failure or worse means that the character was not even close to hitting the target. If there is a friendly ship in the same Arc when a Significant Failure or worse occurs roll a die on a 5 or 6 the friendly ship is hit and damage is then rolled for as normal. This is normally used with the Weapons System skill.

Increased Weapon Damage (Very Difficult): By adding more power to the guns and aiming more carefully the character attempts to inflict more damage in a shorter amount of time. This is used after targets have been selected but before the damage for the shots has been resolved. If successful all weapons grouped under one Fire Control have one added to their damage totals. This means that each weapon (even pulse weapons) are guaranteed to do at least one point of damage. In the event of a Significant Failure or worse, the character has overloaded the guns and they may not fire next round. This is normally used with the Weapons System skill.

Intercept Pulse Fire (Very Difficult): The character attempts to utilize an offensive Pulse Battery in the roll of an anti-pulse Interceptor. This must be attempted when the ship is being fired upon. If successful, the main weapon acts as if it were an Interceptor set on anti-pulse mode for that turn. If a Significant Failure or worse occurs the shots are not stopped and there is a chance that the fire from the cannon meant to be defensive actually hits a friendly ship. Roll a die, on a 5 or 6 it hits a friendly vessel and deals damage as normal. This is normally used with the Weapons Systems skill.

Increase Weapon Range (Difficult): The character tries to augment the computer's firing solution and enhance it with human intuition to increase the range of the shot. This is attempted after targets have been declared but before damage has been resolved. If the character is successful, the guns under this Fire Control are considered to be one MU closer than they actually are (just subtract one full MU from the measured distance to the target). A Significant Failure or worse indicates that the character was wrong and the distance is considered to be one MU further away than normal (add on full MU to the measured distance to the target). This is normally used with the Weapons Systems skill.

Fazil has been aboard the Achilles since its commission, and is one of the best gunners in Earthforce. He has a skill of 5 in Weapons Systems with a Specialty in Ship for a total of 7. Thanks to the repairs that Teresa made, Fazil can open fire with the class 6 Beam Battery on the Light Cruiser in the front. The Centauri ship is 12 MU away, which is normally a penalty of -2 (twelve is two full multiples of six away from the Achilles). In an attempt to do more damage, Fazil tries to increase the range of the laser. This is a Difficult task so has a difficulty number of 11. Fazil's Ability is a 14 (Coordination of 7, skill in Weapons Systems of 5 with a Specialty in Ship). Bill rolls the

dice and gets a -1 result, which makes the total a 13 and is successful. As a result the range is reduced by one to 11 MU, which is less than two full multiples of six away, so the penalty is only -1. Fazil decides to shoot a full blast of 6 Energy Points at the enemy ship. He rolls 6, 3, 5, 2, and 1, which translate to 5, 2, 4, 1 and 0 because of the -1 range penalty to each die. He then gets to re-roll the 6 and add it to his total without modifying the re-roll for range. He gets a 4, which brings the total up to 16. The Centauri vessel was hit hard earlier in the fight by starfuries and cannot take 16 points of damage. Escape pods scurry to flee the Centauri cruiser as brilliant orange explosions dot the surface of the cruiser in the wake of Fazil's blast.

Increase Tracking (Tricky): The character attempts to aid the Fire Control system and increase the ship computer's ability to track and lock enemy ships. This is attempted before targets are chosen during the Weapons Fire phase. If successful, the character has allowed the ship to target one extra ship for the turn. On a Significant Failure or worse, the tampering with the system has caused problems and the ship may target one less ship than normal. This is normally used with the Weapons Systems skill.

Helm

The person at the helm is actually controlling the movements of the ship. Much different than piloting a fighter or shuttle, piloting a large space vessel is more a matter of controlling a large slow moving powerful craft than harnessing the speed and maneuverability of a small vessel. There are very few stations from which the ship can be steered and only one of these is active at any given time.

Minimize Damage (Next to Impossible): The character attempts to position the ship using maneuvering thrusters so the incoming fire hits less vulnerable locations. This is attempted after a ship has taken enough damage to warrant a Threshold

Check. If successful, the helmsman has decreased the collateral damage of a particular shot and the Threshold number for that check is increased by one (never above 6). On a Significant Failure or worse the ship was in a worse position and the Threshold number is decreased by 1. This is normally used with the Shiphandling skill.

Extreme Thruster Burn (Very Difficult): The character overrides normal safety mechanisms and applies more thruster burn than the ship would normally allow. This task must be resolved before orders are written. If successful the ship may use one extra thrust point to push or rotate this turn. A Significant Failure or worse means that the ship does not have the extra thruster point and that the ship is tearing itself apart from the effort, which causes the ship to take 1/10 of its original damage capacity in damage (round down). This is normally used with the Shiphandling skill.

Hiroshige is at the helm of the EAS Charon. The Charon is in the same battle as the Achilles and is currently fighting against a Centauri Battle Cruiser. In the next Movement Phase the Charon and the Centauri will pass each other. Normally the Charon would not be able to bring its fore Beam Battery to bear. Luckily Hiroshige is a superb helmsman. His Ability is a 14 (Coordination of 7, skill in Shiphandling of 5 and Specialty in Capital Ship). Hiroshige attempts an extreme thruster burn, which has a difficulty number of 15. Jeff rolls the random modifier and gets a positive three. This gives Hiroshige a total of 17, which is a success and allows the ship to turn one extra Course Point. As a result the Centauri Battle Cruiser is now in the ships main weapon arc and Jose can open fire.

Increase Main Drive Output (Very Difficult): The character positions the ship in a manner to better benefit from the use of its main drives. This is resolved before orders are written. If successful the ship has one extra main drive unit to use for this turn. In the event of a Significant Failure or worse, the ship does not receive the extra

unit, but instead loses one unit of main drive thrust for the turn. This is normally used with the Shiphandling skill.

Ramming (Tricky): The character executes one final act of valor and attempts to plow their ship into an enemy vessel. This roll is made once all of the following criteria have been met: The intention to ram be mentioned in the orders; the ship must end the Movement Phase 3 MU from the enemy vessel; and the ship must have at least one drive unit left. There is an additional increase of 2 to the difficulty for every drive unit the enemy ship has above the ramming ship. If successful the ram occurs as per the ramming rules (page 89). A Significant Failure or worse means that the ship makes contact but it is a glancing blow which only damages the ramming ship. The ship takes one fourth of the normal ramming damage (rounded up) and the target ship is not harmed. This is normally used with the Shiphandling skill.

Payload

There are many jobs that deal with the payload of a ship. Mainly they interact with the ship's fighter complements or ammunition fed weapons. Instead of working at a console, a character working on payloads must be in the appropriate area of the ship.

Scramble Fighter Group (Next to Impossible): The character oversees the operation of emergency Fighter Group scrambling. This task must be resolved in place of the normal roll to scramble Fighter Groups in response to an attack. If successful, the ship scrambles as many Fighter Groups as it can normally launch in one turn. A Significant Failure or worse indicates that no Fighter Groups are launched and in fact a catastrophe has occurred. Roll a die for each Fighter Group that tried to launch, on a 5 or 6 the group is destroyed. This is normally used with the Engineering, Electrical skill.

Launch Extra Fighter Group (Very Difficult): The character attempts to speed up the process of launching Fighter Groups.

This task is attempted when Fighter Groups are launched. If it is successful then one extra Fighter Group may be launched in this turn. On a Significant Failure or worse the extra Fighter Group does not make it out and may be damaged along with the Launch Bay. Roll a die, on a 5 or 6 the Fighter Group collides into the docking bay walls and both the Fighter Group and Launch Bay are considered destroyed. This is normally used with the Engineering, Electrical skill.

Recover Extra Fighter Group (Very Difficult): The character tries to streamline the workings of the landing process so that the ship can recover Fighter Groups at an accelerated rate. This task is attempted when Fighter Groups are recovered. If the task is resolved successfully then one extra Fighter Group may be recovered that turn. If a Significant Failure or worse occurs there is a problem and only the normal amount of fighters are recovered. There is also a chance that the extra Fighter Group and the Launch Bay may be damaged. Roll a die, if a 5 or 6 is the result the fighters collide with the Launch Bay and both the Fighter Group and the Launch Bay are destroyed. This is normally used with the Engineering, Electrical skill.

Reload Weapon (Difficult): The character attempts to feed ammunition to a certain weapon system that needs it. This roll is made right after beam weapons are recharged. If successful the weapon receives one extra piece of ammunition if it was missing any. In the case of a Significant Failure or worse the ammunition has become jammed in the weapon and the weapon can no longer fire. This is normally used with the Engineering, Mechanical skill.

Piloting

Unlike other combat duties, pilots cannot control their craft from a console—they must actually be inside of the craft. Fighters have a high level of maneuverability and can do things impossible for large capital ships. Player character pilots may attempt these tasks and they also receive all of the benefits of a normal fighter Ace (see Aces, page 87).

Evade Fire (Next to Impossible): The pilot attempts to maneuver around incoming Weapons Fire. This may be used when the pilot's ship would normally be hit. If successful the pilot dodges out of the way

Fighter Group had gotten through defenses and attacked. The Fighter Group may only incidentally fire on one ship in this manner. This is normally used with the Piloting skill.

Blindside Fighter Group (Very Difficult): The character employs a tactic in which the enemy Fighter Group either cannot see his or her Fighter Group or cannot fire upon it. This is attempted after Fighter Groups declare their targets but before anything is resolved. If successful the target Fighter Group may not fire back on the character's Fighter Group when Weapons Fire is resolved. If the result is a Significant Failure or worse the player's Fighter Group is in the wrong spot and the enemy Fighter Group is able to fire without the friendly group returning fire. This is normally used with the Tactics, Space Combat skill.

Lieutenant Commander Petra Guderevich is the squadron leader for the main assault Fighter Group in the EAS Charon. While the battle of the Capital ships rages on around them Petra must take his Fighter Groups and keep the enemy Fighter Groups at bay. In the heat of the combat Petra notices a Centauri Fighter Group on an intercept path with the EAS Achilles. Petra quickly plots a path that will keep them out of notice of the Centauri until the last moment. Petra has an Ability of 13 (Coordination of 6, skill in Piloting of 5 with a Specialty of Fighter). This is a Very Difficult maneuver and the target number is a 15. Bob, the player controlling Petra, rolls the random modifier and gets a result of +5 for a total of 18. It is a success so Petra and his Fighter Group may fire on the enemy without fear of return fire. There are six other fighters in Petra's Fighter Group and they roll a 2, 2, 4, 6, 3, 5. The 6 is rerolled and scores a 1. This kills a total of 5 enemy craft. The remaining Centauri fighter had no idea anything was happening until all of his allies were obliterated and has not yet determined where the attack came from. Therefore he cannot return the fire on Petra's Fighter Group, though he may still fire on any other legal targets.

and the shot passes harmlessly by. In the case of a Significant Failure or worse, the pilot's craft is not only destroyed but the pilot, who decided to stay at the controls at the last moment, may not attempt to eject. This is normally used with the Piloting skill.

Anti-Pulse Interceptor (Very Difficult): The pilot attempts to use his pulse cannons to deflect pulse fire aimed at a nearby capital ship within 6 MU of the fighter. This must be attempted before damage is determined on the ship. If successful, the Fighter Group the pilot is in acts as if it were an Interceptor on anti-pulse mode (it is not limited to protecting the Fire Arc it is in, though it may only cover one Fire Arc per turn). On a Significant Failure or worse the spray of shots from the fighter may hit friendly ships. If there are any friendly ships within 6 MU (including the ship the group is attempting to protect), roll a die on a 5 or 6 the ship is hit just as if the

First Fire (Difficult): The character attempts to gain the edge in a dogfight and fire before the enemy can react. This is attempted after Fighter Groups declare their targets but before fire is resolved. If successful, the player's Fighter Group may fire on the enemy Fighter Group before the enemy can fire. Then the remaining enemies may fire on the player's Fighter Group (the damage is not simultaneous and the enemy may very well lose fighters before they can fire). This is normally used with Tactics, Space Combat skill.

Eject (Average): The character tries to punch out of their cockpit before their craft is destroyed. This is attempted immediately as a character's ship is being destroyed or crippled. If successful the character is able to eject with no problems. With a Significant Failure or worse the ejection system fails entirely and falls apart (such as the handles falling from the ceiling of a Starfury). This is normally used with the Piloting skill.

Tactical

It is the job of a tactician to outthink the enemy. These tasks can be performed from any location where the character can gain significant information about the ongoing battle. Given these pieces of information and the enemy type a good tactician can often predict what an enemy will do in combat.

Anticipate Fleet Maneuvers (Miraculous): The character tries to figure out what each ship in the enemy's fleet is going to do. This task is attempted after the opponent has written down orders and before the friendly orders are written. If successful, the opponent must give a general idea of what the ships are doing (accelerating or decelerating and moving port or starboard). On a Significant Failure or worse the opponent may give the player any information at all, correct or not. This is normally used with the Tactics, Space Combat skill.

Anticipate Ship Maneuvers (Very Difficult): The character tries to figure out what

a particular ship in the enemy's fleet is going to do. This task is attempted after the opponent has written down orders and before friendly orders are written. If successful, the opponent must give a general idea of what that ship is doing (accelerating or decelerating and moving port or starboard). On a Significant Failure or worse the opponent may give the player any information at all, correct or not. This is normally used with the Tactics, Space Combat skill.

Increase Initiative (Difficult): By predicting the moves of the enemy the character tries to position his or her ship in a way that it has the upper hand in firing. This task is attempted before the die roll to determine who fires first in Phase 4. If successful the player adds one to the die roll. On a Significant Failure or worse the player is in a worse position and subtracts one from the die roll. This is normally used with the Tactics, Space Combat skill.

Command

Command of a vessel works differently than any of the other jobs listed here. Instead of having a set list of tasks that someone at the command console can perform, it is assumed that the command console can access any of the ship's functions. Using the command console a character may attempt any of the tasks listed in this section. They can also use the command console to assist any character that is trying to execute one of these tasks. This makes it easier for the Commander of a space ship to personally coordinate the particular effects that they desire.

Using Fortune Points in Battle

Fate has as much influence on a starship battle as it does in other roleplaying encounters. Therefore players whose characters are involved in a battle (even those on a ship not directly involved in a particular attack or task) can use Fortune Points in order to affect the outcome. There are three different ways characters can use fortune points while involved in ship-to-ship battles.

First, a character may try to excel at something. As in the basic rules, the character can spend Fortune Points to increase their chances of succeeding on a certain task.

Second, if a ship's Damage Track is filled up, any player with a character on board may spend 2 Fortune Points to keep the ship from being destroyed. This does not keep the ship operational, merely disabled but intact, with far fewer casualties.

Finally, if Catastrophic Damage and Chain Reaction occurs, any player with a character aboard the ship may spend 2 Fortune Points to negate the effects of any failed Catastrophe Check.

Keep in mind that only player characters and very important NPCs have Fortune Points. These abilities represent the fact that these characters are fated for something more than just dying on a crippled starship.

The Charon, which has been drawing fire away from the Achilles during the battle, is in a more dire situation than its sister ship. The elimination of one of the Centauri warships lessens the amount of fire the Charon must take. However the remaining Centauri ship, a Battle Cruiser, is infuriated by its losses and redoubles its efforts against the Charon in an attempt to bring vengeance to their fallen comrades. The Charon has only two damage points left in its second row. The Centauri deliver 15 points of damage, which forces the Charon to make two Threshold Checks, one at 5 or higher and one at 4 or higher. Before normal Threshold Checks, the Charon must make a test for catastrophic damage because it was forced to make two Threshold Checks in one round. If it rolls a four or higher it will lose another entire row of damage and be forced to check again. Rob rolls a 5. Normally the ship would be in a great deal of trouble but Sarah (one of the players with a character aboard the ship) decides to spend 2 Fortune Points to negate this effect. This means that unlike normal it does not take an additional row of damage and does not have to make another Catastrophe Check. It

passes the first Threshold Check with all systems still up, and only loses a few minor systems during the second check leaving it in adequate fighting condition.

In the next round the EAS Achilles and the EAS Charon are able to destroy the final Centauri Battle Cruiser while suffering only minimal damage themselves. The fight was long and hard but the destroyers succeeded against the odds in destroying the enemy and protecting the merchants.

Sample Ships

This section provides a brief overview of the ship technologies of Earth Alliance, Narn, Centauri and the Minbari. It also contains the game info for the primary ships of each of those races as well as a few extra ships from Earth Alliance. Detailed information for ship-to-ship combat is displayed on each class' Ship Control Sheet, at the back of this book.

The Earth Alliance

The ships of the Earth Alliance are the benchmark around which the standard rules have been developed. Most EA ships use Reaction Drives under the normal rules and their weaponry is a mix of Pulse Batteries and Beam Batteries with Interceptor batteries for defense. The one exception to the normal rules is the *Nova*-class dreadnought.

***Omega*-class destroyer/carrier**: One of the more rugged Earthforce vessels, the *Omega*-class features a jump drive, a powerful (class 6) Beam System, eight Pulse Batteries, and four Interceptor Batteries. It carries four fighter groups.

***Nova*-class dreadnought**: An older class of ships, the *Nova* features a jump drive, eight Pulse Batteries, four Interceptor Batteries, and four fighter groups.

***Hyperion*-class heavy cruiser**: *Hyperion*-class ships feature a Beam System, four Pulse Batteries, and four Interceptor Batteries, and carry two fighter groups. Unlike most ships, the *Hyperion's* launch bay is not mounted in the fore of the ship. Instead it is in the middle of the ship. When fighter groups are launched from a *Hyperion*, instead of having them go 6 MU along the Heading of a ship then moving the Velocity of the ship along the ship's Course, one fighter group launches 6 MU to the Port and then the ship's Velocity along the ship's Course and the other fighter group launches 6 MU to the Starboard and then the ship's Velocity along the ship's Course.

Olympus-class corvette: *Olympus*-class vessels are fast and very deadly. Despite their small size they carry an impressive amount of firepower, including a Beam System, 8 Pulse Batteries, and four Interceptor Batteries.

Cotten-class long-range tender: The *Cotten*-class long-range tender resupplies and supports combat vessels. Though not designed for direct participation in combat action, it is equipped with four Pulse Batteries and four Interceptor Batteries. In ship-to-ship combat, each full line of damage boxes crossed off indicates that 20% of cargo space (and cargo) is destroyed.

CAS-958 "Condor" troop transport: A transport vessel for carrying GROPOS, the CAS-958 has several anti-personnel weapons clusters, as well as a large cargo bay for troops and vehicles (these have no impact on space combat, so are not listed on the Ship Control Sheet). For defense against hostile ships, the Condor has one Pulse Battery.

CS-244 "Porcupine" Starfury transport: The Porcupine carries fighters, but has little combat capability itself (limited to a single Pulse Battery). The fighter bay is not enclosed, therefore the fighters can launch in any direction. When launching during ship-to-ship combat, move the fighters the initial 6 MU in any direction desired, then move them the ship's Velocity along the Course of the ship.

EA CAS-320 "Shepherd" Starfury transport: Like the Porcupine but atmosphere-capable, the Shepherd carries fighters but has little combat capability itself (limited to a single Pulse Battery). The fighter bay is not enclosed, therefore the fighters can launch in any direction. When launching during ship-to-ship combat, move the fighters the initial 6 MU in any

direction desired, then move them the ship's Velocity along the Course of the ship.

The Centauri Republic

Despite the decay of their Republic, the Centauri's technology is advanced enough to give them a small edge over other younger races, particularly in maneuverability—their ships use the standard Reaction Drive movement rules, with one modification described below to account for their gravimetric drives. For weapons, the Centauri make little use of beams, preferring a large concentration of powerful Pulse Batteries. Though this can limit their potential to deliver massive damage in a single shot, the aggregate effect can be equally devastating—and they are not limited by problems of recharging or power storage.

Centauri Battle Cruiser: A very heavy vessel, the jump-capable Centauri Battle Cruiser features fourteen powerful Pulse Batteries (seven class 4; seven class 3) and three Anti-Fighter Batteries, along with four fighter groups.

Centauri Light Cruiser: Another commonly-encountered Centauri vessel, the Light Cruiser is equipped with eight Pulse Batteries (four class 3; four class 2), one Anti-Fighter Battery, and one fighter group.

The Narn Regime

Narn technology is at a similar level to that of the Earth Alliance, and a little bit (though not significantly) behind that of the Centauri. Their ships are powerful and rugged, though not terribly maneuverable. They employ a mix of Pulse Batteries and Beam Batteries (similar to the EA), plus a launched-weapon system known as the Energy Mine for which special rules are given below. In all other respects, Narn ships follow the standard game rules.

Narn Battle Dreadnought: Comparable to the EA *Omega*-class, the Battle Dreadnought features a jump engine, a Beam System, five Pulse Batteries, two Anti-

Fighter Batteries, Energy Mine launchers, and four fighter groups.

Narn Heavy Cruiser: The Heavy Cruiser features jump engines, a somewhat underpowered Beam System, five Pulse Batteries, an Anti-Fighter Battery, an Energy Mine launcher, and four fighter groups.

The Minbari Federation

The technology level of the Minbari is significantly higher than that of the other races given in these rules. For this reason, there are a number of special rules and systems that apply only to Minbari ships. In most battles between Minbari craft and those of the younger races, the Minbari will almost certainly have a massive superiority. If a single Minbari ship is ganged upon by several of younger-race warships, it can be killed—but not without cost.

Minbari War Cruiser: A very powerful warship, the Minbari War Cruiser is equipped with jump engines, a Jamming System, a Plasma Net, an extremely powerful Beam System that can fire in every direction, an EMP Cannon system, and four Fighter Groups.

Civilian Ships

Warships aren't the only types of vessels to see combat in a dangerous universe—civilian ships sometimes find themselves the target of raiders or in the middle of war zones. Some typical types of ships, as representative of any of the younger races as they are of Human designs, are covered here with Ship Control Sheets at the end of this book.

Typical Large Freighter: Civilian freighters are almost never jump-capable, and go armed with, at most, a single light Pulse Battery. In ship-to-ship combat, each full line of damage boxes crossed off indicates that 20% of cargo space (and cargo) is destroyed.

Typical Interstellar Liner: Like freighters, liners are rarely jump-capable, and are armed with, at most, a single light

Pulse Battery. In ship-to-ship combat, each full line of damage boxes crossed off indicates that 20% of the passengers are killed.

Systems

This is a glossary of the systems used on the ship diagrams.

Anti-Fighter Batteries

These clusters of guns are designed to track down and destroy enemy fighters. Normally the clusters consist of several very small pulse cannons capable of extremely high rates of fire. These are reactive weapons that are an integral part of the ships defense grid to keep it safe from incoming fighter attacks. For more detail see page 84.

Antiquated Power Grids

This energy source is not as efficient or powerful as the newer models. As a result, if the ship's weapons are powered up and firing then each Main Drive unit may be used to generate either Main Drive thrust or Thruster Points, but not both.

Beam Batteries

This weapon is one of the weapons with the most potential for damage. At close range a shot from a Beam Battery can tear a ship into pieces. These systems require a large amount of energy and must recharge between shots. This limits their overall effectiveness but does not make them useless by any means. Ships have been outfitted with a wide array of Beam Systems ranging from a class 1 to a class 6. The smaller systems tend to deal less damage but are much more reliable and have an increased rate of fire. Fore more detail see page 81.

Centauri Drive Systems

While the drive systems of Centauri warships are basically the same as those of the Narn and the EA (and use the normal Reaction Drive rules), the Centauri have developed advanced technology that make their ships more maneuverable than those of the other races. Therefore, Centauri ships have a Thruster power that is equal to the total output of their drive units, rather than half value as in the standard rules. With this advantage, Centauri ships are able to rotate much faster than under the normal rules, and can apply a side push or retro thrust equal to the power of their main drive burn. They are still not able to perform the radical maneuvers of a true Grav Drive ship like the Minbari, but will often be able to outfly Narn or EA ships. They are also able to keep their main weaponry trained on an enemy much more easily while they maneuver, which can be of great use.

Energy Mines

The Energy Mine is a weapon system used mainly by Narn warships (though the Earth Alliance has been known to use similar systems for the defense of space installations). Strictly speaking it is not really a "mine," but more of an area-effect energy projectile which is launched from the firing vessel and detonates in the vicinity of the target, causing damage to all craft within the effect radius of its detonation.

Each Energy Mine Projector system on a ship may launch one mine per turn, but has a limited supply of mines (three per projector) which are crossed off the system symbol as they are expended. Once a projector has fired all three of its mines it may not be used again in that battle. Each ship carries more mines but their loading time makes it impractical to reload during combat.

Energy Mines are fired at the beginning of the Ship Movement Phase of the game turn rather than in the normal Weapons Fire Phase—that is, they are launched after all players have written their orders for movement, but before the ships are moved. The mines detonate at the end of the Movement Phase.

An Energy Mine projector has a maximum range of 20 MU; when it fires, the player simply places a Mine marker at the desired detonation point (and crosses one mine off his ship record card). This point of aim can be anywhere up to 20 MU from the firing ship, but must fall within the Fire Arc through which the projector is mounted (a projector mounted in a ship's Fore arc can only aim mines at target points within that arc).

Mines detonate at the end of the Movement Phase. Ships that are unlucky enough to be close to a mine will take damage; the amount depends on how close the detonation is to the ship. When a mine detonates, any ship that is within 1 MU of the mine will take six dice of damage. Each MU further away reduces damage by one die, so at a distance of 3 MU the damage will drop to four dice, at 6 MU away only one damage die is rolled, and further than 6 MU there is no damage.

The total number rolled is the number of damage points inflicted, with no modifiers applied. Die results of 6 allow a reroll.

Energy Mines require a Fire Control system to be used, and this Fire Control system may not be used to fire other weaponry in the same turn. One Fire Control system can, however, be used to fire any number of Energy Mine launchers provided that all the mines are targeted at points no more than 6 MU apart from each other.

Rob and Fred decide to play a strictly tabletop game, just for fun. Rob is playing a Centauri task force sent to harass the Narn and Fred is playing the Narn defense force. Two of Rob's Centauri ships are caught in the burst of one Energy Mine. The first is only 2 MU away from the detonation point, and thus takes five dice of damage. Fred rolls the dice and scores 5,5,4,3 and 1, resulting in eighteen damage points (a crippling score against all but the biggest of ships). The second Centauri is slightly luckier, being 5 MU from the burst center. Fred only gets to roll two dice, which score 2 and 6 (plus a reroll score of 1) for a total of 9 damage points—not as catastrophic, but still bad enough.

Fighter Groups

Fighter Groups are a team of six fighter craft that work together in combat. These ships are much smaller and more agile than the larger capital vessels and are able to perform a variety of tasks due to their flexibility. At any time the Fighter Group can be called on for defense or offense. Each Fighter Group has its own hanger bay onboard the ship it is stationed on. For more detail see page 85.

Fire Control Systems

These systems are used to track and fire on enemy vessels. The Fire Control system is much more than just the system used to aim the weapon. It also locks on to target ships and produces firing solutions. For more detail see page 79.

Gravimetric Drives

Ships using Grav Drives use a different movement system than those that use Re-

action Drives.

When Movement Orders specify a Velocity change (acceleration or deceleration), then the change in Velocity is added to or subtracted from the previous Velocity and the ship is moved the new distance. So if a ship traveled at Velocity 6 in the last turn, and applies an acceleration of 3, it will move 9 MU in the current turn.

If a Course change is ordered, the ship is moved straight forward along its present Course for half its total movement distance for that game turn, then the counter is rotated by the amount specified in the orders before moving it on the new Course by the remainder of its total move distance. For instance, if a ship moving at Velocity 10 receives orders to turn 2 points to Starboard, it moves 5 MU, then turns 60 degrees Starboard, then moves its remaining 5 MU.

Grav Drive ships do not require a Direction Arrow counter, as a ship using a Grav Drive will always move in the direction that the counter is actually facing.

If a ship under Grav Drive does not change Course or Velocity in its written orders, then it is simply moved straight forward (in the direction it is currently facing) by its current Velocity in MU.

Any ship with a Grav Drive that does not move at all in a turn—that is, its Velocity is zero at both start and end of turn—may be rotated on its axis to point in any desired direction, provided orders have been written to this effect. This rotation may exceed the normal Course change limitations, and on the next turn the ship may begin to accelerate in its new direction if desired.

Movement orders for Grav Drive ships should be written in a similar way to those for Reaction Drives, with MD+ for a main drive acceleration, MD- for a deceleration, and RP or RS for turns to port or starboard. Thus an order to accelerate by 2 and turn 2 points (60 degrees) port would be MD+2, RP2; and order for deceleration of 6 with no Course change would be MD-6.

As with Reaction Drive ships, each Grav Drive Unit can produce a thrust of 2 and the sum of all the thrust of the drive units is the ship's Main Drive Rating. A ship may change its Velocity (accelerate or decelerate) by any amount up to its Main Drive Rating each turn. However, Grav Drive ships don't have thrusters—they use main drive power to turn. Thus, a Grav Drive ship may change its Course by up to half its Main Drive Rating each turn. Changes of Course and Velocity may be combined in one turn, but the total number of thrust points used in the changes must not exceed the drive rating available. Thus a ship with Main Drive Rating 4 could change Velocity by up to 4 MU, or could change Course by up to two points with two left over for Velocity change. It could not, however, change Course by three points (as this would exceed half the Main Drive Rating) and similarly could not apply two points to Course change and then accelerate by 4 (as this would total 6 points of thrust).

Interceptors

Interceptors are a much more versatile form of defensive weaponry than Anti-Fighter Batteries. While they are capable of shooting down Fighter Groups, Interceptors may also be used to lessen the effectiveness of Pulse Batteries. When used in this mode, they rapidly fire pulses at the incoming fire in an attempt to disrupt it and render the shot useless. For more detail see page 83.

Jump Engines

These massive drives are used to create a jump point. It is necessary to travel through a jump point or a jumpgate in order to reach hyperspace. A Jump Engine basically rips a hole in real space and holds it open long enough for the vessel that opened it to go through and begin travel in hyperspace. These engines are quite large and require a massive amount of energy to power them and therefore may not be mounted on a smaller vessel. For more detail see page 75.

Launch Bays

This is the area of the ship used to launch and recover smaller craft. The most typical use on a military vessel is for deploying Fighter Groups, though the launch bay is also used for shuttlecraft as well. This is a different location than the hanger bay where the smaller ships are stored. It is possible for a ship to have undamaged fighters and shuttles but have a damaged launch bay and not be able to get them out of the ship. For more detail see page 85.

Minbari Beam Systems

Minbari ships are armed mainly with beam weapons. These weapons are of a significantly higher technology level than those used by the EA and Narn. A Minbari warship has a single Beam Power System in the same way as any other beam-equipped ship, as well as a number of Projectors spread around the ship in its different Fire Arcs. The system can store up to twelve Energy Points at full capacity. This energy may be fired through any number of the ship's Projectors just as a normal beam weapon can. This beam causes one die of damage per energy point fired with a minus one penalty to each die for every full multiple of 6 in the range (sixes are rerolled and rerolls are not modified for range). The only limitation is that any one Projector cannot handle more than six dice of energy in one turn. When the Recharge roll is made for a Minbari ship, instead of recharging at a normal rate, roll one die and double the result, thus recharging between two and twelve points per turn.

A Minbari beam may also be fired as an anti-fighter weapon at any Fighter Group within 6 MU of the ship. In this mode, roll one die per Projector, with the number of damage points scored being the number of fighters destroyed. Firing in this mode does not require the expenditure of a stored Energy Point, and can be done by any functioning Projector even if the Beam Power System is discharged, damaged or knocked out—in the anti-fighter mode the beam Projectors are drawing the small amount of energy they need from the ship's general power grid. Each beam Projector may only fire at one Fighter Group per turn, and if it does so it may not be used again in another role in the same turn.

Minbari Electromagnetic Pulse Weapons

The EPW is a special weapon system unique to the Minbari. It is a short-range projector (capable of all-round fire) that can disable all the systems and electronics on another craft, putting it out of action. An EPW is powered from the ship's Beam Power System, and a single shot from the EPW consumes three stored Energy Points from the beam system. The EPW may only be fired once per turn, and then only if the required power is available.

The EPW has a maximum range of only 6 MU, but any ship fired upon must immediately take a Threshold Check for each of its onboard systems, with each system being knocked-out on a roll of 4 or above. The EPW may be fired at a Fighter Group, in which case each fighter rolls once — it is knocked out on a roll of 4 or above.

Note that the EPW does not cause any actual physical damage to its target. Any system which failed the Threshold Check is still physically there but is considered unusable. These systems may be repaired just as a system knocked out by conventional means. The ship is still intact, and its crew is alive (though probably stunned for a short time). For the next turn of the game the ship may not take any actions at all. On the turn following that, the ship may attempt to use any systems that survived the EPW attack as normal. Fighters knocked out by EPW attacks are effectively lost to the group, though players may wish to record the positions of the disabled fighters (floating dead in space) for subsequent recovery of their pilots.

Minbari Plasma Nets

More than any other weapon system, the Minbari plasma net exemplifies their mastery and superiority in technology. This system is much subtler than most weapons and has a very limited ability to do actual physical harm to a starship. The plasma net is a synthesis of plasma and gravitic technologies.

Using the plasma net, the Minbari have the ability to push and or pull other ships.

This weapon works much differently than any other weapon system. Instead of firing in the Combat Phase, it fires at a very specific point in the Movement Phase. After all ships have moved their Velocity along their Course and have applied all of their maneuvers, but before the Velocity and Course for next round has been determined (i.e. before the Direction Arrow is moved) the plasma net may fire. Firing this weapon does require the use of a Fire Control and that Fire Control may not be used again on the same turn. The plasma net is a gravitic device and therefore is fueled by the ship's Grav drives. When the system fires, any amount of unexpended main drive units may be applied to the shot. The target ship is moved either directly towards or away from the firing ship a number of MU equal to the amount of main drive units devoted to the fire. After the plasma net has moved the target ship, calculate its new Course and Velocity (a plasma net does not alter the Course or Velocity of another ship with a full Grav drive system).

This system is based on the same technology used to create the Grav drives that run the Minbari ships. It can affect ships of most sizes, from a fighter group up to a dreadnought. The plasma net does not affect ships or space stations that are much larger than the vessel with the weapon.

Pulse Batteries

These are by far the most common weapons with which ships are outfitted. They are reliable and have a quick rate of fire, which makes them very dependable. The rules for these systems have already been detailed (page 80).

Class 4 (Super Heavy) Pulse Battery: Maximum effective range is 40 MU; roll 4 dice for hits/damage at up to 10 MU, 3 dice up to 20 MU, 2 dice up to 30 MU and 1 die to 40 MU

Class 3 (Heavy) Pulse Battery: Maximum effective range is 30 MU; roll 3 dice for hits/damage at up to 10 MU, 2 dice up to 20 MU and 1 die to 30 MU.

Class 2 (Medium) Pulse Battery: Maximum effective range is 20 MU; roll 2 dice for hits/damage at up to 10 MU, 1 die up to 20 MU.

Class 1 (Light) Pulse Battery: Maximum effective range is 10 MU; roll 1 die for hits/damage.

Reaction Drives

Races that have not yet achieved a technological mastery of Grav Drives use this form of propulsion. Instead of harnessing gravity, a Reaction Drive works off of thruster power. The vessel can maneuver by using a series of thrusters place along the entire ship to produce force. For more detail see page 75.

Stealth Defenses and Jammers

Minbari ships carry very advanced jamming devices that can disrupt the targeting of other races' Fire Control systems, making it difficult for an opponent to get a positive firing solution on a Minbari ship. To reflect this in the rules, whenever a Minbari ship is fired upon by a ship of another younger race the Minbari player may roll a single die: if the result is a 4 or better, the attacking Fire Control cannot lock on due to the jamming, and no Weapons Fire is possible. If the roll is 3 or less, the fire is resolved as normal. This roll is made once for each Fire Control system that is attempting to control the attack, not for each individual weapon system firing. It is permissible for an attacking ship with two separate Fire Control systems to try and target a Minbari ship with both systems, in which case the Minbari player rolls once against each attempt. However, the attacking player must specify before the attack exactly which of his weapons are being directed by which Fire Control system. Thus if one locks on and the other fails, only the weapons directed by the successful Fire Control system may be used. A Fire Control system that is jammed is considered to have already fired and cannot be used again on the same turn.

The jamming system may also be used against fighter attacks. In this case one roll is made to attempt to jam the attack of an entire Fighter Group—it will either jam all or none. Minbari fighters themselves are capable of limited short-range jamming against enemy fighters, but no rolls are necessary in this case—the ability is factored into the numbers on the Dogfight Kill Table (p. 87).

The Minbari jamming unit is depicted as a system icon on the ship, and may be lost due to damage in the same way as any other system. If this occurs, the ship may no longer attempt to jam enemy Fire Control systems.

Chapter 4: Earthforce Personnel

Those within Earthforce are special because of the oaths they have taken to serve and protect the Earth Alliance, but some within the ranks have distinguished themselves more than others. Whether through family ties, acts of valor or sheer persistence, there are some within Earthforce who have gained a measure of respect within the ranks and whose names are recognized widely. This chapter contains details about some of those characters, from those on the front lines to the Joint Chiefs of Staff, whose orders are the law for the military.

Your characters may meet some of these people during their adventures as they travel through the Alliance. They may take orders from one of them, meet one or more in the course of routine duty, or even become embroiled in the plots and machinations of the politics that are practiced at the highest levels of EF Command. In 2250 and 2251 a great power struggle was taking place among the halls of EarthGov, and many of the higher ranking officers in Earthforce became willing or unwilling participants in that struggle. This information is a resource and a guide to who's who within the ranks of the EA military during that time.

Notable Ground Officers

Those who have served in the ground forces of Earthforce have come from a variety of backgrounds. From career military officers dedicated to their jobs to those who saw Earthforce as the best option left to them, they serve as best they can.

Major General Richard Franklin

COMMANDER, 201st EA INFANTRY DIVISION

Born: Atlanta, North America, Earth 2197 (Age: 53). 180 cm, 95 kg, black hair, brown eyes.

Major General Richard Franklin is the most experienced infantry commander in Earthforce. He has served in every major conflict of the past thirty years, including the reduction of Cooke II, the Dilgar invasion, the liberation of the African bloc in 2234, and the Canal Wars. A master of infiltration tactics and combat engineering, Franklin has become the first choice of EarthGov to command difficult assault operations.

Franklin is both a decisive commander and a stern disciplinarian. He will not tolerate insubordination and has had at least one officer shot on the

Franklin

field of battle for refusing to obey a direct order. However, while he will win no popularity contests, he is respected by the troops under his command, who have nicknamed him "Old Firestorm."

Cammann

Although he has seen long service, General Franklin has no plans to retire. The recent Minbari War has already cost Earthforce many senior officers. Veteran commanders such as Franklin are highly valued by EarthGov, which has been forced to promote young officers to high rank, sometimes too soon. General Hague, Franklin's immediate superior, has therefore entrusted "Old Firestorm" with training the younger generation of officers within Proxima Command. It is a responsibility the veteran takes seriously.

The general is a career officer. He knows no life but the military, and that has caused him to treat his family as if they too are enlisted. He has four daughters, Juanita, Katherine, Maria and Celia, and a son, Stephen. His relationship with Stephen, who is a doctor with Earthforce, is strained. They argued over Stephen's work during the Minbari War, and now seldom speak. Juanita has followed her father into the military and is presently a captain in the 71st EA Armored Division. The younger children are still at home, which is currently Proxima III, where the 201st Infantry is based. Like many military families, they live a vagabond life at the whim of EF Command.

When roleplaying him, remember that General Franklin is a stern man, with little time for anything other than his job. He is always direct and authoritative, even when it is unnecessary. But he is not unkind, and it is very easy to trust his loyalty to Earth.

Chm: 4	Int: 6	Str: 5
Fin: 5	Ins: 6	Agl: 4
Pre: 6	Wit: 5	End: 5
Xen: 4	Per: 5	Cor: 5

Primary Skill: Strategy, Ground
Major Skills: Tactics, Troop
Combat, Ranged
Combat, Unarmed
Main Characteristics:
Command Rank, Veteran

Colonel Paul Stefan Cammann

COMMANDER, 21ST EA CAVALRY BRIGADE, THE STEEL GUARD

Born: Earthdome, Switzerland, Earth, 2223 (Age: 27). 185 cm, 81 kg, blond hair, green eyes.

Paul Cammann commands the gallant 21st EA Cavalry Brigade, the "Steel Guard," an independent quick reaction force currently stationed at Proxima III. The Steel Guard draws its recruits primarily from Europe, especially from France, Germany and Italy. The 21st is a lightly armored, fast moving strike force formed in 2231 during the war with the

Dilgar, although the unit actually gained its reputation in the fierce battles around Ganymede during the Minbari War. The last Earth properties to come under attack before the Battle of the Line were the Io Station and the Ganymede Outpost. The Minbari detached a strike force from their armada to secure Earth's jumpgate before the remainder of the Minbari forces attacked the EA Fleet at the Battle of the Line. The 21st Cavalry thrown forward to counter the threat to the Jovian system was almost completely destroyed in a week of fierce fighting. The Battle of the Line began almost immediately after the jumpgate off Io was taken, but the Minbari were unable to secure Ganymede before the surrender.

At the end of the Battle for Ganymede, the 21st had just 136 effective troopers, out of an initial force of over 1500. The senior surviving officer was Captain Paul Cammann. He was promoted and granted the Earth Alliance's highest distinction, the Alliance Medal of Valor, for continuing the fight in the face of overwhelming odds. This victory did not come without a personal cost, however. Cammann lost the use of his left hand and has severe scars on the left side of his body as a result of a Minbari "bubble mine."

Cammann is Swiss by birth and spent much of his early life in and around Earthdome. His mother was a career EarthGov auditor in the Ministry of Science. His elder sister joined the Psi Corps in 2228 and is currently reported to be a P8. Cammann has not seen her in several years. Paul was pressured by his mother to follow her into EarthGov as he grew older. He was not interested in staying in Geneva, however, and had grown cynical about the politics that dominated EarthGov. After his basic schooling he obtained an appointment to Earthforce Academy: Sandhurst and opted to join the EA Ground Forces.

After graduation Lieutenant Cammann was assigned to Fleet Support Detachment 12, attached to the heavy cruiser *EAS Ravana* serving on patrol in the Orion area. Cammann saw his first action when the Ravana responded to a raid on the colony world at Ceti II. He located the raiders' mothership and captured it without loss, then ambushed the raiders as they attempted to flee the rest of the detachment. For his initiative, he received the Bronze Combat Medal. Cammann received an early promotion to captain after just one year of active service, and was transferred to the 21st Cavalry Brigade as commander of its heavy weapons company, shortly before the Minbari war. Then came the Battle for Ganymede.

He remains strictly neutral in earth politics and does not tolerate political interference with his command. He tolerates but dislikes Psi Corps personnel. Because Cammann has attained high rank so young, he avoids strong personal relationships. Instead, he works hard to maintain his image as a commander. In spite of his personal injuries, he has no hatred for the Minbari.

As a commander, Cammann is quick and decisive in his actions. While this can lead him into difficult situations, he believes strongly in retaining the initiative. Cammann will act even with sketchy intelligence and limited supplies, and this recklessness has put him at odds with his commanding officers on more than one occasion.

When roleplaying him, remember that Cammann is a dashing and elegant man of slightly over medium height. He moves with some hesitation due to his injuries, but is always ready with a dazzling smile. His temper is quick to ignite, but also quick to cool. Cammann cares strongly about the troopers under his command.

Chm: 8   Int: 4   Str: 3
Fin: 7   Ins: 5   Agl: 5
Pre: 4   Wit: 5   End: 4
Xen: 5   Per: 4   Cor: 5

Primary Skill: Strategy, Space
Major Skills: Tactics, Space Combat
              Savvy
              Shiphandling
Main Characteristics:
              Impulsive

Lieutenant General William Hague

COMMANDER, ORION COMMAND

Born: Ontario, North America, Earth 2203 (Age: 47). 181 cm, 81 kg, brown hair, blue eyes.

The sudden end of the Minbari War has left Earthforce confused and uncertain in a dangerous time, and General William Hague knows it. He may not be the best field commander in the EA Ground Forces, but he is devoted to the Earth Alliance, and the concepts of honor, duty and freedom that it promotes. He worries that those freedoms are now in jeopardy from those who would insulate the alliance from alien influences in the name of protecting Earth.

Along with General Kelly Ashe, the Vice Chairman of the Joint Chiefs, Hague has aligned himself with EA Senator Luis Santiago. While Hague has his doubts, he believes Santiago offers the alliance its best chance to recover from the thrashing it took at the hands of the Minbari. He fears the xenophobia within

Hague

113

EarthGov and has seen what hatred of the Minbari can do to discipline even within the ranks of his own forces. Hague especially fears the influence of Admiral Jason Ashvin Singh, who has pushed strongly for vast increases in the EA Fleet.

Hague commanded the 4th EA Army during the last half of the Minbari War, and was named commander of Orion Command in 2249, replacing Vice Admiral M'benga. Hague is responsible for protecting the border colonies and watching both the Centauri Republic and the Narn Regime. Hague hopes to use the high profile that his present job offers as a springboard to the Joint Chiefs of Staff, with a little help from General Ashe and Luis Santiago.

Although ambitious, Hague has concerns about Earthforce being too politicized. While he is a savvy player in the power games surrounding EarthGov, he wants less government influence, not more, in the day-to-day affairs of Earthforce. Therefore, Hague has quietly built up a network of reliable and patriotic officers who hold similar views to himself about the rampant expansionism and isolationism currently in vogue within Earthdome. Hague hopes that if a crisis comes, he and his fellow officers will be able to act to save Earthforce from itself.

When roleplaying Hague, remember that he is very involved in the politics of EarthGov and as such chooses his words very carefully when speaking. He is quite accomplished at it, though, and his loyalty and passion serve him well in conversations with others.

Chm: 6	Int: 5	Str: 4
Fin: 7	Ins: 6	Agl: 4
Pre: 4	Wit: 6	End: 4
Xen: 5	Per: 4	Cor: 4

Primary Skill: Diplomacy
Major Skills: Tactics, Space Combat
Savvy
Strategy, Space
Main Characteristics:
Command Rank, Ally

Major Tyler Poole

ATTACHE, EMBASSY TO THE NARN REGIME

Born: Earth Embassy to Narn Regime, 2220 (Age: 30). 186 cm, 81 kg, blond hair, brown eyes.

Major Tyler Poole has a difficult job. Not only must he serve as the official "spy" in the alliance embassy on Narn, he also must be diplomat, scapegoat or arms dealer depending on the circumstances. Luckily, few humans have more experience dealing with the aggressive Narn than Tyler Poole.

Poole's parents met while serving in the same embassy where Poole now works. They married in 2219, and Tyler was born a year later. Poole grew up on Narn until the age of 8, when his parents sent him to Earth to get his schooling. During that time, Poole's playmates were Narn, and there are several among them who consider Tyler to be a "pouchbrother." Poole has remained proud of his childhood on Narn ever since.

After joining Earthforce in 2242, Poole was sent to graduate school where he received a degree in Xenosociology. He then received an assignment to the Directorate of Military Intelligence, where he served as an analyst studying Narn-Centauri relations. Poole, however, disliked sitting behind a desk in Earthdome and managed to get himself assigned to the Narn embassy as a newly promoted captain in 2245, just prior to the outbreak of the Minbari War.

The war caused a significant change in relations between Earth and Narn. Prior to the war, the close relationship of Earth and Centauri had led to cool relations between the Earth Alliance and the Narn Regime, but the Narn had a reputation as technology brokers. Years of trying to close the gap with their former Centauri masters had helped the Narn develop an extensive arms trading network with their neighbors, not all of it completely legal. Earth needed equipment that could help them defeat the technologically superior Minbari forces. It was Captain Poole, with his intimate knowledge of the Narn, who arranged the pipeline with the Kha'ri that helped the Earth Alliance survive three years of defeats by the Minbari.

Since the war, Major Poole has continued to be the leading expert on military relations between the Narn Regime and Earth. His successes during the war have impressed his superiors. His almost half-Narn personality, however, has raised doubts about his loyalty to the Earth Alliance, especially amongst the more xenophobic members of EarthGov. Poole's career in Earthforce is basically over.

Poole is loyal to Earth, but not slavishly so. He has a love of Narn culture and a respect for the Narn people that color his attitudes. He dislikes his position as in-house embassy "spy" and would prefer to retire from Earthforce and join the civilian staff of the embassy. Earthforce has put Poole in a peculiar position, however. Unwilling to promote him, Earth Central is also unwilling to let him leave Earthforce. Instead, they have authorized a special bonus to his salary to cover "special expenses" for Poole while he is on Narn. He resents Earthforce's manipulation of his life, but up to this point Poole is making the best of a bad situation.

When roleplaying Poole, remember his extensive Narn upbringing. He is very comfortable in the confrontational Narn method of negotiation, and as such can sometimes act too overbearing in human situations. He holds no ill will toward other EF officers and enlistees, but he sometimes forgets how much more subtle human society can be.

Chm: 6	Int: 5	Str: 4
Fin: 5	Ins: 5	Agl: 5
Pre: 5	Wit: 4	End: 5
Xen: 6	Per: 4	Cor: 5

Primary Skill: Diplomacy
Major Skills: Unarmed
Then'sha'tur
Savvy
Main Characteristics:
Proud, Stubborn

Notable Fleet Officers

The EA Fleet is a recovering organization. The loss of most of the fleet to the Minbari has weakened Earth's position, but most within the Senate realize the need to rebuild the fleet, which was much of what saved the Alliance from the Minbari. The fleet now relies on the few strong and resourceful leaders who survived the Minbari War. Eccentric and innovative, this collection of warriors represents the best of the fleet.

Vice Admiral Thierry Moreau

COMMANDER, THREE SUNS BATTLEGROUP

Born: French Enclave, Nereid Station, Jupiter 2212 (Age: 38). 187 cm, 83 kg, brown hair, green eyes.

Poole

During the Minbari War, someone had to watch the "back door." Earth was overmatched, and a number of the worlds bordering the EA knew it. By 2246, losses against the Minbari were already stretching fleet resources to the breaking point, and the situation would only grow worse over the next two years. Captain Thierry Moreau was dispatched with just two cruisers to hold down the threat from the Ch'lonas Corporate. The Ch'lonas planned to snatch the mineral rich Kapteyn System from the Alliance while Earth was too weak to resist.

In a lightning campaign lasting just under a month, Moreau raided six Ch'lonas encampments and destroyed four enemy cruisers at the Battle of Three Suns. The Ch'lonas were enraged, but they called off the attack against the alliance, no longer sure they could win. Moreau, promoted to Rear Admiral, received command of a scratched together squadron of ships. Un-

Moreau

til the end of the war, Moreau's squadron, now called the *Three Suns* Battlegroup, would fight off every threat to the alliance from worlds seeking to take advantage of Earth's preoccupation with the Minbari.

Unconventional, willing to use diplomacy and deception as well as force, Moreau has never been easy to predict. He loves the uncertainty of battle, and the challenge of doing the most with the least. He thrives on diversity. During the war, he studied as much as he could on the psychology and sociology of the worlds bordering the Alliance. This knowledge gave him an edge in his campaigns. Fascinated by what he found, Moreau continued the work after the war, and is nearing completion of a doctorate of xenopsychology from the prestigious Kedigan Institute.

The officers who have served with Moreau all seem to have different opinions of him. To some, he is a martinet, insistent on discipline and form. To others he is a relaxed and liberal commander who granted wide latitude to his subordinates. The truth appears to be that Moreau is a little of all of the above. He quickly analyzes his officers and determines what type of commander he must be to best utilize their talents. This chameleon-like ability allowed him to hold together a very mixed force throughout the war, but has caused resentment and unease with some of his officers, who think him more an actor than a commander.

Since the end of the war, Moreau received command of a task force centered on the dreadnoughts *EAS Ark Royal* and *EAS Australia*, and the cruiser *EAS Persephone*. He was promoted to Vice Admiral in late 2250, but it seems unlikely that Moreau will ever be promoted higher. His unconventionality is prized by his superiors, but they do not want Moreau to disrupt the command structure of Earthforce with his rapid changes of focus and his seeming need to be challenged.

When roleplaying Moreau, remember that he is a very good judge of character and will talk to a group the way he thinks they need to be addressed. He will seem open and friendly off duty, and will inspire great loyalty.

Chm: 6	Int: 5	Str: 4
Fin: 8	Ins: 6	Agl: 5
Pre: 5	Wit: 5	End: 4
Xen: 6	Per: 4	Cor: 5

Primary Skill: Tactics, Space Combat
Major Skills: Diplomacy
Medical, Psychiatry
Navigation, Aerospatial
Main Characteristics:
Leadership, Famous

Commander Gil Hendricks

WING COMMANDER, EAS AUSTRALIA

Born: Guam, Pacific Ocean, Earth 2217 (Age: 33). 181 cm, 78 kg, brown hair, hazel eyes.

Gil Hendricks is considered by many to be the best fighter commander in Earthforce. He is brave, decisive, confident, talented, and resourceful. He is also arrogant, undisciplined, insubordinate, and has been court-martialed twice, once for being absent without leave during a battle. Only the support of his own superiors at the trial saved his career.

Hendricks joined Earthforce in 2235, at the age of 18. Interestingly, he joined as a private in the 86th EA Infantry Division. He trained as an atmospheric assault ship pilot. It was as a ground forces Sergeant that Hendricks earned the Alliance Medal of Valor at the Battle of Dra'Tel 5 in 2238.

Recognizing Hendricks' talents as a pilot and his leadership skills, Earthforce assigned Hendricks to Officer's Candidate School and trained him as a starfury pilot. Hendricks joined the 29th Tactical Fighter Squadron as an ensign in 2239.

By the start of the Minbari War, Hendricks was a lieutenant commander and leader of the 29th TFS. Hendricks proved to be completely fearless under fire and incredibly quick to grab a tactical advantage. He earned his second Alliance Medal of Valor at the Battle of Signet in 2245. Fly-

Hendricks

ing cover for the last ships evacuating from Delphi and Vega through Signet, Hendricks saved the *EAS Hecate* and the *EAS Moskva* from destruction and personally destroyed four Minbari fighters.

Hendricks' antics away from battle were ignored during the war, because Earthforce needed him. But once the war ended, Hendricks became a liability. Hendricks has an open distrust of all aliens, and passionately hates the Minbari. He also is a vocal critic of his superior officers, and has made several enemies within Earthforce's higher echelons. To his credit, however, Gil Hendricks is a patriot, devoted to the Earth Alliance and all of humanity.

In 2249 Hendricks was given command of the fighter wing aboard the *EAS Australia*, part of the *Three Suns* Battlegroup commanded by Admiral Moreau. Moreau has a reputation for handling difficult officers, so Earth Central sent him Hendricks. Hendricks and Moreau have managed to forge a working relationship. While the admiral does not always manage to control Hendricks, he does have Hendricks' respect and has made it clear that he will not tolerate insubordination from the junior officer.

Unfortunately, Hendricks does not have the same level of respect for the *Australia's* captain, Annette Flint, as he does for the admiral. The two barely talk, and the *Australia's* pilots have become undisciplined and scornful of Flint. When the situation explodes, Hendricks will be at the center of it. The only question left is, will Hendricks' career survive another explosion?

When roleplaying Hendricks, remember that his biggest assets, as well as his biggest liabilities are his ego and bravado. In the field of battle he is unmatched and he knows it. He is not afraid to speak his mind, nor to boast, and he will always assume that he is better than you are until you beat him at something he considers a forte.

Chm: 6	Int: 5	Str: 4
Fin: 6	Ins: 5	Agl: 5
Pre: 4	Wit: 5	End: 4
Xen: 3	Per: 5	Cor: 7

Primary Skill: Piloting
Major Skills: Tactics, Space Combat
Gambling
Engineering, Electrical

Main Characteristics:
Impulsive,
Insubordinate

Commander Jeffrey David Sinclair

COMMANDER, 51ST TACTICAL FIGHTER WING

Born: Mars Colony 2218 (Age: 32). 193 cm, 80 kg, brown hair, brown eyes.

Jeffrey Sinclair is a born pilot. There is no place he prefers to the cockpit of a starfury, out amongst the stars. It is a family tradition. Sinclairs have been flying in combat since the Battle of Britain in 1940. Jeff is no different. Except that no other Sinclair led an entire squadron to their deaths in battle.

Sinclair is also a hero. At least that is what everyone keeps telling him. He survived the Line. One of less than 200 men and women who did. Unlike the rest of them, Sinclair has no memory of how he survived. No matter how hard he tries, there is a 24 hour gap in his memory. He knows he led his squadron against the Minbari armada, that the responsibility for the lives of twelve pilots were his, and he cannot even remember how they died. The guilt is eating Sinclair apart.

Born on Mars Colony in 2218, Sinclair joined Earthforce in 2237, determined to become a pilot. He finished flight school in early 2240, and was named acting squadron leader at the end of 2241. By the beginning of the Minbari War he was a lieutenant commander and experienced squadron leader.

Through three years of war, Sinclair led the 361st Tactical Fighter Squadron, "Death's Hand," against the Minbari. Though his Mitchell-Hyundyne SA-23A "Novas" were inferior to the Minbari starfighters they

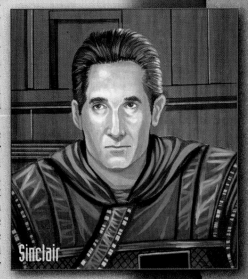

Sinclair

faced, Sinclair learned how to anticipate the enemy tactics, and compensate for the stealth and performance advantages of the enemy ships. His men died, but they usually took their share of Minbari fighters down before they went. Few other squadrons could claim the same.

The 361st TFS was destroyed at the Line. Rather than try to reconstitute the squadron, Earth Central retired the unit designation, to honor the dead. Sinclair was promoted, granted leave, and then given command of the 51st Tactical Fighter Wing, three squadrons stationed on the Mars Colony's Phobos Station.

When roleplaying him, remember that Sinclair continues to be a solid commander and his squadrons are among the best trained units in Earthforce. Jeffrey Sinclair is, however, just going through the motions. His ambition gone, he lives in a tangle of rage at the Minbari and haunted guilt over his own failures. Sinclair searches for redemption, a chance to make up for those missing 24 hours on the Line. Given the chance, he will do anything to find out what happened that day.

Chm: 7	Int: 5	Str: 3
Fin: 7	Ins: 6	Agl: 4
Pre: 4	Wit: 4	End: 4
Xen: 6	Per: 4	Cor: 7

Primary Skill: Piloting
Major Skills: Diplomacy
Navigation, Aerospatial
Main Characteristics:
Haunted, Decorated

Captain John Sheridan

CAPTAIN, EAS ENDYMION

Born: Iowa, North America, Earth 2219 (Age: 31). 190 cm, 88 kg, brown hair, brown eyes.

John Sheridan is one of the few surviving heroes of the Minbari War, and one of Earthforce's finest ship commanders. His decisive thinking under pressure and innovative tactics propelled him to command rank in just six years of service with Earthforce, and made him the youngest captain in the fleet at the age of 29. Now, two years after the war that made him famous throughout the Earth Alliance, Captain Sheridan continues a career expected by many to eventually take him to the corridors of power of Earth Central.

John Sheridan, a descendant of the famous American Civil War cavalry commander Phillip Sheridan, was born in 2218 on his family's property in Iowa, North America. His father, a career diplomat, traveled often, and on occasion the young John Sheridan or his sister Elizabeth traveled with their father. One memorable moment for Sheridan was his meeting with the Dalai Lama in Tibet in 2240.

Two years later Sheridan graduated third in his class at Earthforce Academy: Sandhurst and joined the Moon-Mars patrol under Commander Jack Maynard. Maynard,

Starkiller   BAB/COM

In early 2246, the EA Fleet was desperate. In every encounter with the Minbari, more officers and men died, yet never could Earthforce claim a win. At best they held on doggedly, managed to trade even in a skirmish, or to stay in the fight long enough to evacuate another base–give ground on yet another world. Then John Sheridan gave Earth its first true victory.

Commander John Sheridan was the XO of the *EAS Lexington* when the Minbari made its first attack on Dakota. After Captain Sterns' death, he did not sit by and wait, but instead took a cue from the Minbari, luring the *Drala Fi* into a trap and destroying it just as his ship had been lured. Through his quick thinking he scored Earth's only true victory of the war.

He also gave the Minbari a personal enemy. The *Drala Fi*, which translates to *Black Star*, was one of the Minbari's best ships with a proud and honorable captain. Its death gave the Minbari a personal enemy, someone who deserved to die for his cowardly attack. Although they did not at first know his identity, John Sheridan was the target of a special hatred. Among the Minbari he became known as Starkiller.

currently captain of the exploration vessel *EAS Lepanto*, and Sheridan remain close friends. Sheridan left the Moon-Mars patrol after receiving his Lieutenant's bars in 2243.

The outbreak of the Minbari war forever changed Sheridan's career. Newly promoted to Commander, Sheridan was assigned to the *EAS Lexington* as XO under Captain Sterns shortly before the war broke out. It was the *Lexington*, with Sheridan in command after Sterns' death in the battle, which destroyed the Minbari cruiser *Black Star* just a few months later.

The *Lexington* was scrapped for salvage after the battle, and Commander Sheridan was transferred to top secret diplomatic duties which he carried out for the rest of the war. More recently, the promoted Captain Sheridan has been named as CO of the *Hyperion*-class cruiser *EAS Endymion*. The *Endymion*, stationed out of Io, routinely cruises the Solar system on defensive patrol when not detached on a more important mission.

Sheridan and his wife Anna live on Ganymede Outpost when he is not aboard the *Endymion*. John is a devoted and responsible husband, but he and Anna lead largely separate careers. Sheridan is grateful that the Io assignment allows him more time at home, while still allowing him to pursue the career he loves.

John Sheridan is respected by all the officers who have served with him for his calm under fire and his great personal courage. His devotion to Earthforce and the Alliance is unquestioned by his superiors. When EarthGov wants a critical mission handled smoothly and efficiently, it is the *Endymion* and Captain John Sheridan that will be first on the scene.

Chm: 6	Int: 6	Str: 4
Fin: 6	Ins: 6	Agl: 5
Pre: 5	Wit: 5	End: 4
Xen: 4	Per: 5	Cor: 5

Primary Skill: Strategy, Space
Major Skills: Tactics, Space Combat
Diplomacy
Investigation
Main Characteristics:
Command Rank,
Dedicated

Captain Jack Maynard

CAPTAIN, EAS LEPANTO

Sheridan

Born: Kansas, North America, Earth 2211 (Age: 39). 182 cm, 83 kg, brown hair, brown eyes.

"Smiling" Jack Maynard is known throughout the fleet for his easygoing nature, and his large and well cared-for cowboy boots. One of the more experienced captains to survive the Minbari war, Maynard now serves with DSX, the Deep Space Exploration Command. He commands the long range scout ship *EAS Lepanto*, currently on deep patrol beyond Minbari space.

Jack Maynard joined Earthforce in 2231, the year the conflict with the Dilgar began. During the conflict, he served as a third-shift bridge officer aboard the corvette *EAS Diego* on scout duty along the Dilgar frontier. It was during this assignment that Maynard discovered he enjoyed the freedom that went with scouting missions and exploration.

Maynard served in a variety of posts before the Minbari War. From 2240-2243, Commander Maynard served on the Moon-Mars patrol, where he became friends with a young ensign named John Sheridan, later to become famous as commander of the *EAS Lexington* during the war. In 2243 Jack Maynard was promoted to captain, given command of the *EAS Prokofiev* and sent on a cruise deep into

Maynard

the Taurus Arc. The *Prokofiev* returned to EA space for the first time in 2246. By then the Minbari War was in full swing and experienced captains were needed. Maynard was given command of the cruiser *EAS Arethusa* and he served capably through the remainder of the war.

Only after the end of the Minbari War could Maynard return to duty with DSX. He spent 2249 serving as Deputy Program Director for the new *Explorer*— ships and is considered a strong candidate to command one of the first three examples upon their completion beginning in 2253.

In the meantime, Maynard has been given command of the *EAS Lepanto*, an older *Nova*-class dreadnought rebuilt as an exploration vessel. He is currently midway through a two-year mission surveying beyond Minbari space, a job few in Earthforce would feel comfortable commanding. But Jack Maynard is eager to discover the unknown. Commanding the *Lepanto* gives him that chance.

When roleplaying Maynard, remember that he is a dreamer at heart, and his job makes him very happy. He commands by becoming friends with his crew, and has a very laid back manner. His trademark snakeskin cowboy boots and the nickname "Smiling Jack" best illustrate his personality.

Chm: 7	Int: 5	Str: 4
Fin: 6	Ins: 5	Agl: 5
Pre: 4	Wit: 5	End: 4
Xen: 5	Per: 5	Cor: 5

Primary Skill: Savvy
Major Skills: Management
Navigation, Aerospatial
Diplomacy
Main Characteristics:
Curious, Veteran

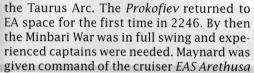

Hyatt

Notable Base Commanders

It is almost impossible to serve in Earthforce without serving at one of the military's two largest bases, the Gate Complex in Jupiter's orbit, the sole port of entry into Earth's solar system, and the Wolf V shipyards, the center of new fleet building efforts. The commanders of these two important bases, as well as others, have their own stories to tell.

Rear Admiral Carter Hyatt

COORDINATOR, EA GATE COMPLEX

Born: Auckland, New Zealand, Earth, 2205 (Age: 45). 181 cm, 72 kg, blonde hair, gray eyes.

The EA Gate Complex is a large series of Earthforce protected facilities scattered throughout the Jovian system. The Io jumpgate is Earth's most important link to the outside, and Earthforce has taken every precaution to defend it. Admiral Carter Hyatt is the present Coordinator of the Io Gate Complex. His responsibilities include supporting the EA Fleet ships stationed around Jupiter, managing logistics for the Gate Complex, command of the defenses at Barbican Point and control over the shipyards. He also heads a council of the commanders from Ganymede Outpost, Ganymede Station, Io Station and Saturn Station.

Hyatt is a spare, middle-aged man with a fussy manner and an eye for detail. He lives by a very tight schedule, and does not appreciate those who circumvent proper channels. His rear admiral's rank is a result of his administrative skills, not his command abilities, and his subordinates know it.

Because of Hyatt's lack of leadership, the Earthforce organization in the Jovian system has become partisan and riddled by personal rivalries. Although Hyatt has managed to put together an efficient organization on paper, he cannot make his officers work together and they often ignore him completely. Colonel Tompkins, commander of the Io Station's garrison troops, considers Hyatt worthless and runs the EA Ground Forces contingent without even consulting his superior. The colonel is pressing for Command to make the garrison a separate organization, not responsible to the coordinator.

The heads of the civilian posts in the system dislike Hyatt's nit-picking. Admiral Hyatt has also failed to mediate key trade issues between Sirius Station and Io. Personnel from the two stations have already become involved in altercations and even caused a riot that killed two people. Hyatt does not know how to handle the situation, except by issuing security directives. The directives have only increased the discontent.

Hyatt is frustrated and short tempered, because he can feel the situation falling apart. He is under increasing pressure from EA Command, who are worried that the fleet rebuilding program is in jeopardy, and is in a position he is ill equipped to handle. Until he is replaced, the situation in the Jovian area will continue to rot away from within, even as Hyatt keeps them outwardly running smoothly.

When roleplaying him, remember that Hyatt is constantly on edge, and badly out of his league. He is a man sinking in a mire of duties that he cannot control. He is often distracted, and meetings with him never go for long without being interrupted by one minor crisis or another.

Chm: 5	Int: 6	Str: 4
Fin: 5	Ins: 7	Agl: 4
Pre: 4	Wit: 5	End: 4
Xen: 4	Per: 6	Cor: 5

Primary Skill: Management
Major Skills: Law
               History
               Engineering, Mechanical
Main Characteristics:
               Stubborn, Enemy

Major Sabrina "Angel" Webber

COMMANDER, WOLF V SHIPYARDS

Born: Suffolk, United Kingdom, Earth, 2222 (Age: 28). 175 cm, 80 kg, blond hair, green eyes.

Major Webber is a patriotic woman whose career is on the rise. During her childhood, her father served at the helm of the EAS Susan B. Anthony during the Dilgar War, and although she didn't share his love of space, she did learn from him a sense of pride in the Alliance and a desire to serve.

She enlisted in Earthforce immediately upon graduation from secondary school, training for logistical positions at Earthforce Academy: Sandhurst and graduating at the top of her class in 2242. She asked for and received assignment to Earthdome, where she served as a Supply Officer until the War.

Webber

When the War started, Lieutenant Webber was promoted and made Chief Operations Officer for the Earthdome Situation Room. There, she proved her abilities to the Joint Chiefs and others in Command. Chairman Mazuk referred to her as their "angel," keeping the room running smoothly, a nickname which has stayed with her.

She was there during the final days of the War, and was one of the few outside of the Joint Chiefs and their advisors who knew exactly how badly outclassed the EA forces were by the Minbari fleet. She has become a vocal advocate of rebuilding the fleet, stronger and better, so that a tragedy like this never happens again.

Her views on the fleet along with the recommendations of several of the Joint Chiefs earned her a plum assignment: the command of the Wolf Shipyards. Devastated after the war, completely without staff, one of the primary goals of the fleet's rebuilding program was to reform the Wolf Shipyards. Major Webber, still young and energetic, is up for the challenge. Although many outside the Joint Chiefs doubted her abilities, she has proven a capable leader and has brought the shipyards a remarkably long way in just a few short years. What was a ruined husk after the War is now once again the foremost facility in the Alliance, and the home of the *Omega*-class destroyer.

When roleplaying her, remember that Sabrina is coming into the peak of her career and she knows it. She is full of confidence and energy, ready to meet the challenges ahead. She's used to being treated well due to her position and contacts in the Alliance, and although she wouldn't use her position against someone, she's not above implying that she would if it got the job done.

Chm: 6	Int: 5	Str: 4
Fin: 6	Ins: 6	Agl: 4
Pre: 4	Wit: 5	End: 4
Xen: 4	Per: 5	Cor: 6

Primary Skill: Management
Major Skills: Acumen
Savvy
Business
Main Characteristics:
Proud

Captain Georges Oyono

COMMANDER, DELPHI IV RESERVE YARDS

Born: Cameroon, Earth, 2209 (Age: 41). 185 cm, 79 kg, brown hair, brown eyes.

Oyono is a man without a future, and with a past he would rather forget. Once one of the EA Fleet's brightest and best ship commanders, Oyono now hides on a forgotten supply station on the outskirts of alliance territory, and drinks his life away.

At the outbreak of the Minbari War, Oyono commanded the cruiser *EAS Bouvines*. Survivor of the disasters at Signet and at Hell Run, Oyono and the *Bouvines* developed a reputation as a "lucky ship." Many men and women requested transfers to the *Bouvines*, hoping to increase their chance to make it through the war.

Only a year into the War, the *Bouvines'* luck ran out. On patrol

Oyono

near Leonis, the *Bouvines* responded to a distress call from the Kandhi III Colony, under attack from a small Minbari raiding force. Oyono arrived on the scene and engaged the Minbari raiders, only to receive a second distress call from Leonis reporting a Minbari strike led by a cruiser. Faced with a devilish choice, Oyono chose to break off and abandon Kandhi and face the more serious threat to Leonis.

The *Bouvines* raced for Leonis, but not quickly enough. Oyono arrived only to witness the destruction of the Earthforce outpost near the gate. Enraged that he had left Kandhi to be decimated for nothing, Oyono attacked the Minbari cruiser furiously as it turned for home. The *Bouvines*, an older *Nova*-class dreadnought, was no match for the Minbari force. In the short struggle that followed, the *Bouvines* was pounded into debris. Oyono was wounded early in the flight and hauled to an escape pod by one of his crew. He was one of the few survivors.

Captain Oyono was cleared of any wrongdoing by Earthforce's investigation into the battle, but Oyono knows he could have saved Kandhi and the crew of the *Bouvines* if he had chosen differently. He cannot forgive himself, nor will he just give up. Instead he punishes himself, by working himself to death at an almost meaningless job in order to atone, at least a little, for those who died. And when the pain gets too much for him, Oyono drinks. Heavily.

Oyono has actually turned the Delphi IV Reserve Yards into an efficient and well-run station, if not a happy station. He punishes only himself, not those around him. The tragedy of Georges Oyono remains confined, so far, to just one man, and that is the way Oyono wants it to remain.

When roleplaying him, remember that Oyono is a defeated man. His emotions, when they manifest themselves, are repressed and kept at bay, and he finds nothing left in life to enjoy. Beyond his duty to Earthforce, he has and wants nothing.

Chm: 6	Int: 6	Str: 5
Fin: 6	Ins: 4	Agl: 5
Pre: 4	Wit: 4	End: 4
Xen: 4	Per: 5	Cor: 6

Primary Skill: Management

Major Skills: Savvy
               Shiphandling
               Tactics, Space Combat
Main Characteristics:
               Addicted, Haunted

Joint Chiefs of Staff

The Earthforce Joint Staff attained its current form in 2226, when the Director of Military Intelligence's staff was added to the Joint Staff. Until the Minbari war, the role of the Chief of Colonial Forces had been rapidly shrinking, but the destruction of much of the EA Fleet has emphasized the need for auxiliary defense forces funded directly by the earth colonies, but kept strictly under Earthforce supervision.

The Chiefs are loyal to Earth every one, but each has his or her own ideas about how best to serve the Alliance. Within their council a struggle brews, one that could erupt at any time, dividing the military and causing untold harm to innocent lives.

Fleet Admiral Garik "Gary" Mazuk

CHAIRMAN OF THE JOINT CHIEFS

Born: Ukraine, Earth 2189 (Age: 61). 179 cm, 83 kg, gray hair, blue eyes.

Fleet Admiral Mazuk is a shattered man. An entire generation of brother and sister officers were wiped out at the Battle of the Line. Mazuk cannot forgive himself. He, with Admiral Singh, drew up the battle plans for the final defense of Earth, and he watched as the Minbari wiped out all he had built over 37 years in Earthforce.

Gary Mazuk has chaired the Joint Chiefs for eight years, and served as acting Chief of Fleet Operations during the war with the Dilgar. He began his career after graduating from Earthforce Academy: Olympia on Mars in 2212. In 2226, as commander of the cruiser *EAS Bangkok*, Mazuk directed the evacuation of Myoto during the Karthedo Conflict. His steady rise to the highest position in Earthforce was a result of his calm, consensus building leadership style and an uncanny ability to sense political trends.

The Minbari War has worn away Mazuk's confidence and destroyed many of his most trusted and capable subordinates. Mazuk's son was killed in 2245 while serving with the EAS Warspite, and his daughter was a Starfury pilot on the Line. His wife Amanda divorced him in 2228. She blames Mazuk for the death of their children.

Mazuk

Mazuk plans to retire, but he is determined to start the rebuilding of Earthforce before he departs. His attention is no longer focused on directing and mediating between the other chiefs, instead he spends his time in the halls of EarthGov, lobbying senators and speaking to the press to gain public support for another cruiser or to purchase more technology through the Narn Regime.

Without Mazuk to control them, the other chiefs are engaged in an increasingly nasty and divisive struggle for power. The two most powerful of the chiefs are Admiral Singh, Chief of Fleet Operations and General Ashe, the Vice Chairman. General Ashe now runs most of the day-to-day operations of the Joint Staff, while Admiral Singh is a vocal and hawkish supporter of Earthforce expansion.

When roleplaying Mazuk, remember that he is at the end of a long, hard road. He still carries the burden of thousands of lost lives including his own children. Despite this, he is still committed to the Alliance and is determined to finish the work in front of him. His temper is growing shorter and he tolerates few distractions.

Chm: 5   Int: 6   Str: 4
Fin: 6   Ins: 7   Agl: 5
Pre: 4   Wit: 5   End: 4
Xen: 5   Per: 4   Cor: 5
Primary Skill: Savvy
Major Skills: Strategy, Space
               Diplomacy
               Management
Main Characteristics:
               Dedicated,
               Command Rank

Lieutenant General Kelly Ashe

VICE CHAIRMAN OF THE JOINT CHIEFS

Born: Seadome, Orion VII, 2201 (Age: 49). 175 cm, 57 kg, brown hair, brown eyes.

Perhaps Kelly Ashe should not be the most powerful of the Joint Chiefs, but she is. Her rise to the vice chairman's post is a result of talent, ambition, determination, and most importantly, powerful friends. General Ashe is a close friend of Senator Luis Santiago, a power broker in EarthGov and likely presidential nominee in the 2253 elections. She was also a protege of Admiral Mazuk prior to the war.

Ashe served as commander of Earth's ground defenses during the Minbari war. She organized what would have been the final and probably futile ground defense of the planet if the Minbari had not surrendered at the Line. Her calm and steady handling of frantic senators and their staffs during the last days before the Line impressed many in EarthGov, and won her the promotion to the vice chairmanship when General Hosni Salah al-Din retired.

Ashe is the junior member of the joint chiefs in rank. She has been nominated for full general but her promotion is being blocked in the Senate by Senators Renault and Clark. She sus-

Ashe

pects that Admiral Singh is responsible. Ashe is not hawkish enough for Singh, who believes that Earthforce must prepare now to fight a second war with the Minbari. Ashe dislikes Singh's xenophobic attitudes, and while she has no liking for the Minbari, she believes Singh and his supporters will only force a war that Earth is not ready for, and which they cannot win.

To counter Admiral Singh's influence in Earthforce, Ashe has become the center of a strong faction throughout Earthforce dedicated to a strong and secure peace with Earth's neighbors. Along with Lt. General Hague, commander of Orion Command, Ashe is involved strongly in EarthGov politics. Her strategy is to get Senator Santiago elected president, and hopefully then succeed Admiral Mazuk as chairman. She believes Santiago will support her aims for peace with Earth's neighbors and reasonable expansion of Earthforce.

When roleplaying Ashe, remember that she is very driven and optimistic. She doesn't blame anyone for the past with the Minbari, but she does hold a grudge against those who would want to fight them again. She is friendly and open at first, but that changes if she believes that you are not on her side.

Chm: 6   Int: 5   Str: 4
Fin: 7   Ins: 6   Agl: 6
Pre: 5   Wit: 5   End: 3
Xen: 4   Per: 4
Cor: 5
Primary Skill: Strategy, Ground
Major Skills: Diplomacy
               Geography
               Tactics, Troop
Main Characteristics:
               Ally, Enemy

Admiral Jason Ashvin Singh

CHIEF OF FLEET OPERATIONS

Born: Jamshedpur, India, Earth 2194 (Age: 56). 176 cm, 79 kg, black hair, brown eyes.

Coldly charming, a calculating and precise thinker, Admiral Jason Ashvin Singh is a dominant power within Earthforce. Ambition and a driving hunger have made

Singh the most powerful man in the EA Fleet, and he is determined to use that power to mold the fleet into his image.

To that end, Singh has always cultivated powerful allies. Senators Clark and Renault are old friends of Singh's, and in the years leading up to the Minbari War he established a close working relationship with Fleet Admiral Mazuk. Now, however, with Mazuk's influence on the wane, Singh sees a chance to push his agenda to expand Earthforce in preparation for a second war with the Minbari.

Jason Ashvin Singh has always carefully managed his career. While his rise to flag rank was not quick, it was steady, and every transfer was arranged to support his ambitions. Singh has served as a ship commander, director of fleet construction, and as a special aide to the president advising her on fleet issues. Singh was promoted to full admiral and named as Chief of Fleet Operations in 2246, during the early stages of the Minbari War. Singh proved to be a capable planner; it was he who helped Admiral Mazuk plan the ill-fated Battle of the Line. Unlike Mazuk, Singh carries no guilt over the losses at the Line. Singh knows the Line was a futile attempt to stop a superior enemy.

Singh does not trust the recent peace with the Minbari. He sees the Minbari as an obstacle to the Earth Alliance's future. Therefore they must be removed as a threat. So Singh has worked hard to encourage Mazuk's fleet rebuilding campaign, and often aligns with General Romano, the Chief of Staff of the EA Ground Forces, to push for more money and resources. He also is aggressively pursuing weapons technology programs designed to close the gap with the Minbari, and purchasing equipment from the Narn and Centauri, as well as accepting Minbari "help"—anything he can think of to push the EA ahead of its rivals technologically.

Lieutenant General Ashe, the new Vice Chairman of the Joint Chiefs, he sees as an obstacle to his plans. It is because of his influence that Ashe has not been promoted to full general. Ashe advocates a continuing and strengthened peace with the Minbari which Singh cannot countenance. Their recent clashes have divided the joint chiefs.

Admiral Singh continues to quietly accumulate power throughout Earthforce and the halls of Earthdome. Senior to all of the chiefs except Admiral Mazuk and Admiral Kim, who is not considered politically powerful, Singh hopes to succeed to the chairmanship when Mazuk finally retires. Only General Ashe and a few disorganized alliance senators stand in his way. From the chair, Jason Ashvin Singh would become architect of a second Minbari War. And this war, unlike the first, the Earth Alliance would win.

Singh

When roleplaying Singh, remember that although he is at heart cold and calculating, he can put on a very friendly face when necessary. His vast network of contacts keeps him informed on many things, and he rarely agrees to meet someone before he knows everything that he can about them, and he is willing to use that knowledge as leverage if it will help.

Chm: 5	Int: 5	Str: 4
Fin: 6	Ins: 6	Agl: 5
Pre: 5	Wit: 6	End: 4
Xen: 3	Per: 6	Cor: 5

Primary Skill: Diplomacy
Major Skills: Savvy
                 Acumen
                 Philosophy
Main Characteristics:
                 Heartless, Militaristic

Admiral Lee Hwan Kim

DIRECTOR OF MILITARY INTELLIGENCE

Born: Kimchaek, Korea, Earth 2197 (Age: 53). 172 cm, 70 kg, black hair, brown eyes.

Lee Hwan Kim has served as Director of Military Intelligence for almost 5 years, taking over after the previous director was removed by the Senate for failure to obtain adequate intelligence on the Minbari in the early stages of the Minbari War. Kim's selection for the post was unexpected, as he was a relatively junior Vice Admiral, but he has proved to be an excellent director. His staff anticipated the main Minbari thrust towards Earth in 2248 in time for Admirals Mazuk and Singh to draw up plans for the defense at the Line. Though the battle was disastrous for Earthforce, Kim's talents were recognized and he is a popular director, with broad support throughout EarthGov.

Kim

Kim is a pleasant and thoughtful man in person. He is known for his quick understanding of intelligence issues. He supports the rapid expansion of Earthforce by Admiral Mazuk, but is a fence sitter in most confrontations between General Ashe and Admiral Singh. Kim's immediate staff is efficient, however much of Military Intelligence's work remains shrouded in secrecy and suffers from a confusing organization and many layers of security and bureaucracy.

What EarthGov does not know, and few even suspect, is Psi-Corps' hand in almost all of Kim's success. Kim's eldest son is a P-10 in the Corps. Psi-Corps recognized Kim's fatherly pride in his talented son early, and enlisted Kim as an ally, quietly supporting him by supplying Psi-Corps intelligence to him in return for his advice and help in facilitating matters of interest to Psi-Corps. Kim trusts the Psi-Corps' leadership, and shares information out of a sense of collegiality. However, he owes the Corps for his career and he knows it.

When roleplaying Kim, remember that he is a quick learner, and picks up on things quite well. In addition to being a pleasant conversationalist, he has a very quick wit. He will always steer conversation away from the Psi-Corps and will usually refuse to meet with people when a telepath is present.

Chm: 6	Int: 6	Str: 4
Fin: 8	Ins: 7	Agl: 4
Pre: 3	Wit: 5	End: 3
Xen: 4	Per: 5	Cor: 5

Primary Skill: Acumen
Major Skills: Strategy, Ground
Strategy, Space
Management
Main Characteristics:
Ally, Proud

General Jennifer Romano

CHIEF OF STAFF, EARTH GROUND FORCES

Born: New Rockville, Europa, Jupiter 2198 (Age: 52). 174 cm, 55 kg, brown hair, green eye.

Jennifer Romano is a hard case. It is rumored through the halls of Earth Central that if they fired General Romano out of a launch tube, they could take out a Minbari cruiser in one shot. When Earthforce Command Sergeant Major Gates was informed of the rumor, he offered his pension to any GROPO who could put Romano IN the launch tube. There were no takers.

Romano is known for her quick temper and attacking style. In the ground campaign for Ross in 2246, Romano managed to hold off an entire Minbari strike force by counterattacking with just two armored divisions, long enough for the colony to be evacuated. She was decorated for her heroism. Over 11,000 troopers died in two days.

Senator Natawe of Nigeria called publicly for Romano's court martial after Ross. Romano angrily defended her actions, asking Natawe whether he thought she should have had two divisions of troops join hands and sing peace songs to stop the minbos.

Many in EarthGov thought Romano a strange choice to become Chief of Ground Forces after the war, but it became apparent very soon after she was nominated to the joint chiefs that Romano had powerful allies throughout Earth's defense industries. Her father, a retired CEO of the Liao Industrial Group, and her brother-in-law, an executive vice president with Mitchell-Hyundyne, lobbied for her nomination with the defense connected senators of North

America, the Pacific Rim and Mars. The senate, ever ready to accommodate powerful business interests, confirmed her assignment easily.

General Romano is a difficult chief. Intolerant, often impolitic, she advocates a rapid expansion of Earthforce. This often aligns her with the chairman and Admiral Singh. But she also wants a larger slice of the pie for ground forces, and will make common cause with General Ashe to cut back Singh's budget when she wants more promotion slots, another battalion of tanks, or wants a GROPO officer in a key assignment.

Unfortunately for all concerned, Romano is not a good manager. She is a field officer, with little respect or liking for her senior logistics and acquisition officers. To her, they are bureaucrats who would rather give excuses than deliver the goods. While she has managed to get more equipment for her troops, some of it is of inferior quality, or has been designed to poor specs. General Ashe has attempted to compensate for Romano's faults, but Ashe is too often diverted by her struggles with Admiral Singh, and Romano does not tolerate interference in her command by anyone, even the vice chairman.

When roleplaying her, remember that Romano is very no-nonsense. She does not accept less than a person's best and will not tolerate a flippant attitude. Her reputation as a hard case is well earned, and any talking with her will see it.

Chm: 4	Int: 5	Str: 4
Fin: 5	Ins: 5	Agl: 6
Pre: 6	Wit: 6	End: 4
Xen: 3	Per: 5	Cor: 4

Primary Skill: Strategy, Ground
Major Skills: Tactic, Troop Combat, Unarmed Combat, Ranged
Main Characteristics: Impulsive, Decorated

General Felipe Arturo Ruiz

CHIEF OF ALLIANCE COLONIAL FORCES

Born: San Miguel, Guevaria, 61 Cygnus A II 2203 (Age: 47). 195 cm, 99 kg, brown hair, blue eyes.

Felipe Ruiz's latin good looks, tall powerful figure and booming baritone are recognized throughout Earth's colony worlds. An imposing and passionate personality, Ruiz is the voice of the colony worlds within Earthforce. It is a voice too often ignored by those on Earth.

Ruiz became a folk hero in 2231 when he led the Guevarian Home Guard's outmoded SA-15 "Tiger" starfighters against a strong Dilgar task force and destroyed two enemy cruisers. After the war he was recruited into Earthforce, and graduated second in his class at Earthforce Ground School: West Point. Ruiz was from the colonies and he never forgot his roots, choosing to serve as an Earthforce attache with the Signet Colonial Defense Forces after his graduation.

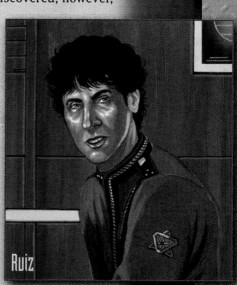
Romano

Ruiz was promoted quickly and often, and in 2249 he was named to the Joint Chiefs. Earthforce realized at the end of the Minbari War they needed colonial support to defend humans throughout space, and Ruiz was seen as a popular choice with the colonial leaders.

General Ruiz has discovered, however, that deep suspicion of the colonies remains in the halls of Earthdome. Many in the senate fear that allowing the colonies their own armed forces, however limited the numbers or equipment, will tempt local governments to rebel against EarthGov. Ruiz has become embroiled in a political battle to get squadrons of older Mitchell-Hyundyne SA-23A "Nova" Starfuries released to the colonial

Ruiz

forces as Earthforce replaces them with the new SA-23E "Aurora" model Starfury. Ruiz is not a politician, and he has been short tempered in key Senate committee meetings. He is supported by Admiral Mazuk, but Admiral Singh wants to upgrade the older starfuries to equip more carriers and cruisers for the EA Fleet. Ruiz does not think the fleet should be expanded to the size wanted by Singh, but he may be forced to compromise and support Singh's expansion plans in order to get those fighters for the colonies.

When roleplaying Ruiz, remember that he has a powerful personality. He is a passionate speaker, led by what he feels is right rather than by political expedience. He appreciates honesty in others and will be more open with those whom he thinks are being honest with him.

Chm: 7	Int: 4	Str: 5
Fin: 6	Ins: 6	Agl: 4
Pre: 5	Wit: 5	End: 4
Xen: 4	Per: 5	Cor:5

Primary Skill: Piloting
Major Skills: Strategy, Ground
               Management
               Diplomacy
Main Characteristics:
               Dedicated, Veteran

General Robert Lefcourt

ASSISTANT TO THE JOINT CHIEFS

Born: Proxima III, 2197 (Age: 53). 183 cm, 74 kg, gray hair, blue eyes.

In another life, Robert Lefcourt would have been a man of peace. Brought up in a very traditional home in the Reagan dome on Proxima, he was instilled with a high regard for the history and traditions of the Alliance and Earth. A high score on his ad-

mission tests placed him in line for the Alliance's best schools, and his wealthy background virtually guaranteed him a spot anywhere he wished.

Despite the fact that his mother wanted him to go into business, he felt a strong sense of duty to the Alliance and his choice of enrollment was the Earthforce Academy: Olympia, where he graduated with honors in record time. When the EA threw in its support with the League of Non-Aligned Worlds, he was captain of the *EAS Atreus*, where he served for the duration of the Dilgar War. A brilliant tactician, he was noticed by Command after the war and transferred to the Academy, where he became one of the top instructors on tactics and command. An entire generation of officers was trained under General Lefcourt's watchful eye.

When the Minbari presence became known, Robert's expertise was sought out by Admiral Mazuk, and he was given the post of Assistant to the Joint Chiefs. He received the post in 2244, immediately assuming the direct supervision of the Minbari Contact Committee.

In a way, he felt responsible for the way the Minbari War started, as he was the one who had assigned Captain Jankowski and the *Prometheus* to the border patrol that led to the war. But that responsibility was not overshadowed by guilt. He continued to pursue the goal of peace throughout the war, though he realized that the goal was a long shot.

Since the war, he has been a vocal advocate of rebuilding the fleet, supporting Chairman Mazuk and General Ashe. It is expected that when Mazuk retires Lefcourt will be on the top of the list to join the Joint Chiefs, but he has privately decided that he will retire.

When roleplaying him, remember that Lefcourt is a very confident man. He is used to being in command and having a measure of superiority over others from his years as a teacher, and he tends to treat people as students. He is not overbearing, though, and can be very friendly.

Chm: 5   Int: 6   Str: 5
Fin: 6   Ins: 5   Agl: 4
Pre: 5   Wit: 6   End: 4
Xen: 4   Per: 5   Cor: 5
Primary Skill: Management
Major Skills: Strategy, Space
               Tactics, Space Combat
               Diplomacy
               Combat, Ranged
Main Characteristics:
               Veteran, Command Rank

Assistants to Notable Characters

As your characters are performing their duties to the Alliance (or whatever other tasks and motivations they might pursue), they might well run across one or more of the characters outlined in this chapter. However, for characters who have not yet made a name for themselves, especially early in an epic campaign, most interactions with these important persons will happen at a distance—the player characters will see them only in passing, meet them briefly, or deal with them only after working through a morass of bureaucrats and assistants. This is not to say that player characters won't meet these notable figures—only that they probably won't be rubbing elbows with them on a regular basis when, as well known and busy as they are, they have subordinates to deal with the relatively minor issues that player characters bring to them. These subordinates deserve some attention here; not individually, of course, but in general.

Three types of characters generally working for notable personnel—and those most likely to interact with player characters on a day-to-day basis—are aides, secretaries and receptionists. A general overview of each role, along with some sample game stats, are covered here.

Aides

Aides are generally other officers in Earthforce assigned on a long-term basis to the staff of major commanders and other important officers. On a station or ship this might be the second in command or XO. Only command rank or higher officers have aides. Those who do have them usually have enough responsibilities that the aide is often the only one available in an office, and aides usually have some limited authority to speak in the officer's name when he or she is not around. In a well-run organization, aides are usually efficient and capable—but sometimes they have their own agendas, which they can exercise by limiting the access of others to their principal.

Chm: 6   Int: 5   Str: 4
Fin: 7   Ins: 4   Agl: 5
Pre: 5   Wit: 4   End: 4
Xen: 5   Per: 5   Cor: 4
Primary Skill: Diplomacy
Major Skills: Law
               Savvy
Main Characteristics:
               Authority

Secretaries

Secretaries are people responsible for executive management of the affairs of officers and other important figures, which generally includes day-to-day paperwork, correspondence, and schedule management. In Earthforce they are generally enlisted personnel, but can also be non-Earthforce contractors, depending on the office or posting. Officers posted on ships or minor stations do not generally have secretaries, but instead the duties a secretary might perform are tasked to a number of technicians on the bridge or in the command and control center.

Chm: 6   Int: 6   Str: 4
Fin: 5   Ins: 5   Agl: 4
Pre: 4   Wit: 5   End: 4
Xen: 5   Per: 4   Cor: 5
Primary Skill: Management

Major Skills: Writing
               Diplomacy
Main Characteristics:
               Authority

Receptionists

Receptionists are people whose primary responsibilities with regard to the officer in question are to make sure that only people who actually have a reason to meet with or talk to the officer. Unless the base to which the officer is stationed has a security requirement, receptionists are gener- ally non-Earthforce contractors, but enlisted personnel can sometimes fill this role. As with secretaries, ships and stations task these duties to bridge or C&C crew.

Chm: 7	Int: 5	Str: 4
Fin: 5	Ins: 5	Agl: 4
Pre: 4	Wit: 5	End: 4
Xen: 5	Per: 4	Cor: 4

Primary Skill: Savvy
Major Skills: Acumen
               Acting
Main Characteristics:
               Attractive

Appendix: Ship-to-Ship Combat Components

The last few pages of this book contain the components needed to use *The Babylon Project's* ship-to-ship combat system— whether run during a roleplaying session or as a standalone battle. Included are Ship Control Sheets for eight classes of Earthforce warships (the *Cotten*, *Hyperion*, *Olympus*, *Omega*, and *Nova*-classes, along with the "Cotten," "Porcupine," and "Shepherd" transports); five types of alien ships (the Centauri Battle Cruiser and Light Cruiser, the Narn Battle Dreadnought and Heavy Cruiser, and the Minbari War Cruiser); and two typical civilian ships (a large freighter and an interstellar liner). Ship Order Sheets are also provided, along with a sheet of cut-out counters.

The Ship Control Sheets and Ship Order Sheets may be photocopied for use with the game—they come two to a page; photocopy as many as you might need and cut them apart before play. Photocopying a ship's Order Sheet onto the back of its Control sheet is convenient for keeping paperwork under control during the game—if you have access to a double-sided copier (or a local copy shop that will do that), you'll find it handy to do so. Either way, remember that you do need one Ship Order Sheet per ship in play.

The counters are printed in color on heavy stock. Remove them from the book by carefully cutting their page out—for best results, place a sheet of heavy cardboard under the counter sheet, then use a straight edge and a sharp art knife to trim the sheet out, cutting close to the spine of the book. Carefully trim the counters out, again using a sharp art knife for best results.

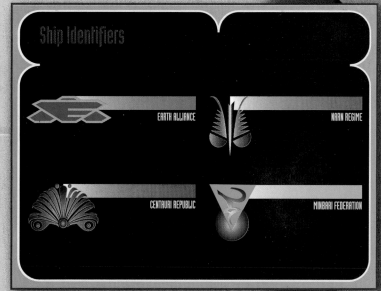

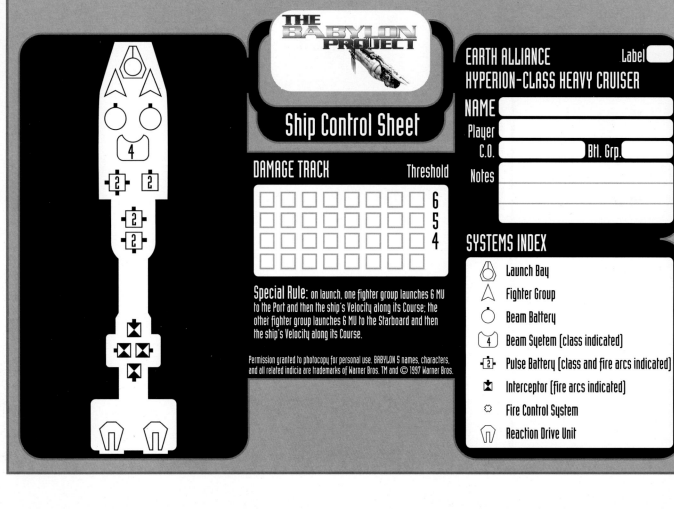

THE BABYLON PROJECT

Ship Control Sheet

EARTH ALLIANCE
HYPERION-CLASS HEAVY CRUISER

Label

NAME

Player

C.O. · Btl. Grp.

Notes

DAMAGE TRACK — Threshold

6
5
4

Special Rule: on launch, one fighter group launches 6 MU to the Port and then the ship's Velocity along its Course; the other fighter group launches 6 MU to the Starboard and then the ship's Velocity along its Course.

SYSTEMS INDEX

- Launch Bay
- Fighter Group
- Beam Battery
- 4 Beam Syetem (class indicated)
- 2 Pulse Battery (class and fire arcs indicated)
- Interceptor (fire arcs indicated)
- Fire Control System
- Reaction Drive Unit

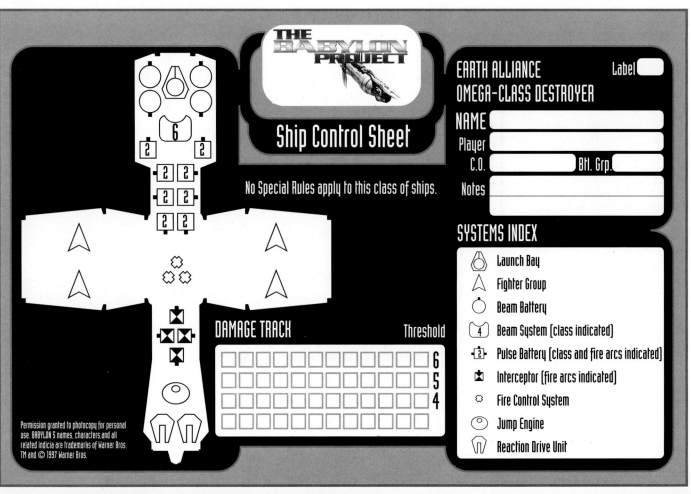

THE BABYLON PROJECT

Ship Control Sheet

No Special Rules apply to this class of ships.

EARTH ALLIANCE
OMEGA-CLASS DESTROYER

Label

NAME

Player

C.O. · Btl. Grp.

Notes

DAMAGE TRACK — Threshold

6
5
4

SYSTEMS INDEX

- Launch Bay
- Fighter Group
- Beam Battery
- 4 Beam System (class indicated)
- 2 Pulse Battery (class and fire arcs indicated)
- Interceptor (fire arcs indicated)
- Fire Control System
- Jump Engine
- Reaction Drive Unit

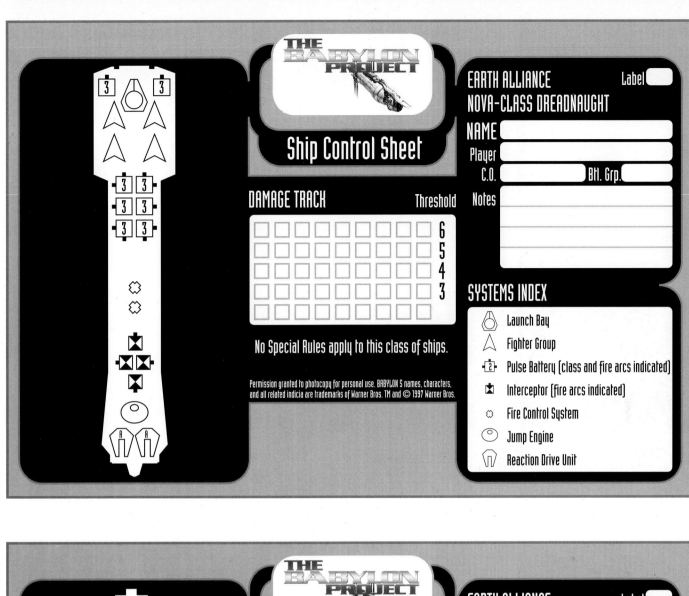

THE BABYLON PROJECT

Ship Control Sheet

**EARTH ALLIANCE
NOVA-CLASS DREADNAUGHT**

Label ▢

NAME ▢
Player ▢
C.O. ▢ Btl. Grp. ▢
Notes ▢

DAMAGE TRACK

Threshold

6
5
4
3

No Special Rules apply to this class of ships.

Permission granted to photocopy for personal use. BABYLON 5 names, characters,
and all related indicia are trademarks of Warner Bros. TM and © 1997 Warner Bros.

SYSTEMS INDEX

- Launch Bay
- Fighter Group
- Pulse Battery (class and fire arcs indicated)
- Interceptor (fire arcs indicated)
- Fire Control System
- Jump Engine
- Reaction Drive Unit

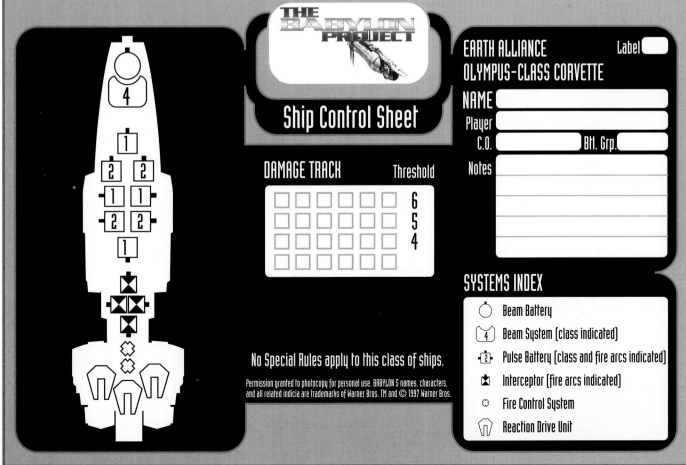

THE BABYLON PROJECT

Ship Control Sheet

**EARTH ALLIANCE
OLYMPUS-CLASS CORVETTE**

Label ▢

NAME ▢
Player ▢
C.O. ▢ Btl. Grp. ▢
Notes ▢

DAMAGE TRACK

Threshold

6
5
4

No Special Rules apply to this class of ships.

Permission granted to photocopy for personal use. BABYLON 5 names, characters,
and all related indicia are trademarks of Warner Bros. TM and © 1997 Warner Bros.

SYSTEMS INDEX

- Beam Battery
- Beam System (class indicated)
- Pulse Battery (class and fire arcs indicated)
- Interceptor (fire arcs indicated)
- Fire Control System
- Reaction Drive Unit

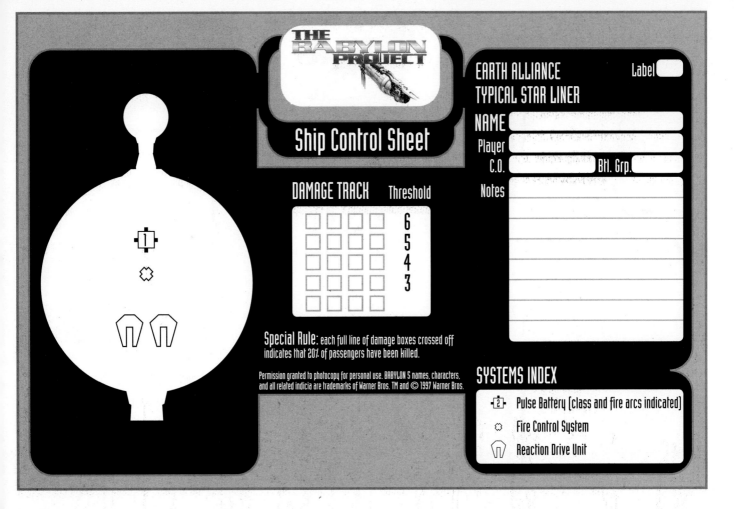

THE BABYLON PROJECT

Ship Control Sheet

EARTH ALLIANCE
TYPICAL STAR LINER

Label ⬜

NAME _____
Player _____
C.O. _____ Btl. Grp. ____
Notes _____

DAMAGE TRACK

Threshold

6
5
4
3

Special Rule: each full line of damage boxes crossed off indicates that 20% of passengers have been killed.

Permission granted to photocopy for personal use. BABYLON 5 names, characters, and all related indicia are trademarks of Warner Bros. TM and © 1997 Warner Bros.

SYSTEMS INDEX

⊡2 Pulse Battery (class and fire arcs indicated)
⬦ Fire Control System
⊓ Reaction Drive Unit

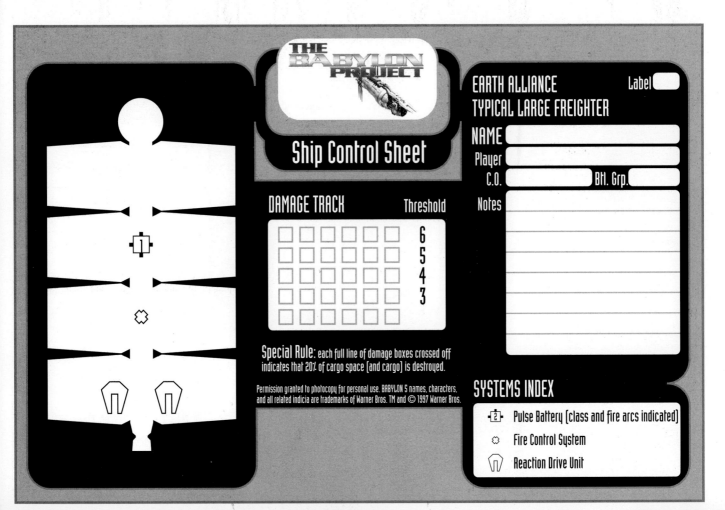

THE BABYLON PROJECT

Ship Control Sheet

EARTH ALLIANCE
TYPICAL LARGE FREIGHTER

Label ⬜

NAME _____
Player _____
C.O. _____ Btl. Grp. ____
Notes _____

DAMAGE TRACK

Threshold

6
5
4
3

Special Rule: each full line of damage boxes crossed off indicates that 20% of cargo space (and cargo) is destroyed.

Permission granted to photocopy for personal use. BABYLON 5 names, characters, and all related indicia are trademarks of Warner Bros. TM and © 1997 Warner Bros.

SYSTEMS INDEX

⊡2 Pulse Battery (class and fire arcs indicated)
⬦ Fire Control System
⊓ Reaction Drive Unit

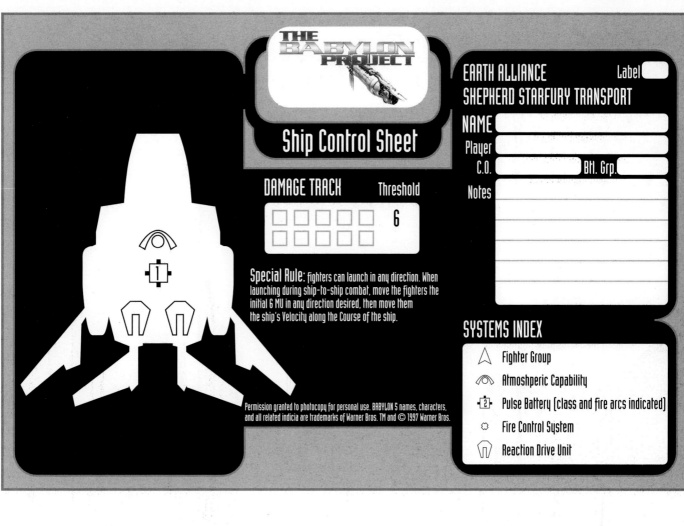

Ship Control Sheet

THE BABYLON PROJECT

EARTH ALLIANCE
SHEPHERD STARFURY TRANSPORT

Label ☐

NAME
Player
C.O. _____ Btl. Grp.
Notes

DAMAGE TRACK   Threshold

6

Special Rule: fighters can launch in any direction. When launching during ship-to-ship combat, move the fighters the initial 6 MU in any direction desired, then move them the ship's Velocity along the Course of the ship.

Permission granted to photocopy for personal use. BABYLON 5 names, characters, and all related indicia are trademarks of Warner Bros. TM and © 1997 Warner Bros.

SYSTEMS INDEX

△ Fighter Group

◠ Atmoshperic Capability

⊡ Pulse Battery (class and fire arcs indicated)

◇ Fire Control System

⌂ Reaction Drive Unit

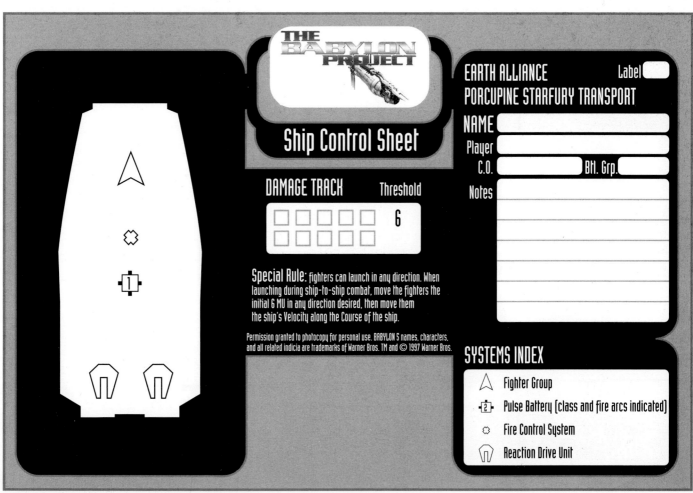

Ship Control Sheet

THE BABYLON PROJECT

EARTH ALLIANCE
PORCUPINE STARFURY TRANSPORT

Label ☐

NAME
Player
C.O. _____ Btl. Grp.
Notes

DAMAGE TRACK   Threshold

6

Special Rule: fighters can launch in any direction. When launching during ship-to-ship combat, move the fighters the initial 6 MU in any direction desired, then move them the ship's Velocity along the Course of the ship.

Permission granted to photocopy for personal use. BABYLON 5 names, characters, and all related indicia are trademarks of Warner Bros. TM and © 1997 Warner Bros.

SYSTEMS INDEX

△ Fighter Group

⊡ Pulse Battery (class and fire arcs indicated)

◇ Fire Control System

⌂ Reaction Drive Unit

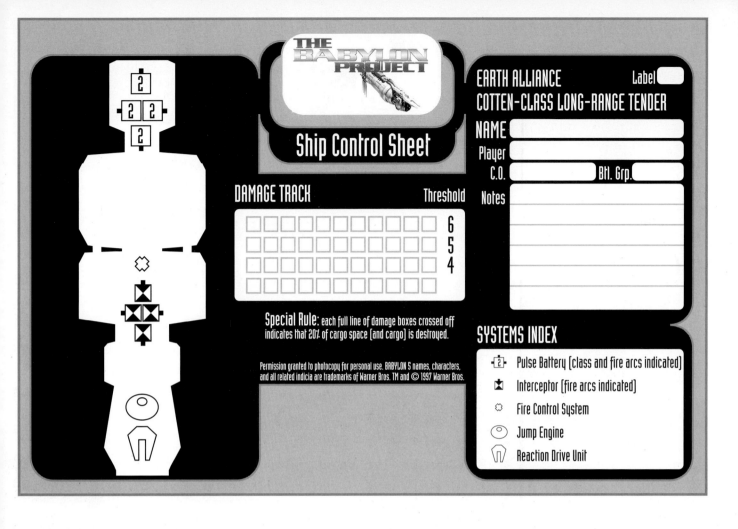

THE BABYLON PROJECT

Ship Control Sheet

EARTH ALLIANCE
COTTEN-CLASS LONG-RANGE TENDER

Label

NAME

Player

C.O.   Btl. Grp.

Notes

DAMAGE TRACK   Threshold

6
5
4

Special Rule: each full line of damage boxes crossed off indicates that 20% of cargo space (and cargo) is destroyed.

Permission granted to photocopy for personal use. BABYLON 5 names, characters, and all related indicia are trademarks of Warner Bros. TM and © 1997 Warner Bros.

SYSTEMS INDEX

- 2 Pulse Battery (class and fire arcs indicated)
- ⊠ Interceptor (fire arcs indicated)
- ✛ Fire Control System
- ◉ Jump Engine
- ⬱ Reaction Drive Unit

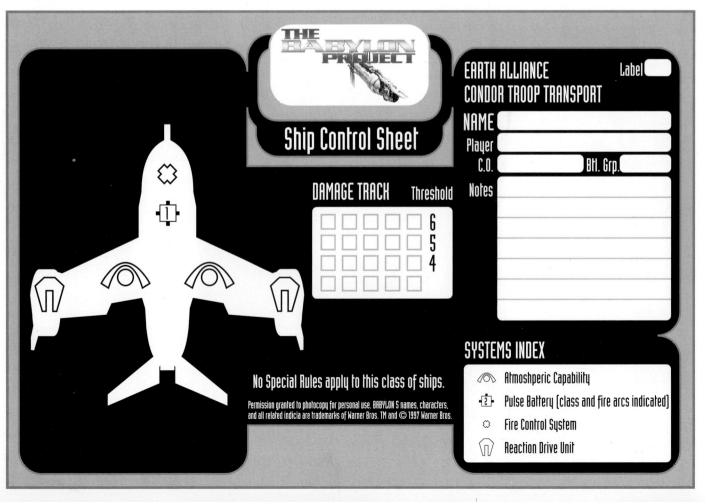

THE BABYLON PROJECT

Ship Control Sheet

EARTH ALLIANCE
CONDOR TROOP TRANSPORT

Label

NAME

Player

C.O.   Btl. Grp.

Notes

DAMAGE TRACK   Threshold

6
5
4

No Special Rules apply to this class of ships.

Permission granted to photocopy for personal use. BABYLON 5 names, characters, and all related indicia are trademarks of Warner Bros. TM and © 1997 Warner Bros.

SYSTEMS INDEX

- ⌒ Atmoshperic Capability
- 2 Pulse Battery (class and fire arcs indicated)
- ✛ Fire Control System
- ⬱ Reaction Drive Unit

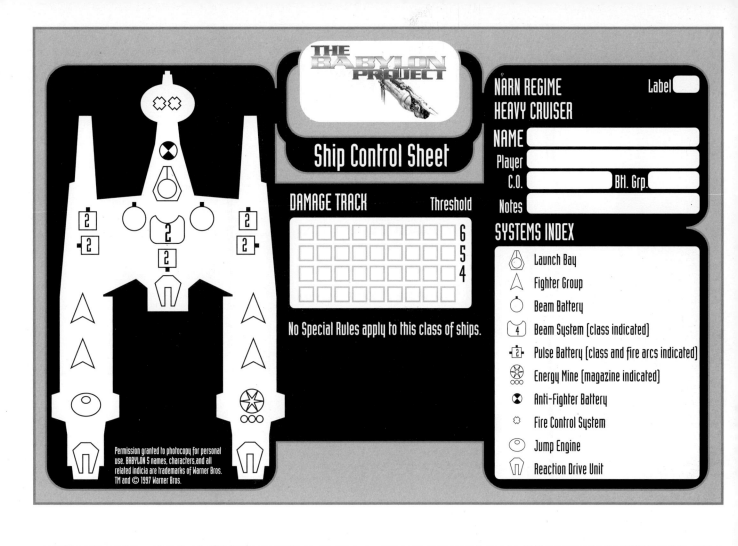

THE BABYLON PROJECT

Ship Control Sheet

NARN REGIME
HEAVY CRUISER

Label ☐

NAME
Player
C.O.   Btl. Grp.
Notes

DAMAGE TRACK   Threshold

6
5
4

No Special Rules apply to this class of ships.

SYSTEMS INDEX

- Launch Bay
- Fighter Group
- Beam Battery
- Beam System (class indicated)
- Pulse Battery (class and fire arcs indicated)
- Energy Mine (magazine indicated)
- Anti-Fighter Battery
- Fire Control System
- Jump Engine
- Reaction Drive Unit

Permission granted to photocopy for personal use. BABYLON 5 names, characters, and all related indicia are trademarks of Warner Bros. TM and © 1997 Warner Bros.

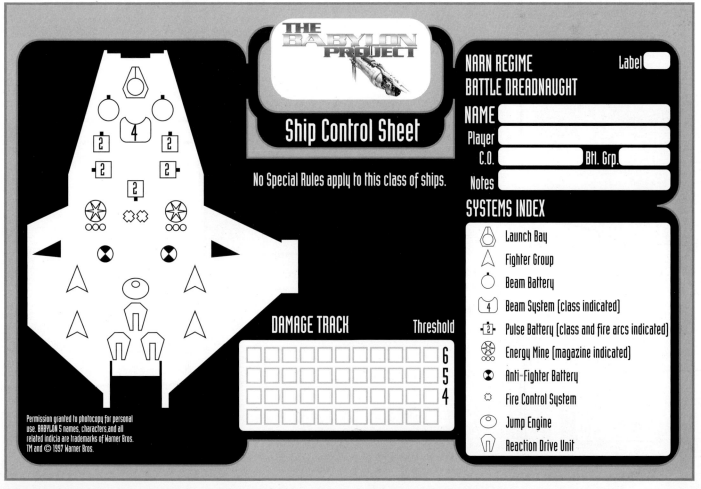

THE BABYLON PROJECT

Ship Control Sheet

NARN REGIME
BATTLE DREADNAUGHT

Label ☐

NAME
Player
C.O.   Btl. Grp.
Notes

No Special Rules apply to this class of ships.

SYSTEMS INDEX

- Launch Bay
- Fighter Group
- Beam Battery
- Beam System (class indicated)
- Pulse Battery (class and fire arcs indicated)
- Energy Mine (magazine indicated)
- Anti-Fighter Battery
- Fire Control System
- Jump Engine
- Reaction Drive Unit

DAMAGE TRACK   Threshold

6
5
4

Permission granted to photocopy for personal use. BABYLON 5 names, characters, and all related indicia are trademarks of Warner Bros. TM and © 1997 Warner Bros.

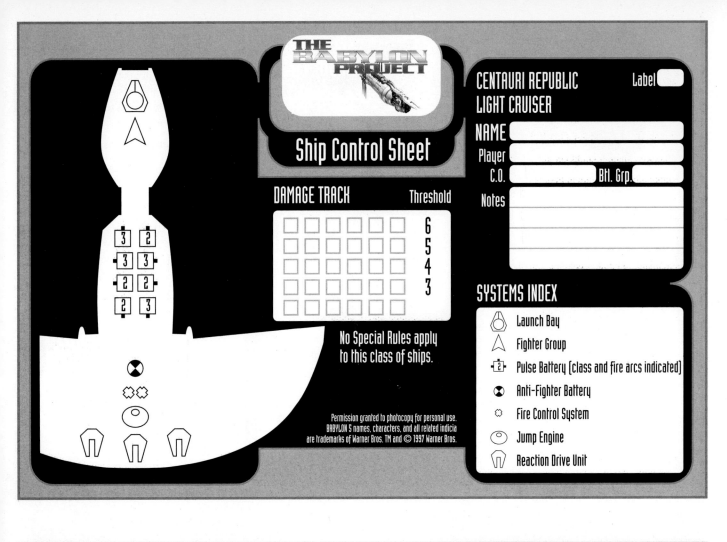

THE BABYLON PROJECT

Ship Control Sheet

CENTAURI REPUBLIC LIGHT CRUISER — Label

NAME

Player

C.O. — Btl. Grp.

Notes

DAMAGE TRACK — Threshold

6
5
4
3

No Special Rules apply
to this class of ships.

SYSTEMS INDEX

- Launch Bay
- Fighter Group
- Pulse Battery [class and fire arcs indicated]
- Anti-Fighter Battery
- Fire Control System
- Jump Engine
- Reaction Drive Unit

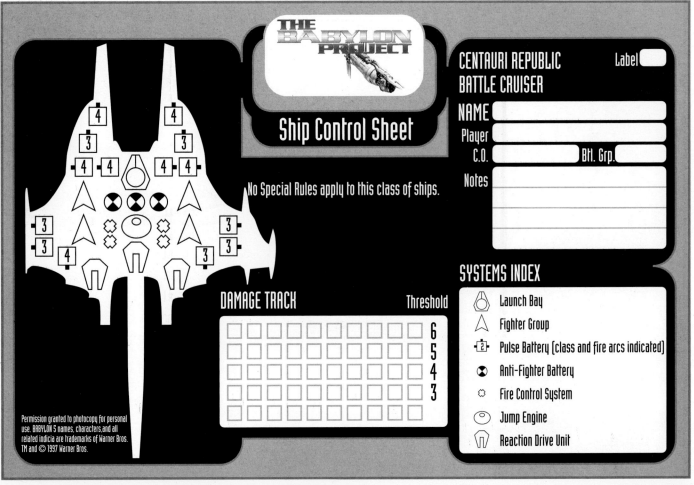

THE BABYLON PROJECT

Ship Control Sheet

CENTAURI REPUBLIC BATTLE CRUISER — Label

NAME

Player

C.O. — Btl. Grp.

Notes

No Special Rules apply to this class of ships.

DAMAGE TRACK — Threshold

6
5
4
3

SYSTEMS INDEX

- Launch Bay
- Fighter Group
- Pulse Battery [class and fire arcs indicated]
- Anti-Fighter Battery
- Fire Control System
- Jump Engine
- Reaction Drive Unit

SYSTEMS INDEX

⬡ Launch Bay

△ Fighter Group

○ Beam Battery

⬡4 Beam System [class indicated]

⬡12ₘ Minbari Beam System [class indicated]

⊡2 Pulse Battery [class and fire arcs indicated]

⬚ Interceptor [fire arcs indicated]

✪ Anti-Fighter Battery

⊛ Energy Mine Launcher [magazine indicated]

⦿ Jamming System

◇ EMP Weapon

✧ Fire Control System

⬠ Plasma Net

◠ Atmospheric Capability

◉ Jump Engine

⬠ Reaction Drive Unit

⬠G Gravimetric Drive Unit

Ship Combat Reference Sheet

TURN SEQUENCE

1 Order Phase. Players write down orders for all ships.

2 Ship Movement Phase. All ships move.

3 Fighter Movement Phase. Fighters move.

4 Combat Phase. Ships and fighters fire weapons.

  4a Ship Selection. Choose Active Ship and resolve fighter attacks against it.

  4b Weapons Fire. Active Ship fires on other targets.

REACTION DRIVE MOVEMENT SEQUENCE

1] Move ship according to final vector from previous turn (direction as indicated by Direction Arrow, distance as recorded Velocity).

2] Apply any ship maneuvers (main drive, rotations and pushes in the orders written).

3] Measure distance from Direction Arrow to new ship position, note this as new Velocity.

4] Turn and move Direction Arrow up to ship to show new Course.

ORDERS OPTIONS

MD [X]: Main Drive [X] moves the ship X MU along its Heading.

RP [X]: Rotate Port [X] rotates the ship X Course Points to port.

RS [X]: Rotate Starboard [X] rotates the ship X Course Points to starboard.

PP [X]: Push Port [X] moves the ship X MU directly to port.

PS [X]: Push Starboard [X] moves the ship X MU directly to starboard.

PA [X]: Push Aft [X] moves the ship X MU directly to the aft.

LFG [X]: Launch Fighter Groups [X] launches X Fighter Groups (X cannot exceed the maximum number of Fighter Groups the ship can launch per turn).

LEM [X]: Launch Energy Mine [X] launches X Energy Mines.

R: Ram indicates an intentional attempt to ram another ship.

JP: Jump Point begins the jump point formation process (this will keep guns offline for two rounds and the point will not open until the beginning of the next round).

AP: Anti-Pulse sets the ship's Interceptors to anti-pulse mode.

AF: Anti-Fighters sets the ship's Interceptors to anti-fighter mode.

THE BABYLON PROJECT

Ship Control Sheet

Permission granted to photocopy for personal use. BABYLON 5 names, characters, and all related indicia are trademarks of Warner Bros. TM and © 1997 Warner Bros.

No Special Rules apply to this class of ships.

MINBARI FEDERATION WAR CRUISER

Label ▭

NAME ▭

Player ▭

C.O. ▭ Btl. Grp. ▭

Notes ▭

SYSTEMS INDEX

⬡ Launch Bay

△ Fighter Group

○ Beam Battery

⬡12ₘ Minbari Beam System [class indicated]

⦿ Jamming System

◇ EMP Weapon

✧ Fire Control System

⬠ Plasma Net

◉ Jump Engine

⬠ Gravimetric Drive Unit

DAMAGE TRACK

Threshold

□□□□□□□□□□□□□□□□	6
□□□□□□□□□□□□□□□□	5
□□□□□□□□□□□□□□□□	4
□□□□□□□□□□□□□□□□	

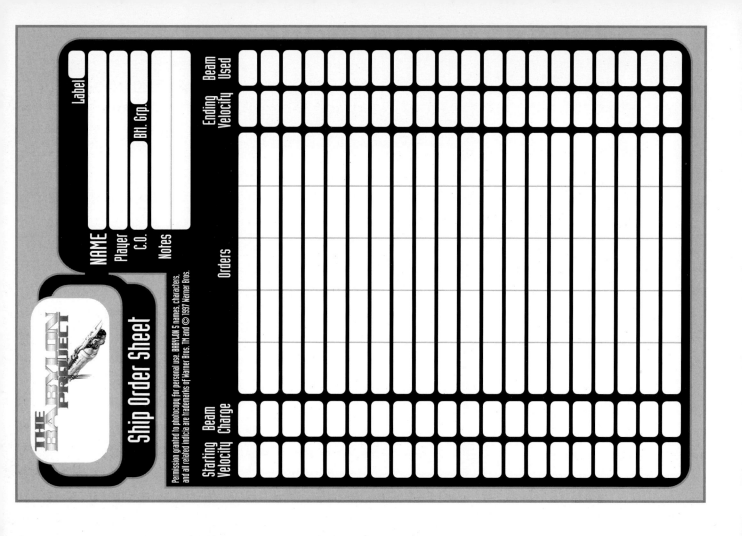

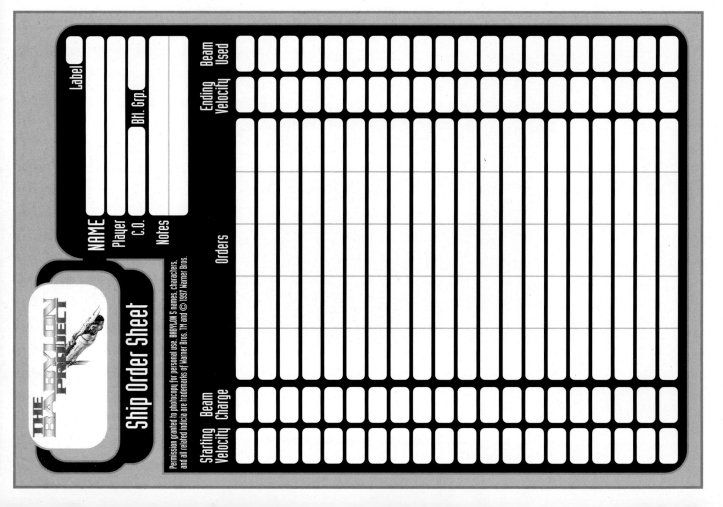